Economic Issues, Problems and Perspectives

What/Who Are We after the Transition?

Focus on Romania

ECONOMIC ISSUES, PROBLEMS AND PERSPECTIVES

Additional books in this series can be found on Nova's website
under the Series tab.

Additional e-books in this series can be found on Nova's website
under the e-book tab.

ECONOMIC ISSUES, PROBLEMS AND PERSPECTIVES

WHAT/WHO ARE WE AFTER THE TRANSITION?

FOCUS ON ROMANIA

MARIN DINU,
DOREL AILENEI,
ANCA DACHIN,
CĂTĂLIN HUIDUMAC-PETRESCU,
MARIANA IOVIȚU,
MARIUS CORNELIU MARINAȘ,
CHRISTINA-MARTA SUCIU
AND
DUMITRU-ALEXANDRU BODISLAV
EDITORS

nova
publishers
New York

Library of Congress Cataloging-in-Publication Data

Names: Dinu, Marin, editor. | Bodislav, Alexandru, editor.
Title: What/who are we after the transition? : focus on Romania / editors, Marin Dinu, and Alexandru Bodislav and others.
Other titles: What are we after the transition? | Who are we after the trasition?
Description: Hauppauge, New York : Nova Science Publishers, Inc., 2015. | Series: Economic issues, problems and perspectives | Includes bibliographical references and index.
Identifiers: LCCN 2015037925 | ISBN 9781634839471 (hardcover)
Subjects: LCSH: Romania--Social policy--21st century. | Right of property--Romania. | Structural adjustment (Economic policy)--Romania. | Romania--Population.
Classification: LCC HN643.5 .W43 2015 | DDC 306.09498--dc23 LC record available at http://lccn.loc.gov/2015037925

Published by Nova Science Publishers, Inc. † New York

CONTENTS

FOREWORD

MODELS AND REALITY

The 20th century ended in an opening; that is the 21st century debuting with a crisis. Between the two paradoxical states of the world's evolution, new hopes have emerged. The peaceful collapse of a totalitarian regime, namely the geopolitical experiment referred to as communism, brought new hope to the inhabitants of Central and Eastern Europe (CEE). The hope was that they could win the development competition without any act of violence and the avoidance/delay of social consequences of the financial crisis nurtured the hope for a capitalism protected against the risk of dystopia.

CEE countries are part of the group that went through both developmental stages of the world in the past two and a half decades. They should be subject to the study on how mankind could become a winner after seemingly being doomed to utter failure and how everything can be lost when victory appeared within reach. Reflecting on these realities is inevitably related to the mainstream theories that inspired the transition. To jumpstart this transformation, we should consider bypassing mankind's exit from primitive tribalism and this could also be a challenge to making the science-society relationship work.

In time, post-communist transition is still the only episode that closes a deviant loop of the world's evolution on a significantly inhabited area. Communism was a side-track, a detour from the normal course that had been couched as a shortcut to progress, but proved a leap into the void, an illusion of improving human nature through constraints. The part that science should dwell upon is how one can resume the normal course of development by precluding a topsy-turvy experiment, with all interventionist/authoritarian ingredients, in what regards obviating the conditioned reflexes attributed to the structures imposed by communist reality.

There was a belief at work which stated that the mere targeting of capitalist values is capable of patterning transformational behaviors and human nature in general. The ideal of compliance, even by mimicking, proved its influential power on the path of education/re-education, during long cycles, yet far too long for the claims of the standard transition model.

Beneath the surface of day-to-day life, many delicate implicit questions and further topical issues could arise with no surprise. Of these, one could detect against the backdrop of analyses in this book some issues with an epistemological attachment for more broad-based academic contexts. In any case, the approximation of answers pertains to the recurrent principle of accurately testing the manner in which reality—shaped by the theories deemed as adequate—works at 100% and also reaches the principle of leaving the door open to the penetration of elements from beyond the meaning of the main theory.

The stake exceeds the endeavor to establish how relevant one theory or another is because, undoubtedly, though it is quite simple to explain how a theory changes, it is not quite clear how reality changes. It could be a rift between trendy theories and the natural reference to scientific ideas. Theoretical and practical experience of the post-communist transition could be a relevant epistemic chapter in correcting the way society refers to the cycle of theoretical preferences, above all via the conclusion on the underlying data, which defines the consistency and concordance of the reality cycle itself.

Certainly, the new challenge to the epistemology of social sciences will, to a large extent, capture the understanding and push the explanation to the level implied by the formulation of social change strategies that, relying on the ideality and idealism inherent to theories, should not materialize in utopic structures.

What/Who are we after the transition? is not only an expression fit for a book title, but also a tense issue whose rational solutions are slow in coming amid the vibrating emotion for the life-changing consistency differential. The prospects of long processes cover a life expectancy, but in Romania, where generations of sacrifice succeeded one after another, time doesn't have enough patience to run smoothly.

The assessment made in this book is an attempt at decoding what has been done by the last generation, i.e., the transition generation, from communism to capitalism. The authors reunited under the Research and Economic Analysis Centre which is the research side of the Department of Economics and Economic Policies from the Faculty of Theoretical and Applied Economics that is part of the Bucharest University of Economics.

The topics referred in the book come with a bit of historical flavor, but they are approached starting from the need to explain why things happened this way, why is it so, and not as we expected, from the standpoint of hopes of higher individual and societal amenities. The authors were driven by the moral burden to identify a progress-generating formula even under tough external constraints stemming from any arrangement, conditionality or commitment undertaken by an open-economy country with Western geostrategic options.

In an explicit manner, one accepts the assumption that such starting conditions may help to leave behind the postwar political dependencies, but are unusual when attempting to go beyond underdevelopment. The assumption that there should be an exit, a knob for opening the outlet of energies to beat the gravity, which generates realities inconsistent with the mainstream model, is felt throughout the concluding remarks.

Moving away from the fringes by discouraging and disengaging with an emergence from the status of a consumption market, which is where Romania is now due to an economy unable to bring about a competition-driven market, proves the failure in innovating a society engaged on the post-communist path. Of course, there was no alternative to the impending opening-up of the economy, and acknowledging this truth implies that the effects brought by the displacement of the native economic forces should be mitigated in an open market in order to have real development. The emerging gap between domestic consumption and foreign supply was not a promise incorporated in the transition model.

What needs to be done, however, is to deal with the issue of the model for escaping underdevelopment in non-conflicting terms, also by means of the theoretical inspiration of global decisions. An honest opinion looks at balancing the benefits in the external balance of change, which is a good thing for the post-communist transformations in their effort to resume the path of modernity that CEE countries had embarked upon prior to being trapped in the pitfall of communism. This is the only way for post-communist transition to keep the pace with the global society correction movement in the aftermath of the ongoing economic crisis. This also happens when the pendulum of theoretical preferences changes from globalization slippages to accountability assumed by countries in strategies centered on a fairer access to action, respect for societal innovation (of the roads to success!) and participation in development consequences.

* * *

The focus on Romania, a country still facing radical systemic changes in its attempt at inserting into regional trends, reveals a more pronounced refining of developments, with varying degrees of conclusiveness relative to the model standard, as well as of societal innovation breakthroughs.

The case of Romania is emblematic for a manner in which transformation is made, as the emancipation path that had been reopened by post-communist transition at both individual and country level was marked by the complete change in domestic and external political links and lingering uncertainty about economic links. Market economy functionalization still falls short, *inter alia*, of social insertion, since the most active part of its population works in the European Union's advanced economies.

The potential for real convergence is riddled with structural gaps, in terms of both capital utilization, especially financial capital, and yield use. Post-communism generated, at least in Romania, a state-of-affairs that should be bypassed, i.e., capitalism devoid of local capitalists.

It is beyond the shadow of a doubt that the transformations might ultimately be rendered effective, but the time lapsed from the beginning of the change, which already covers the expectations horizon specific to a generation, poses novel challenges and the most delicate issues relate to the identity embedded in the original transition projection. The benchmarks of a case study on the development of a post-communist country presented in the form of questions and going beyond national specifics, even beyond the transformation model, are chiefly the following:

- Did Romania have any development strategy in the past 25 years and were its overriding economic problems accurately identified? How were the solutions found and how were they implemented? How did the body of the economy react to the treatment imposed via Washington Consensus recipes, IMF conditionalities, and so on? Compared to other CEE countries, how much did the initial conditions weigh and how much did the consistency of the implemented policies weigh (also in terms of the quality of those who formulated and implemented them)? Did economic, social, well-being indicators, etc. make any progress from 1989? Why do people still get the feeling of running round in circles?
- Does the privatization of resources and strategic companies constitute the backbone of the restructured economy? Did the change in ownership structure and economy structure entail a transfer of competencies or strategic responsibilities? Transfer of ownership versus creation of property, the ratio of foreign capital and domestic capital and the trends in capitalization; Deindustrialization, reindustrialization and tertiary sector development; How profitable was for the Romanian economy the

companies' shift from the state into private hands? Is renationalization one of the feasible solutions for directly engaging development sources? Reform of state-owned companies; Private management – how much relevance, how much an experiment? What is the adequate speed for structural adjustment? Are regulatory agencies "captive"? Is reindustrialization the engine for stronger potential growth?

- What should be the adequate speed for fiscal adjustment? What should be the proper government deficit threshold? How can we deal with the tradeoff between fiscal consolidation and growth-boosting policies? How is the transfer from quantitative adjustment to qualitative adjustment to be made? What are the steps to be taken to achieve an efficient fiscal adjustment? How does capital account liberalization affect the exchange rate and the Romanian economy's competitiveness? Capital account liberalization in Romania: how much and how fast? What are the effects of early capital account liberalization on external balances? How to financially secure the external imbalance and to adjust macroeconomically during the financial crisis?
- Romania's intricate European integration – narrow room for maneuver – core standards, peripheral means; Which countries that made a successful European integration are an inspiration? How can we circumvent the constraints in order to develop? Making restrictions fuzzy by observing the rigors of the EU body of laws. Can the expected effect be improved under the EU's current tight rules? How can the competitiveness gap be bridged?
- Due diligence of the demographic picture in Romania; The economic and social impact of migration; Geostrategic losses – and less power in the EU! The lack of economic and social cohesion; What should be done to remedy the situation? Can New Developmentalism-type programs be implemented in Romania? What should they allow for?

* * *

Since tearing down the Berlin Wall to the end of "Occupy Wall Street," one could detect the post-communism chances to pass entirely into the desired reality, which was the driver of its original drive, but whose purpose must be confirmed in order to be a real winner. The CEE countries' peoples should look at the post-communist goal by protecting themselves from the illusions of the confidence stemming from the access to the values once prohibited by the former regime. Romanians can no longer look today to ideology-prone mirrors in order to comprehend themselves, but should look to evolve in the regained landscape of a world from where they were brutally cast out by the geopolitical aftermath of World War Two.

Memory is the strongest force on which the direction of post-communist transition could rely. Some kind of energy from the pre-communism past clashed with the communist past, but in order to exit post-communism, like a battlefield of more remote or more recent past, other dangerous traps should be avoided. The opening-up manifest in the final decade of the century of the most hideous crimes against humanity may not annihilate social memory, but is able to take it out of the cycle of violence, gearing post-communist transformation towards actual development, along its human, economic and social lines.

The actual development model involves its approximation based not necessarily on theoretical, even changing, principles, but also on people's direct perception of the functional reality of a shock-free Western society. All in all, post-communist transition was also fueled by individuals' will to no longer be different in terms of options and opportunities from their fellow men in the developed societies.

The authors hope that taking a more or less subjective approach to the Romanian reality is a good occasion to ponder on the chance that mankind has today, more than two decades from the collapse of the communist regime, to boldly turn to account for its true potential.

REAC/DEEP
Research and Economic Analysis Centre
Department of Economics and Economic Policies
22 December 2014

In: What/Who Are We After the Transition? Focus on Romania ISBN: 978-1-63483-947-1
Editors: M. Dinu, D. Ailenei, A. Dachin et al.

Chapter 1

Post-Communist Capitalism

Anca Dachin**, PhD, Cătălin Huidumac-Petrescu, PhD, Marin Dinu, PhD, Amalia Cristescu, PhD, Magdalena Manole, PhD candidate, Roberta Stanef-Puică, PhD, Andreea Claudia Şerban, PhD and Daniela Livia Traşcă, PhD

Bucharest University of Economics Studies, Bucharest, Romania

Romania followed the joint historical path of Central and East Europe (CEE) both after World War II and after the fall of the Iron Curtain. The set-up of the communist regime under the umbrella of the Soviet occupation as well as its collapse in this region was in the same year are key events of a common historic destiny. The year 1945 was the kick-off of a most significant deviation in the development of modern societies, due to its radicalism and geographical extent: the introduction of economic and social collectivism. The year 1989 marked the start of a geostrategic correction of this bubble in CEE. In essence this imposed historical interval was distinctively marked by the opening and closing of a social experiment that was ideologically motivated; overcoming it meant the return to an evolution which had been abruptly interrupted.

Apart from the mainstream ideas and visions, the global context, the legal linkages between the states as well as the more transparent international climate in terms of attitude and behavior of national and international decision-makers were relevant in order for fully understanding the transformational mechanisms in this European region [1]. It is clear that neither in 1945 nor in 1989 was there a valid theory on how to impose the change of the course of history beyond the standard assumptions, based on ideological adversity and on visible geopolitical or international order factors. Moreover, for both moments the perception of an imminent, radical change that was set to materialize failed to exist at the level of social decisions. In the post-war framework the expectations regarding the observance of the deals between the allies seemed solid, with leaders prone to a chemistry of agreements on various matters in the long run. In post-communist times the expectation related to a collapse of the bipolarity and the stability of the areas of influence had yet to materialize.

---

* Corresponding author: ancadachin@yahoo.com

From the perspectives of real results, the heightened expectations had a say in laying the theoretical fundamentals for both models of change. In the first case it was the expectation that a long-term functional reality could be build based on the illusory assumptions of scientific socialism. In the second, the expectation was that abstract principles would pave the way for a democratic society and functional market economy to naturally emerge in the CEE region in the context of a permissive globalization. In reality, the developments have failed to follow these theoretical projections: a society that was forced to adopt communist rules had definitively and violently rejected the 1989 experiment.

1. A Return to the Market Economy

1.1. The Decisive Role of the Social Memory

As for the post-communist change, after a quarter of century, it is worth mentioning that it went somehow different compared to what had been solicited by the implemented scenarios, especially the one on shock-therapy [2]. Such a discrepancy does not refer to the strategic goal, but to the way in which the transformational forces got involved, how the contributions of the agents of changes have materialized. In summary, it can be said that the post-communist change in the CEE region, Romania including, had triggered the development through the reactivation of a factor that seemed to have been eradicated by the violence of the collectivist regimes, but which proved to be the most relevant propeller of the exit from communism: *the social memory*. The most spectacular effect of the social memory was the adoption of measures that led to post-communist changes which aimed to restore the fundamental benchmarks of the pre-communist social experience – private property first of all.

In terms of actions, social memory resisted more than four decades despite a systemic repression that sought to create the communist new man. The ousting of the communist parties from the political scene has accelerated a rise from the ashes of the social memory, whose first mission was extremely important for the push towards a democratic society and market economy. That factor was decisive in the structuring of the pro-capitalist political option, especially given the scarcity of individual experiences in terms of political or economic alternatives to communism. This led to big outcomes in countries such as Romania where private property was liquidated and replaced by the unique state property or the people's property.

The social memory explained and explains the achievement of a critical mass towards change in the right direction as well as its role in guiding the individual attitude and decisions amid the confusing moments of the start, especially as the new political leaders seemed inspired by Gorbachev's model of a socialism with a human face. Coming back on the public scene as a street movement reflecting the will to put an end to the communist experiment, the social memory had pressured the post-revolutionary political institutions to favor a transformational process towards capitalism. Thus, unexpectedly for the theoreticians of post-communist reforms, the real author of the scenarios of the shift towards capitalism was the social memory. The transformational force stemmed from the extraordinary fact that social memory had generated a specific formula to erase the consequences of this deviant bubble in history, induced by the Soviet regime in this part of Europe.

In principle post-communist transition in CEE fully confirmed that the development of the human society does not follow radical, abstract ideological scenarios. The communist utopia failed in the dystopia of CEE's collectivist prison. The post-communist change, moderated by the social memory of the failure of the top-down social life change, stayed away from the experiment and allowed the natural energies of change to act. These energies were the ones that allowed the rebuilding of the profound links with the pre-communist historic path and brought to light an already-tried pattern of social action, instead of one rejected by history.

In corrective terms for a rather hesitant formula such as the post-communist transformation, which assures us that it is exiting communism, but leaves us wondering about the essence of the target, the social memory was pivotal in configuring within the CEE region a capitalism strongly dependent on its pre-communist functioning, which had been brutally interrupted by the Soviet occupation. The general result of these changes substantiates a certain type of capitalism in CEE, one that tried to exploit the experimental advantages of a capitalist past, advantages that became an opportunity in the context of closing of the deviant bubble of communism. It is a post-communist capitalism that transcends the communist desertification to reconnect the development of society to the natural mechanisms of its own history and to the new trends of the world amid globalization.

The reconnection to the solid historic experience through a restoration of property rights, a complete redemption in case of Romania, has a compensatory role even though frequently there was too much of a consumption of energy in pushing towards overcoming the intricacies of the reset of legal rights. The going forward force of the changes specific to the post-communist capitalism, aimed at a recoupling of this geographical area to the western world, which was replaced accordingly via the economic globalization channels as well as via those of the political entities from the European Union.

Post-communist capitalism's chance of representing a CEE specific chapter on the road to a lasting recoupling to the global capitalism, even in its European style, hinges on the way in which the return to pre-communist capitalism does not end up lost in the past. At the same time, its success is sustained by the dynamic of the Western vision in managing its own interests, especially those related to the economic aid which may trigger a real exit of this European region from the periphery of development.

No doubt that one may talk about the duty of the Western world, at a great extent as a moral one, for what the CEE region persistently perceives as a post-war abandonment of the region to the communist experiment. The aid policy should have decisively underpinned the creation of development factors, the internal capital first, also required to reach the force of a critical mass. After two decades and a half of post-communist transformation the functionality of market economies in CEE appears to be a delicate issue whose solution lies in the right balance between the economic progress and the social emancipation, between the internal capital and FDI. In moral terms, recovering the capitalist path of development should trigger a change in the perception that it is merely a recuperation of the CEE region as a consumption market for the global capital of the states that had been continuously following the capitalist way.

The experience of performance in global capitalism is earned in time through *seeing and doing*. The advantage of repositioning post-communist capitalism into the global markets comes from its ability to offset the consequences of this type of restoration as long as it manages to intensify the post-communist free-initiative capitalism' cores, as much as it boosts the one deriving from the transfer of property from the state to the individuals (selloffs) or to FDI. Here the transformational role of mentalities is revealed, apart from the mentalities revived by the social memory, in other words the action of agents emerged in the new conditions, which also have the ability to resonate to trends in the global capitalism and remain resilient to its specific challenges. From this viewpoint, post-communist capitalism in the CEE region naturally remains a complex societal process, opened to social creativity towards a destiny that comes to confirm people's expectations of progress.

1.2. Characteristics of the Romanian Transition

Unlike economic thinking in most former communist countries, Romanian economic strategy was predominantly gradualist type, characterized by the slow pace of reforms carried out by the authorities in 1992-1996. This concept has been visible since the early 1990s and can be found in official documents, such as "Draft Strategy of Accomplishing Market Economy in Romania" (1990) [3], as well as in lectures and public statements of government representatives.

Strengthening of economic reforms could be observed after the Helsinki European Council (December 1999) that decided to include Romania (and Bulgaria) in the list of candidate countries destined to join the European Union, and also after the start of accession negotiations (February 2000). Throughout the following timeframe periodic assessments of the European Commission showed the country's progress towards being prepared for accession. These steps demonstrate the propensity to achieve as much as possible the political goals without catching the model consistently and also that political stimulus was perhaps stronger than the efficiency stimulus.

During this period changes have occurred on several levels:

- Economically, the transition can be synonymous with total change of economic paradigm, respectively from the paradigm of centralized economy to one of the market economy governed by the rules of the free market. In Romania, this change has induced a shock to the whole economic system whose operating principles were completely changed.
- Socially, the previously set-in social statuses were redefined and during this process individuals sought to take advantage of the new economic frameworks and institutional contexts. The adaptive behavior of people in the new market economy, consumption patterns that are defined by ambiguity, imprecision in assuming the position of the entrepreneur and the lack of previous guidelines in this regard, appreciable increase in consumption in the first years after 1989 etc. were some of the observable manifestations of social changes.

Economic and social changes were determined not only by the evolution of external context but also by each person's individual characteristics and their ability or lack thereof to capitalize on those individual traits in order to climb the social ladder in tune with the new relative value society placed on these characteristics.

Changes induced by the transition to a market economy have generated changes in the way in which members of society place themselves on the social ladder. Without removing the criteria recognized in communism used for positioning individuals on the social ladder, such as education and occupation, the capitalist model outlines other criteria such as entrepreneurship or the number and value of assets held.

1.3. The Rent-Seeking Behavior of Transition Agents

The slow reforms in the first period of transition in Romania brought as major change with profound negative effects, the emergence of enrichment opportunities for certain groups; often members of the old or new political class have favoured the crystallization of the "*rent-seeking*" behavior. They act to achieve their own interests, the interests of the group and only in the case of the foreign institutions constraint they aimed with syncope, general interests. The lack of interest in carrying out the reform programs was determined by high social and economic costs for a short term, which would have negatively affected the popularity of the political class (the case of Poland) and it would have limited the crystallization of rent seekers. This explains the slow privatization, the Romanian delayed reform of the autonomous bodies such as rail, gas and electricity, aspects that have been favoured by the lack of political consensus on reforms.

The desire of these groups of getting rich quickly hijacked the thinking from the natural orientation towards growth and development that should have characterized the transition to a market economy, thus representing a major constraint of the economic development of Romania. The legitimate social objective of increasing per capita income at the maximum sustainable levels, the concern for general efficiency and social benefit, the sense of social justice conflicts with the objective of maximizing the extraction of rents [4].

A direct consequence of this behaviour is the emphasis on income inequality in society, the redistribution of wealth from those at the bottom of the pyramid to those at the tip of the pyramid. Increasing the inequality was the result of political and economic forces. The rent-seeking behavior is mainly based on political power to increase inequality, but not only the political power is used by them. Economic forces equally, through the creation of market, contributed to growing inequality in the former communist countries. However the political forces have a decisive role in influencing the market through public policies, laws, institutions, regulations, through decisions that bring certain advantages to some groups rather than others by what the government does or not. The economic power generated by various methods, by monopolistic position or by the exploitation of those poorly informed or trained, does not directly involve the use of political power. However governments have an important role in tolerating these behaviors [5]. Therefore, most often economic and political interests reinforce each other, the two types of interest being found in the same groups.

The interest of the political class is primarily related to maintaining the position in the political hierarchy, to be able to control the masses and to use them as instruments of action in achieving personal goals (business, profitable contracts and grants, access to better paid positions in various government or state-owned institutions). Secondly, it was claimed the desire to get rich quickly without the risks of having your own business, especially for developing countries, seeking rent is more profitable than productive activities [6]. This is the explanation of businessmen involvement in the political life in order to extract rents from contracts with the state, from privatization, subsidies, postponements or exemptions from taxes and duties etc. However, the indolence, the natural effect of comfort and stability of their situation, often made and makes them not only ignorant, but incapable of making those judgments that are necessary to establish and understand the consequences of public regulations [7].

During the transition to the market economy, the economic and social environment in Romania experienced new challenges and was characterized by uncertainty and hesitation of the political power in the implementation of specific measures of privatization, restitution of property, promoting the principles of fiscal austerity and market liberalization. This was due to the close relationship of the political class with the fields that provide access to various resources, opportunities or image capital. This statement is sustained by the following [8]:

- The orientation of the public resources for infrastructure projects or social assistance to local governments led by members of the ruling parties;
- The politicization of management positions in various major areas: education, government, healthcare, state-owned companies;
- Relations of the political class with the private sectors dependent on public resources and thus abandoning the national interest in favour of the political one (by investments from the state budget or European funds, purchases of goods and services for the public sector);
- The access to certain areas of social prestige (universities, research institutes, etc.) or to mass media in order to promote the interests and strengthen the image of the political class.

Smith appreciated that summing the actions of the individuals can lead to the welfare of all, beyond the selfish interest, existing in human nature principles that call for the care for the fate of others. Given that rent seekers want to obtain a gain by manipulating and exploiting the economic and political environment, rather than by economic activity capable of increasing national wealth, the moral imperative of capitalism seems to be the maximization of self-interest not welfare. Rent seekers acquire or strengthen their positions due to their ability to sneak by the law or the possibility to influence the law in favour of self-interest as a result of the availability of taking advantage of the poor and uninformed (e.g., abusive lending, deceitful loans) or unfair play. Thus, they take advantage of the political or economic power in order to promote themselves or people in their group, they assume excessive risks because they know (or have the possibility to do so) that the state take their risks; they engage in profitable business with the state [9], they consolidate their positions either by acquiring some assets, resources owned by the State-owned at prices below the current market price (in the privatization process), or by selling goods to the state at overvalued prices (inefficient government procurement).

The guidance of the economic policy decisions of class interests and political clients determined in Romania that *the late and slow start of transfer of ownership and restructuring of the economic activities become ineffective*, given the loss of traditional sale markets in Eastern Europe and the lack of external financing and the deterioration of the main macroeconomic equilibria and galloping inflation.

The political class has acted in Romania in order to 'protect' the role and size of the state in the economy. State-owned enterprises, which the government has given direct or indirect subsidies and which the state banks have granted loans on favourable terms (which were or were not reimbursed), accumulated large arrears to the state budget and the utility providers obtained in this way, funds that they could obtain through favourable contracts, the new private companies 'ticks' - rent seekers [10]. Large companies such as Sidex Galați suffered financial losses and high debt to the state before privatization and had wasteful contracts with hundreds of "tick" companies selling products in the internal or foreign market.

Continuation of subsidizing of state-owned enterprises intended to mask the unemployment, to delay the occurrence of unfavourable social effects, in order to maintain political credibility. The adoption of bankruptcy law was postponed, accepting bank credit of the insolvent companies. Subsequently, the bankruptcy of these companies led to the loss of a significant number of jobs and social imbalances. Promoting the legal framework on collective redundancies, severance payments or early retirement caused other budgetary allocations that targeted the reduction of the social costs in the short term, sacrificing the long term objectives and benefits.

The influence of rent seekers is reflected in the size of the informal sector and low level of tax revenues in Romania, one of the lowest among the new EU member states. Fiscal pressure has supported the development of the informal economy and corruption and caused the redistribution of wealth by transferring income from the good to the bad payers by increasing public debt. To the growth of the informal sector it is estimated to have contributed the intensity of state regulations (state intervention that encourages rent seeking by bureaucracy) and clientelistic relationships that encourage such behaviour of businessmen.

After 2000, the rent seekers had to cope with external constraints and to accept a series of reforms required for fulfilling the EU accession criteria and to obtain external formal financial support form the International Monetary Fund, World Bank and European Union. The delay or opposition to some reforms was motivated by the low level of social supportability due to low living standards. The liberalization of markets and prices have negative effects on the interests of different groups, because they reduce the ability to obtain rents arising from administered prices or lack of competition. The objective of interest groups is increasing profits and not competition, which would reduce the benefit generated by privileged position in the marketplace.

After Romania joined the European Union, the economic reforms meet a new process of slowing down, amid the economic crisis and the political class action that assimilated the laws and values of the European Union at a superficial or declarative level, but, in reality, the political power continued to be in the hands of a small group of players who impose their will on the society [11]. An example in this respect is the ratio of public investment to GDP: during 2005-2008 this was over 5% of GDP in Romania, compared to over 4% in Poland, about 5% in the Czech Republic and between 3 and 5% in Hungary. However, investments in Romania have not at all materialized in the greater infrastructure, meaning highways, railways, harbour complex, irrigation systems, land etc. which required and still requires the modernization of public administration, preventing the diversion of public funds [12].

The behaviour of rent-seeking type associated with different groups or businessmen or politicians have emphasized the polarization of income and the erosion of socio-economic status of the middle class. According to statistics of European Commission (Eurostat), Romania, Bulgaria and Greece recorded in 2013 the highest level of *inequality of income distribution*. Reflecting the rate between the richest 20% of the population and the poorest 20%, this indicator increased in Romania from 4.5 in 2000 to 6.6 in 2013, representing the second highest increase after Bulgaria in this period in European Union. Apart from increasing inequalities in society, rent-seeking behavior led to the backwardness of Romania in terms of per capita income, the level of productivity, investment in human capital and in research and development, gaps that are difficult to reduce and which affect the social and economic development potential in the long term.

1.4. The Crisis of Transformation in Geopoliticial Terms

The consolidation of post-communist changes in the form of a functional post-communist capitalism and its lasting connection to global capitalism mechanisms is a priority of a valid response which the CEE region should offer to the new geopolitical context. This challenge becomes relevant to the path of changes especially when there are attempts, including via violence, to reset links in the region that have originated in the post-war international setting, which was agreed by all allies for the countries taken over by the Soviets. Frankly speaking, post-communist capitalism in the CEE region should not have been hunted by the ghosts of history, this being possible only through a clean-out in each country of the internal links tolerant of rent-seeking political recipes, a clean-out of the political control over the markets - either domestic or external, and through the avoidance of an unbalanced capitalization of the economy or of the weak structuring of the capital in terms of national economy.

Nowadays the political and military developments in the ex-Soviet area are the tip of an iceberg that freely floated on the stormy seas of post-communist changes. Its effects are not only a possible slowdown of the motivational drive towards the strategic target of post-communist capitalism that is the exit from forced inter-dependencies with a power center, but also the tragedy of witnessing a reversal of these changes. After the episode of Russia taking over territories of a sovereign state, a fear of returning into the cruise of successive transitions in the opposite direction was revived in the CEE region.

The fact that after a quarter of a century looms the spectrum of a return to a geopolitical formula of power management, which was considered to be obsolete, underlines the insufficient strength of the social determinants of liberty in this region. Therefore, more than ever there is the need to make functional the mechanisms of distributing prosperity in these countries, as these mechanisms are the only ones able to secure the post-communist capitalism project from its past record and from the revived imperial ambitions.

It is exemplary that such a strategic-risk situation makes counterproductive the rhetoric of the winner in the debate on the fall of communism, present at the start of post-communist transition, the assessment of international affairs in the bivalent winner-looser when the post-war arrangements of the allies were from the start undermined by the adversative thinking which fueled the cold war. Moreover, the geopolitical agreements made at the end of the largest global conflagration seem to be more resilient, and with recent perverse consequences, not only due to their mere reconfirmation in Helsinki in 1975, but also through the current military actions in the areas to the West of Russia's borders.

The fragile state of post-communist changes in CEE, unveiled by the rising geopolitical claims by Russia, comes on one hand from the finalizing of some processes well beyond people's expectations regarding the benefits of a political regime change and, on the other hand, from a bad political management of the functioning of democracy and the state. The reduction at a lesser extent of imbalances between prosperity versus expectations, and in some cases versus the initial promises, but especially versus economic and social model based on equal opportunities that the transition aimed to achieve, is complicating the right perception of what's at stake in the change and risks to induce social tensions, to cloud the adhesion to democratic values and principles. Social action emerges as a crucial issue in the establishment of the transformational processes, along with the respect for the law which demands the law be observed and applied in the day to day life of the society.

The social development deficit, revealed by the scarcity of projects that impact on the image of the change in the way public goods are distributed, is a well-known theme of social sensitivity and the number one issue in the consolidation of post-communist changes.

Significant for what the state of a nation with rightly-deserved expectations of better and solid economic and social development standards stands for is the fact that people are taking the risk to leave their countries to work abroad because the reforms of their economies did not solve the employment problem. If we are to point out a beneficial factor inherited from the collapsed communist system is the people's predisposition to work, to have a paid job, to manage in the end by obtaining subsistence through effort, even in the more complicated circumstances of economic migration. The same predisposition is translated into profit for the nomadic capital as the possibility to obtain a minimum wage job is there. From the structural viewpoint there is a clear risk of getting into a vicious circle of underdevelopment.

2. Central and Eastern Europe Development Map

Transformation processes have led to a certain configuration of development in the group of former socialist countries located in Central and Eastern Europe (CEE). Understanding the paths taken by these countries and highlighting Romania's position in this chapter is based on the selection of representative countries in terms of size and similarity of political and social heritage. The analysis highlights the key moments of the post-communist period: the year 1990 - triggering systemic change specific to transition; year 2000 - the start of negotiations with the EU; the years 2003 and 2006 preceding the first wave of integration for the CEE countries and subsequently for Romania and Bulgaria; the year 2009 that marked the first tangible manifestations of the economic crisis.

2.1. Background of Development in 1989

The differences between the countries of Central and Eastern Europe regarding the level of development reached at the end of the '80s and the previous experience with transformations such as "market socialism" marked the starting position in the transition to a market economy. To highlight these differences some representative countries were selected. Analysis of the situation in 1989-1990 shows the overall state of CEE economies prior to radical transformations.

Table 1.1 shows that the highest level of GDP per capita at the end of the 80's in the group of socialist countries in Central and Eastern Europe selected was reached in the Czech

Republic (state located in part of the former Czechoslovakia until 1992) and lowest in Romania. In socialist countries labor productivity was only 10.1% of the corresponding indicator in countries with developed market economy, and in Romania the indicator had the lowest level.

Export is one of the most important indicators that could provide clues about the development of national economy and its ability to compete in international markets. In 1989 CEE export recorded significantly differentiated values (as % of GDP). Bulgaria had the highest level of exports, 46% of GDP and Romania was far from that level, with only 17% of GDP in 1990.

Inflation and unemployment rates are significant indicators for analyzing the state of socialist economies. In 1989, Poland, with an inflation rate of 244.6%, was at the top of the hierarchy of the CEE countries in terms of inflation, which is largely due to the launch of the reform before 1990. Hungary experienced an inflation rate of 16.9%. Bulgaria and Romania were the only former socialist countries with walking inflation in 1990, due in fact to repressed inflation through price controls. Starting with 1991 however the state of these two countries deteriorated profoundly and they experienced significant increases in the price level.

Regarding unemployment, in 1990 the highest value was also recorded in Poland (6.1%), while the rest of the EEC countries were below 2%. This low level of unemployment was in part telling of masked partial unemployment caused by oversized staff and unrecognized status of the unemployed. In 1991 the unemployment rate was significantly higher in Bulgaria (18.5%), Poland (10.8%), Hungary (10.6%) and Romania (7.8%).

Table 1.1. Main macroeconomic indicators in selected CEE countries, 1989 to 1990

	GDP / capita ($ / capita)		Labor productivity (GDP / worker) ($ / person)		Export (% of GDP)		Unemployment rate (%)		Inflation rate (%)	
	1989	1990	1989	1990	1989	1990	1991	1992	1991	1992
Czech Republic	-	3787	17214	17859	-	39	2.3	3.3	-	-
Poland	2166	1694	12828	12100		26	10.8	13.3	76.7	45.3
Hungary	2783	3186	13275	12626	36	31	10.6	9.9	34.2	22.9
Romania	1790	1651	6454	5744	-	17	7.8	8.6	230.6	211.2
Bulgaria	2450	2377	11942	11334	46	33	18.5	13.8	338.4	91.3
Slovakia	1852	2211	15768	15498	29	27	11.1	10.9	-	-
Slovenia	-	8699	23395	22365	-	91	5.2	4.4	-	-

Source: World Bank Database www.data.worldbank.org.

Peculiarities of the economic and social state of CEE countries in the late 80's and early 1990 include issues such as:

- *The degree of centralization of the economy.* Most centralized economies were those of Czechoslovakia and Romania.
- *Entrepreneurial development in the private sector.* The privately-owned sector generated by entrepreneurial activity had significant shares in Hungary (in trade and

other services) and Poland (in agriculture, where about 75% of all farms had remained privately-owned during the communist period, with additional numerous small joint ventures with participation of capital from Polish emigrates). This feature gave a comparative advantage for the two countries in early transition.

- *The supply – demand balance on the consumer goods and services market.* While shortages were endemic in commodity markets in countries such as Poland and Romania, the markets in Czechoslovakia and Hungary were more balanced.
- *The volume of external debt* and its pressure on the economy, expressed in external debt service. Only three of the communist countries of Central and Eastern Europe faced external debt burden: Hungary, Poland and Bulgaria.
- *The standard of living and quality of life.* Two of the analyzed countries had higher performances in this area due to different circumstances: while in Hungary the standard of living was higher primarily due to the practice of public sector employees seeking a second job since the early 80s, in Czechoslovakia it was a result of a higher level of development relative to all other former communist countries. Also noteworthy is the fact that there was no significant disparity in quality of life between rural and urban areas as a result of a deliberate policy to increase the income of rural workers.
- *Mentality and favorable or hostile attitudes toward market economy.* People in countries that had previously tried reforms were more prepared, whereas in other countries only a small fraction of the population (such as specialist with contacts outside the country or intellectuals) were informed enough to favorably assess Western economies and societies, despite hostile and mystifying propaganda from the communist period.
- *Configuring a homogeneous civil society or, on the contrary, the existence of a divided society with conflicting interests group settings.* In Poland and Czechoslovakia, the presence of political parties with broad popular support (Civic Forum in the former and Solidarity in the latter) has made possible the rapid completion of the painful but necessary stages that underpinned the subsequent construction of the market economy during the first few years of transition. In contrast, in Romania, the crumbling society with numerous interest groups competing to acquire economic power was delayed in the process of law-making and creating of market institutions.
- *Dependence on the CMEA market (Council for Mutual Economic Assistance).* CMEA collapse in 1991 was an external shock that had a different impact on transition economies in relation to both their export dependence on Soviet markets and the supply of energy and raw materials from the USSR – on both counts Bulgaria seems to have been the most affected country.

These data show that Romania began the transition from a disadvantageous position relative to other countries in the same group, was less prepared, and detachment from the initial trajectory was predictably difficult.

2.2. Post-Communist Economic Performance

The negative effects of political, economic and social changes had a more powerful impact in countries that were initially less prepared for transition, such as Romania and Bulgaria. In the first ten years of transition after the initial collapse of production, all analyzed countries experienced short periods of economic growth alternating with periods of economic decline (Figure 1.1). Compared with other countries, Romania and Bulgaria needed several years to achieve the level of GDP/capita of 1990 – the process took 10 years in Romania, while in Bulgaria it took about 13 years.

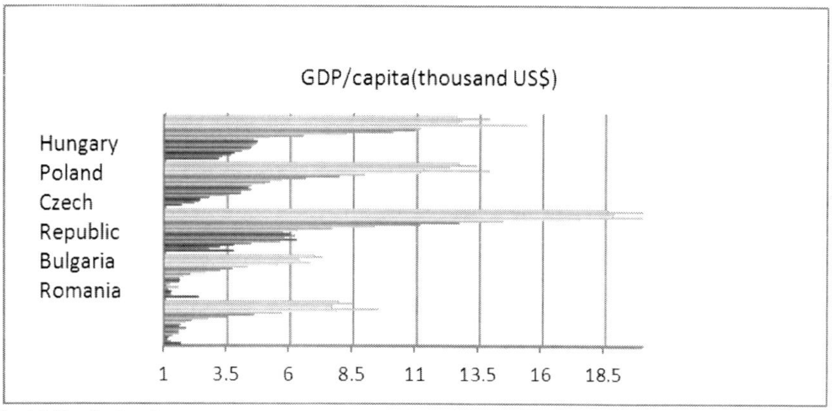

Source: World Bank database.

Figure 1.1. Evolution of GDP/capita, 1990-2012 (US$).

At the beginning of the transition, the most developed countries in the CEE group were Hungary and the Czech Republic, each registering a GDP/capita of over $3,000/capita (Table 1.2). At the end of the period, however, in 2012, it is noted that the Czech Republic maintained its position, while the performance of Hungary was exceeded by that of Poland. Among the analyzed countries, Poland recorded the highest increase in GDP/capita, while Bulgaria registered the worst performance.

Table 1.2. GDP/capita, 1990-2012 (US$)

	1990	2000	2003	2006	2009	2012
Romania	1,651	1,651	2,737	5,681	7,651	7,943
Bulgaria	2,377	1,579	2,642	4,313	6,403	6,986
Czech Republic	3,787	5,725	9,336	14,446	18,806	18,608
Poland	1,694	4,454	5,675	8,958	11,295	12,708
Hungary	3,186	4,543	8,247	11,174	12,635	12,622

Source: Data selected from the World Bank database.

Table 1.3 shows increased performance in regards to the external sector of all analyzed countries. CEE countries that have developed the most after 1990 were those that showed a significant increase in exports by reorienting their trade toward industrialized countries. In 2004, the Czech Republic, Poland and Hungary became EU member states (along with seven other countries in the CEE group). Of these, only Poland has been less prepared, with a share of exports in GDP of only 33% in the year prior to becoming an EU member (Table 1.3). However, Poland's low level of dependence on the exterior significantly reduced the effects of the global financial crisis in 2009-2010, crisis that in the EU turned into a sovereign debt crisis. The situation of Romania and Bulgaria, which joined the EU in 2007, resembles that of Poland from the point of view of the external performance.

Table 1.3. The share of exports in GDP, 1990-2012 (%)

	1990	2000	2003	2006	2009	2012
Romania	17	33	35	30	31	40
Bulgaria	33	50	49	61	48	67
Czech Republic	39	61	59	67	59	78
Poland	26	27	33	40	39	46
Hungary	31	75	61	78	78	95

Source: Data selected from the World Bank database.

The economic performance was also influenced by changes in the structure of the national economy. Table 1.4 reflects a trend of an expanding tertiary sector in the economies analyzed. At the beginning of transition all countries, except the Czech Republic, had a share of less than 50% of services in GDP, while in 2010 the share of services exceeded 50% in all these countries. Romania still has the lowest share of services in GDP, while the remaining countries have shares that are closer to the EU average of 70%.

Table 1.4. The share of services in GDP, 1990-2012 (%)

	1990	2000	2003	2006	2009	2010	2012
Romania	26	51	52	52	54	52	52
Bulgaria	34	61	62	62	64	66	63
Czech Republic	52	60	63	61	62	61	60
Poland	42	63	66	65	65	65	...
Hungary	46	62	66	66	67	65	...

Source: Data selected from the World Bank database.

In Romania, the share of services has increased also due to the lower contribution of primary and secondary sector to the GDP. At the beginning of transition in Romania agriculture had a share of 24% of the GDP, but its contribution to the GDP was significantly reduced to 6% in 2012 (Figure 1.2), which is still three times higher than the EU average. The secondary sector has decreased its relative importance to the GDP creation to 42%.

The GDP decline was considered inevitable in the early stages of the transition because of the increased foreign competition but also because of the dissolution of the CMEA. Data show that while Poland and Hungary have adopted severe measures to adjust employment, other countries avoided drastic cuts in employment. In Romania, in a first phase, the decline of employment in industry was offset by an increase of employment in the subsistence agriculture, with negative effects on labor productivity. After resuming the economic growth, the CEE countries have not returned to the level of employment in 1991, except for Bulgaria (Table 1.5). The evolution of the employment rate in Romania shows that the drastic reduction of the population employed in agriculture after 2000 was not sufficiently compensated by the increase of employment in other activities. Thus, in 2012, the employment rate in Romania was 4 percentage points lower than in 1991.

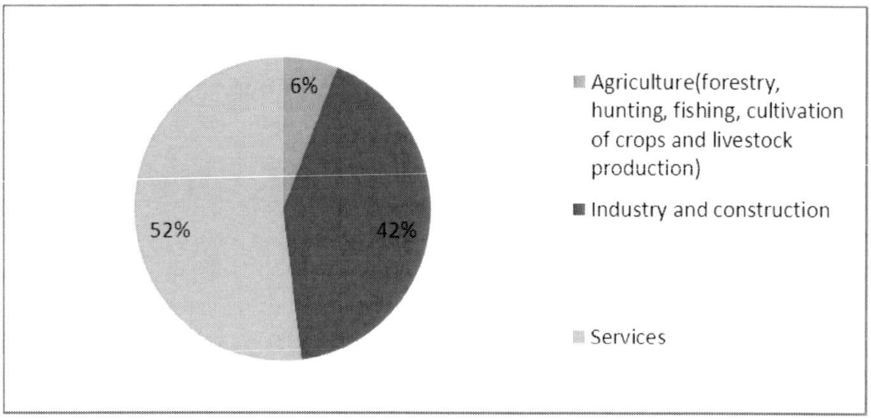

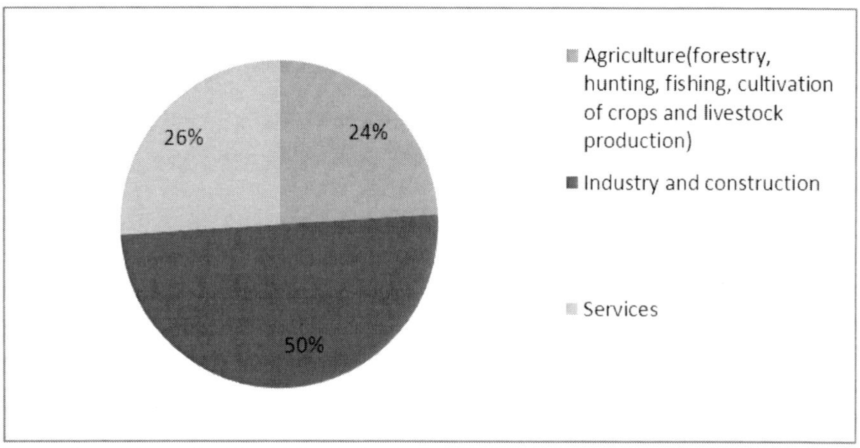

Source: Data selected from the World Bank database.

Figure 1.2. Structure of GDP in Romania, by categories of resources in 1990 and 2012.

Table 1.5. Employment rate, 1991-2012 (%)

	1991	2000	2003	2006	2009	2012
Romania	56	60	53	52	52	52
Bulgaria	47	44	43	48	51	47
Czech Republic	60	55	55	55	55	55
Poland	55	47	44	47	51	51
Hungary	49	46	47	47	45	46

Source: Data selected from the World Bank database.

Table 1.6. Productivity per person employed, 1991-2012 (GDP/person employed, prices constant 1990 PPP$)

	1990	2000	2003	2006	2009	2012
Romania	5744	6350	8352	10442	11315	11584
Bulgaria	11334	13625	15299	16991	17604	20210
Czech Republic	17859	19909	21860	25368	20735	26781
Poland	12100	19480	22163	24085	25219	27502
Hungary	12626	16218	18299	20884	20392	20328

Source: Data selected from the World Bank database.

The tendency to restrict employment, as well as the economic growth after 2000 have positively influenced labor productivity in CEE countries (Table 1.6). Romania and Poland stand out as they doubled their productivity in 1990-2012.

The real convergence for the countries that joined the EU in 2007 was hampered by the social cost of transition. Over the last two decades, the social policy in the CEE countries has had a different evolution specific to the development of each country. Clearly social tensions have raised concerns about the extent to which the Central and Eastern Europe moves towards the European Social Model and the most appropriate path for each country in the context of a diversity of economic and political models.

2.3. Competitiveness and Vulnerabilities of the Romanian Economy

The meaning of the post-communist transformation has been to increase economic competitiveness as a prerequisite for the welfare improvement. The shocks induced by the transition to the market economy and recently by the global crisis starting in 2008 put to the test the potential of economic development and revealed the malfunctions that make the systems vulnerable.

The vulnerabilities of a national economy are currently relevant only when analyzed in the context of the globalization process, driven by trade openness, gradual deregulation of markets, accelerated technological progress, new organization structures of companies etc.

The scientific concept of vulnerability defined by the global change literature is multidimensional and provides a useful framework for analyzing the consequences of these changes on human societies. One of its facets is the economic vulnerability, which has various definitions and interpretations [13]. In the simplest way it can be associated with a disturbance that affects any kind of economic activity as a result of exposure to factors that produce shocks. The risk of a country to be affected by shocks depends on the size and likelihood of shock, the exposure to shocks and the ability of the economy to respond to shocks.

Romania's transition to the market economy and the accession to the European Union occurred in the conditions of growing economic interdependence and competition on global markets. Thus, while becoming an open economy, Romania's economy increased its vulnerability because of its low level of competitiveness and resilience to external or internal shocks.

a. Competitiveness and Internal Vulnerabilities

The review of the first ten years of transition in Romania [14] highlights successive major shocks generated by the transformation process:

1990-1993: "The first transformational recession," characterized by a severe downturn of production and high inflation.

1993-1994: The interest rate shock determined by the substantial increase of the nominal interest rate (the refinancing rate reached 136.6% in 1994), after a period of pronounced negative interest rates until the end of 1993.

1997: "The second transformational recession" as a result of the economic policy shock induced by the liberalization of the foreign exchange market and by a new stage of price liberalization.

The year 1999 was marked by the risk of sovereign default and the danger of a banking crisis as consequential effects of significant non-performing loans and insufficient foreign exchange reserves of the National Bank.

The institutional fragility and the low capacity of structural adjustment in the real economy were the vulnerabilities of the first decade of post-communist transformation. Lack of vision to be followed, insufficient government reform experience, as well as postponing of reallocation of resources to efficient activities because of social costs, have delayed the entering of the Romanian economy on a coherent and sustainable development path.

Since 2000 Romania had enjoyed a period of sustained economic growth and in 2003 capitalized the historic opportunity of entering into partnership for accession to the European Union. In the new context created by the EU by means of pre-accession instruments (PHARE, ISPA and SAPARD programmes) and assistance for increasing the administrative capacity, the institutional building process started with the implementation of the *aquis communautaire* and the modernization of real economy speeded up.

On the eve of its accession to the EU (2006), Romania had a lower global competitiveness level compared to the countries that joined the EU in 2004 (EU10), according to the *Global Competitiveness Index* (GCI). This index proposed by Xavier Sala-i-Martin in 2004 at the World Economic Forum measures the productivity level that a national economy is able to support by means of specific drivers, considering that productivity plays a critical role for growth and prosperity.

The global competitiveness gaps are estimated by using relevant indicators of the competitiveness pillars. The scores measured on a scale from 1 to 7 (where 7 is the best level) show that during the period 2006-2007 Romania had all the specific drivers (pillars) under the EU10 average, as well as under the EU25 average (Figure 1.3). The competitiveness pillar with the nearest value to the EU average was „Health and primary education." Despite these differences, Romania is placed in the second stage of development together with countries where economic growth relies on the improvement of factor use efficiency. Changes during the post-accession period have influenced the competitiveness pillars (Figure 1.4). Recently, the shock caused by the economic crisis contributed to the downturn in business, innovation and institutional capacity. The significant deterioration of the health and education factors, on the one hand, and improvement of the macroeconomic conditions, on the other hand were two major changes during 2006-2012. The Global Competitiveness Report prepared by the World Economic Forum for 2012-2013 shows that Romania ranked 78th out of 144 countries, being behind all EU member countries except Croatia and Greece. Detailed analysis of the pillars that sustain competitiveness (Appendix 1) presents a more nuanced picture of the factors that impede competitiveness improvement and that basically contribute to a certain vulnerability degree both in the short and in the long run. In this subchapter the selection of shortcomings in the case of Romania used the criterion of scores below 3.5 (half of the maximum level 7).

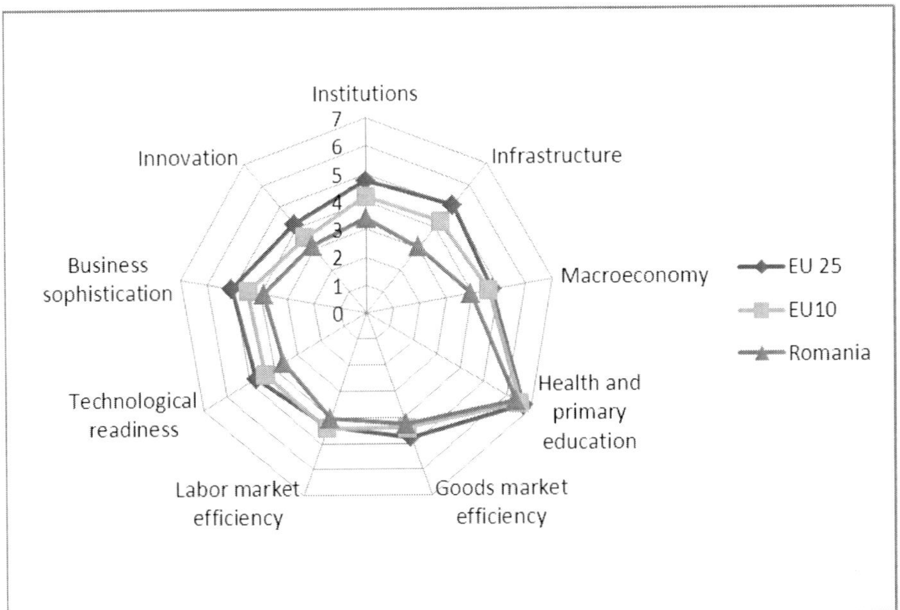

Source: data from the Global Competitiveness Report 2006-2007 and 2012-2013, and [5].

Figure 1.3. The Global Competitiveness Index for Romania compared to EU countries, 2006-2007.

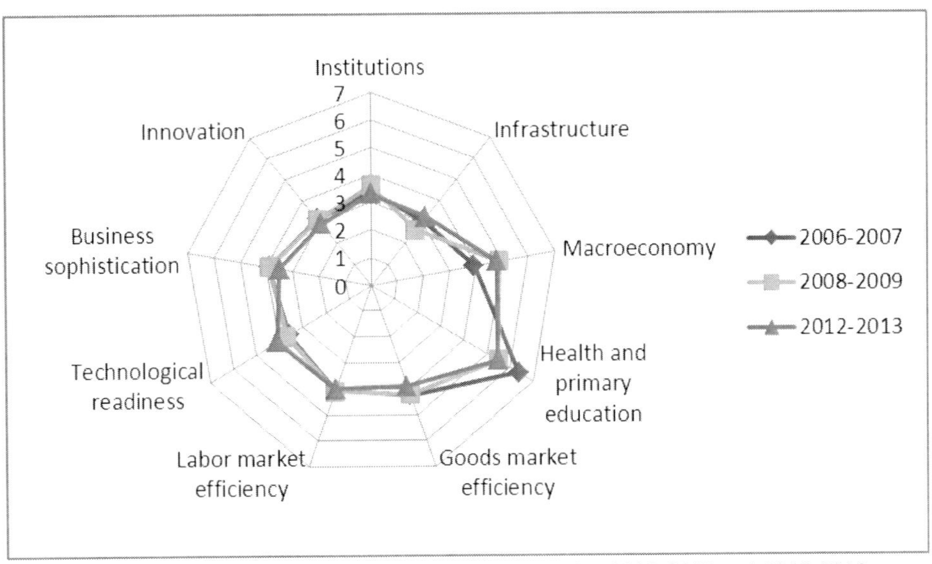

Source: data from the Global Competitiveness Report 2006-2007, 2008-2009 and 2012-2013.

Figure 1.4. The Global Competitiveness Index for Romania, 2006-2007, 2008-2009, 2012-2013.

Thus, referring to the *basic requirements* of competitiveness (weighted at 40% of the overall GCI score), the most deficient components are the institutions and the infrastructure.

The fragility of institutions remains one of the major problems, being associated with low public trust of politicians, favoritism in government officials' decisions, diversion of public funds, interference with judicial independence, waste of public funds etc. The condition of the transport infrastructure hinders the business development and delays the overall economic development. The perpetuation of this situation could be construed as a result of successive inefficient governments given that big infrastructure projects are under their responsibility.

A negative signal about providing the basic requirements of competitiveness is the deterioration of people's health and primary education, even if those scores are still better compared to other components. Changes in recent years reflect the loss of a competitive advantage resulting from the worsening of the functionality and quality of the education and health systems. The course of these components indicates a long term vulnerability, which has been stated in all Romania's development strategies, but empirical evidence show the unwelcomed results of several inconsistent reforms of the two systems.

Factors that are *efficiency enhancers* (weighted at 50% of the overall GCI score) refer to highly educated workforce, market efficiency and competitiveness at microeconomic level.

The highly qualified workforce is seen as key factor of the GCI. In Romania the quality of the educational system is quoted relatively low (score 3.1 out of maximum 7 in 2012), while the postgraduate training is similarly assessed. This situation induces long term vulnerability, since the system does not prepare enough skilled workforce needed to modernize the economy. This fact is aggravated by the severe „brain-drain" process of the last two decades.

Regarding the market for goods and services, the aspects that do not respond sufficiently to the requirements of efficiency enhancement involve the government institutions, especially in the field of agricultural policy costs, efficiency of legal framework and effects of taxation. According to the competitiveness report, the factors that *hindered the most* the efficient running of business were (in 2011): corruption, taxation, bureaucracy, access to loans, fiscal regulations, inadequate infrastructure, inflation and policy instability. Noteworthy is that in 2008-2009 the most problematic factor was the instability of public policies, generating low predictability of the business environment, and in 2011 corruption reached the first place.

The *financial markets* have low sophistication, companies have difficult access to loans and the venture capital is scarce. Lack of domestic capital has been a reality since early '90s. The Romanian banking system has gone through a comprehensive reform process, by trying to introduce financial discipline in the economy. The reinforcement of strong constraints has been postponed all the time under political pressure to back up the state-owned companies by the state-owned banks. The bankruptcy of a large state-owned bank (Bancorex) in 1999 was a clear signal that any bank can get into a similar situation. Like in other areas, on the financial and monetary market the emergence of the private sector started with small initiatives aimed at collecting money from the public. In addition to this source of financing the real economy, on the Romanian market the foreign capital was another major source of private money. The privatization of banks was done mostly with foreign capital (currently there are 39 institutions of the banking system, of which 25 banks with majority foreign capital and 8 foreign bank branches) and solved the problem of financial discipline, but reduced the access of companies to loans. The vulnerability created by the dependency of the economy on foreign capital was obvious during the economic crisis (2009-2010), when the withdrawal of capital by foreign banks could become a dangerous reality for financing the Romanian economy. The development of the capital market and the utilization of this important funding source depended on the ability of entrepreneurs to create national networks. A major advantage was the capacity to collect from the public certificates of ownership and privatization vouchers that could be converted into shares of pre-determined companies. Unfortunately, during the first years of transition the capital market was dominated by the domestic capital, which was totally insufficient compared with the requirements of the economic development. This has prevented the companies from funding through the capital market.

The sophistication of production is another aspect of competitiveness that reveals deficiencies of the production system in Romania. The restructuring of production that took place along with the development of the private sector, due to the initiative of entrepreneurs as well as to the privatization of state-owned companies, led to the fragmentation of previous production chains and sales channels. The new successful companies, many of them privatized with foreign capital, were inserted in the international production chains. These companies rely heavily on imported supplies and re-export most of their production. The low score in this area indicates the predominance of less sophisticated value chain activities, since activities with high value added, such as R&D and innovation, are located abroad. Under this conditions defining the competitive advantage in certain industries is still a problem (score 3.0 in 2012-2013). This strong fragmentation, often justified by the low quality of products that could be supplied by domestic companies, does not allow for a significant development of the domestic market. It was noticed that during difficult periods like the recent crisis the economies with consolidated domestic markets had no downturn of the GDP (i.e., Poland) or recovered faster. In Romania, the export increased as driver of economic growth, but without the building and consolidation of the domestic production chains, it indicated and still indicates competitiveness deficiencies and also vulnerability to external shocks.

The *innovation* component of the Romanian economy's competitiveness (weighted at 10% of the overall GCI score) is the most lagging behind the EU average. Obviously the economy is not prepared for the innovation-driven development stage. The reduced concern of private companies for financing research and the low transfer of knowledge and technology from universities to companies are major causes of stagnation in this field. Chronic underfunding of research and weak demand of the private sector on the market for innovative goods and services undermine the research potential in Romania and encourage „brain-drain" and „brain-waste." In addition, the effect of any economic shock is the reduction in first place of the research funding, followed by the loss of other research resources.

b. Vulnerabilities in Relation to the Foreign Environment

The Romanian economy presents a number of vulnerabilities caused by the imbalance of the relations with the foreign environment. Thus, the first vulnerability is the high level of external indebtedness. While at the beginning of the transition period the external debt was insignificant, at the end of 2012, it reached 98,968 million euro. The structure of the external debt at the end of 2012 shows that most of it was represented by the private non-guaranteed debt (47%), followed by the external public debt (30%) and loans from the IMF (11%). The indebtedness rate of the private sector has increased steadily, on the one hand, because of its low competitiveness, and on the other hand, because of the dependence on imports, since the Romanian society presents a high risk of turning into a society based on consumption.

Also, after 1989 the national economy faced a steady increase in domestic public debt. Thus, according to the data provided by the National Bank of Romania, in 2012 the share of the public debt (internal and external) in GDP reached 37.8%. Although the national economy does not present an excessive level of public debt, given the fact that the Maastricht Treaty established that a debt below 60% of the GDP is sustainable, its growth rate is alarming. A contributing factor to increasing the level of the external debt is the underperformance of the national economy.

One of the problems that the Romanian economy had to face was the insufficient experience in the management of public debt and budget deficits. Related to the improvement of the management of the internal debt, a decisive moment was in 1997 when new regulations were adopted regarding transactions with government securities, the development of the secondary market for government securities, the restriction of access to external sources of financing and also the take-over of a significant amount of non-performing loans to the public debt. The restructuring of the banking sector made it possible that the share of state loans approved by special legislation reach 30% in 1998-1999.

Another external vulnerability is the persistence of the current account imbalance. In the period after 1989, the imbalance between production and consumption widened significantly, being a cause of the worsening of the current account. Imports were paid from the savings of other countries, as an important part of the money in the banks which was lent to the population for consumption or to companies for production came from other countries. These aspects are included in the unfavorable evolution of the external account, which recorded significant deficits of up to 14%, although the economic theory regulates that restrictive measures should be adopted when the negative balance exceeds the 6% level. Although exports have increased in the early stages of the transition period, the import growth outpaced the exports, and this trade deficit caused the increase of the negative balance of the current account.

Another external vulnerability is the low level of foreign investment. Processes specific to the transition such as privatization and liberalization attracted both direct and portfolio foreign investment. In the first decade of the transition, 1997 was marked by the largest volume of foreign portfolio investments attracted by the national economy. The level of the foreign capital was significantly higher than the volume of the local capital and had a higher legitimacy from the public given the fact that it had both a technological and an organizational know-how. In this context, the international financial institutions such as the World Bank and IMF supported the restructuring of the national economy.

CONCLUSION

The pro-capitalist option of the CEE countries after the communist experiment meant the return to an evolution that had been interrupted in 1945. The reactivation of the social memory in connection to the pre-war experience, to private property first of all, was a driving force for reforms. The release of market forces from the major political and administrative constraints of the centralized economy and the gradual enforcement of the functional market mechanisms did not implicitly generate increase of economic competitiveness and welfare according to people's expectations. The social development deficit in the context of rising geopolitical instability indicates the still fragile state of post-communist changes.

During the post-communist transformation process the structures of the real economy faced successive shocks from which the more prepared CEE countries recovered faster. Romania, having significant domestic vulnerabilities, had to bear larger economic fluctuations with more persistent effects. In 2012 the analyzed CEE countries achieved a GDP/capita of about 3-7 times higher than in 1990, representing an important positive result of the transformations.

Despite its deep structural distortions, in conditions of delayed and less consistent reform actions, Romania reached the efficiency-driven development stage in the period of pre-accession to the European Union (according to the Global Competitiveness Report). Even if the macroeconomic environment has improved, mostly under the pressure of the EU and IMF, the drivers of efficiency at microeconomic level are still under the influence of negative characteristics of unfinished post-communist transformations and of the dominance of politics over economy (i.e., extended bureaucracy, corruption, unstable economic policy measures etc.).

The quality of economic growth and the further reduction of vulnerabilities depend on the quality of structural transformations and on the development of the domestic market. Although there are numerous development strategies elaborated over time, the evidence indicates that factors which determine the competitiveness increase in the long-term, mainly human capital, R&D and innovation capacity are neglected by underfunding in favor of other factors with short-run impact, usually of social kind, having implications on the political capital of ruling parties.

APPENDIX 1

Table 1.7. Global competitiveness index, selection of Romania´s most problematic factors within the main pillars, 2006-2007 and 2012-2013 (Scores 1-7)

	EU25	EU10*	Romania	
Indicator	2006-2007		2006-2007	2012-2013
1.Institutions	4.76	4.17	3.40	3.3
Diversion of public funds	5.05	4.22	3.15	2.5
Public trust of politicians	3.41	2.58	1.64	1.8
Judicial independence	5.01	4.26	2.88	2.7
Favoritism in decisions of government officials	3.76	3.06	2.24	2.4
Wastefulness of government spending	3.64	3.21	2.46	2.5
Burden of government regulations	3.21	3.11	3.10	2.8
2.Infrastructure	5.03	4.28	3.05	3.2
Overall infrastructure quality	5.11	4.34	2.36	2.8
Railroad infrastructure development	4.37	3.43	2.86	2.2
Quality of road infrastructure	...	...	...	1.9
Quality of port infrastructure	4.85	4.09	3.12	2.6
3. Macro-economy	4.76	4.62	3.94	4.8
4. Health and primary education	6.71	6.54	6.38	5.5

Table 1.7. (Continued)

	EU25	EU10*	Romania	
	2006-2007		2006-2007	2012-2013
5. Higher education and training	5.15	4.84	4.34	4.4
Quality of the educational system	...	...	...	3.1
Extent of staff training	4.70	4.11	3.29	3.4
6. Market efficiency	4.73	4.44	4.03	...
A. Goods markets				
Agricultural policy costs	3.75	3.71	3.22	3.3
Efficiency of legal framework	4.85	4.11	3.07	3.4
Extent and effect of taxation	3.44	3.69	2.44	2.2
Buyer sophistication	...	...	...	3.0
B. Labor markets				
Cooperation in labor-employer relation	...	...	...	3.2
Brain drain	4.08	3.52	2.16	2.1
C. Financial markets				
Financial market sophistication	5.20	4.36	3.09	...
Ease of access to loans	4.36	3.95	3.41	2.7
Venture capital availability	4.16	3.60	3.04	2.5
7. Technological readiness	4.74	4.38	3.59	4.10
8. Business sophistication	5.07	4.46	3.89	3.50
Production process sophistication	4.96	4.18	3.31	3.2
Willingness to delegate authority	4.51	3.89	3.47	3.2
Nature of competitive advantage	4.69	3.71	2.64	3.0
Value chain breadth	5.20	4.44	3.29	3.3
9. Innovation	4.17	3.54	3.14	2.90
Company spending on research and development	4.11	3.52	3.07	2.9
University/industry research collaboration	4.01	3.47	2.86	3.1
Intellectual property protection	4.99	4.04	3.13	2.9
Capacity for innovation	4.53	3.77	2.87	3.1

* EU10 Accession countries.

Source: The Global Competitiveness Report 2006-2007 and 2012-2013; Jennifer Blanke and Irene Mia – Turkey's competitiveness in a European Context, 2006 World Economic Forum, Switzerland.

References

[1] Dinu, M, Brateş, T. (2014), Răzbunarea trecutului. Capitalismul în cinci luni postdecembriste, Economică Publishing.

[2] Sachs, J. (1993), Poland's Jump to the Market Economy, Cambridge: MIT Press.

[3] Postolache, T., coord.(1990), Schiţa privind strategia înfăptuirii economiei de piaţă în România, INCE, Bucharest.

[4] Croitoru, L. (2010), *A false problem*: the *compromise between external coercion and social imperatives* – Presented at the conference "Romania 2010: Between financial constraints and social imperatives," the 21st of June 2010, National bank of Romania.

[5] Stiglitz, J. (2013), The price of inequality, Publica Publishing House, Bucharest.

[6] Krueger, A. (1974), The Political Economy of the Rent-Seeking Society, *American Economic Review,* Vol. 64, No. 3 (Jun., 1974), pp. 291-303.

[7] Smith, A. (1962), The Wealth of Nations, Romanian Academy Publishing House, Bucharest.

[8] Giosan, V. (2013), How to stop the political assault on democracy?, Romanian Centre of European Policies.

[9] Dăianu, D.; Vrânceanu, R (2006), *Ethical boundaries of capitalism*, Polirom Publishing House, Iaşi.

[10] Cerna, S. (2011), *Transition and interest groups*, ŒCONOMICA no. 2/2011.

[11] Gallagher, T. (2010), *Romania lost decade. The mirage of European integration since 2000*, ALL Publishing House, Bucharest.

[12] Dăianu, D. (2012), *When finance corrodes* the *economy and undermines* the *democracy*, Polirom Publishing House, Iaşi.

[13] Mesjasz, C. (2011), Economic Vulnerability and Economic Security in: Brauch, H. G. et al.(eds.) (2011) – Coping with Global Environmental Change, Disasters and Security, Hexagon Series on Human and Environmental Security, vol.5, Springer Verlag Berlin, Heidelberg, pg.142-143.

[14] Rühl, C., Dăianu, D. (coord) (1999), Tranziţia economic în România. Trecut, prezent şi viitor, Arta Grafică, Bucharest, pg.12-24.

[15] Blanke, J., Irene Mia, I. (2006), Turkey's competitiveness in a European Context, 2006 World Economic Forum, Switzerland, http://www.weforum.org/pdf/Turkey/ Competitiveness.pdf

In: What/Who Are We After the Transition? Focus on Romania ISBN: 978-1-63483-947-1
Editors: M. Dinu, D. Ailenei, A. Dachin et al.

Chapter 2

PRIVATE PROPERTY REFORM

Dorel Ailenei*[*]*, PhD, Dumitru-Alexandru Bodislav, PhD, Liliana Crăciun, PhD, Cosmin Liviu Mosora, PhD, Marius Pană, PhD, Raluca Andreea Popa, PhD and Daniela Vîrjan, PhD
Bucharest University of Economics Studies, Bucharest, Romania

The return to capitalism in Central and Eastern Europe was a unique global experience, both in terms of perspective and size, but also in terms of the complexity of historical dynamics. A central element of these changes was the reform of private property - a process that involved major changes in social institutions and public perspective. The transition from quasi-communist dominance of state property to private property domination was marked by the privatization of hundreds of thousands of businesses, millions of apartments and homes, and the retrocession of an impressive number of buildings and most of the agriculture land in Central and Eastern Europe.

Faced with a huge amount of properties to be privatized and the novelty of such situation Central and Eastern Europe countries tried several methods of privatization that could be summarized as: open and direct sale, privatization to managers or employees, mass privatization, retrocession and bankruptcy/liquidation.

1. PRIVATIZATION OF STATE COMPANIES

The eighth decade of the last century was marked by what the theory of economic development called "free market model counterattack" [1]. Under the influence of the Supply Side Policy promoted by Ronald Reagan in the USA and Margaret Thatcher in the United Kingdom, the countries in Western Europe triggered a major wave of privatization, starting with France and the UK in 1986, followed by Italy, Spain and Germany in 1993. Meanwhile

---

[*] Author passed away

the collapse of communism, triggered by Reagan's military and economic policy, the privatization wave turned into a tsunami in the Central and Eastern Europe countries.

Table 2.1. The share of the private sector in GDP and employment in CEE

Country / year	In GDP				In Employment			
	1991	1995	2002	2010	1991	1995	2001	2009
Albania	24	60	75	75	..	74	82	83
Bulgaria	17	50	75	75	10	41	81	76
Czech Republic	17	70	80	..	19	57	70	..
Croatia	25	40	60	70	22	48	..	70
Estonia	18	65	80	80	11	..	..	..
Latvia	..	55	70	70	12	60	73	..
Lithuania	15	65	75	75	16	...	...	..
Macedonia	..	40	60	..	..	..	..	70
Moldova	..	30	50	65	36	..	..	..
Poland	45	60	75	75	51	61	72	73,9
Romania	24	45	65	70	34	51	55	69
Russia	10	55	70	65	5	..	..	..
Slovakia	..	60	80	80	13	60	75	..
Slovenia	16	50	65	70	18	48	..	..
Ukraine	8	45	65	60	..	..	..	..
Hungary	33	60	80	80	...	71	...	..
Averages	21	53	70	72				

Source: EBRD, Transition Report, 1999, 2003, 2013 [5].

This historical experience proved to be unprecedented and shadowed the privatization in Western Europe, including over 150,000 large, medium and small companies, to which over 5 million apartments and homes were added [2]. The difference between the two processes of privatization was that the Western model of privatization did not work in Eastern Europe [3]. While the privatization in Western Europe aimed at streamlining the public sector and took place within the market economy, the privatization in Eastern Europe aimed to recreate the market economy itself on the ruins of communist systems [3, 4]. However, in a short historical period the private sector increased exponentially, reaching about 70% of the GDP in the former communist countries (Table 2.1.).

We can observe the heterogeneity of the initial state before privatization, the advanced positions of Poland (45% private sector) and Hungary (33% private sector) and the amazing progress of the Czech Republic (where the private sector increased from 17% in 1991 to 70% in 1995, but also in Romania where it reached majority in 1996), the significant difference in performance in the transition towards a market economy.

1.1. Methods of Privatization of State Companies

Given the large number of state companies and their diversity there were used several combinations of privatization methods, depending on the phase of the privatization process. Across CEE countries, the main privatization methods varied depending on economic and social circumstances, the historical communist background, the share of the private sector in early transition, etc. [6]. From this perspective, it is interesting to see the emphasis on these methods in initializing the privatization process as complementary methods (secondary) in stimulating privatization itself (Table 2.2.).

In Romania, the MEBO (Management Employee Buy Out - MEBO) and privatization through direct sale to foreign investors methods were those that were most used. Overall it can be said that all privatization methods were used in Romania, with different impact in time, from the test privatization period between 1991 - 1994, to the mass privatization period between 1995 - 1996 (The Great Coupon). Experiencing these methods, made the private sector greater than the public sector in terms of GDP, reaching 54.1% of GDP in 1996 (RCEP). In the next period (1996-1999) the private sector grew both through direct sales and through the reduction of the state sector as a result of a wave of liquidation/bankruptcy of some large state companies. In 1997 the first privatizations took place through the capital market (Table 2.3.).

Table 2.2. Methods of privatization in CEE countries

Country	Primary method			Secondary method		
	Direct sales	MEBOs	Vouchers	Direct sales	MEBOs	Vouchers
Albania		X				X
Bulgaria	X					X
Czech Republic			X	X		
Croatia		X				X
Estonia	X					X
Latvia			X	X		
Lithuania			X	X		
Macedonia		X		X		
Moldova			X	X		
Poland	X				X	
Romania		X		X		
Russia			X	X		
Slovakia	X					X
Slovenia		X				X
Ukraine			X		X	
Hungary	X				X	

Source: EBRD, Transition Report [5].

Table 2.3. Privatization methods in the period 1996 – 1999

Year	Privatization settled by auction	Privatization through direct sale of companies	Privatization through IPOs	TOTAL
1996	455	1006	-	1461
1997	231	1064	9	1304
1998	991	244	32	1267
1999	1333	272	71	1676

Source: RCEP, Study no. 13 - http://www.cerope.ro/pub/study13ro.htm [7].

After the year 2000 the privatization process increased as a result of starting the negotiations of the chapters for the accession of Romania to the European Union and due to the significant increase in Foreign Direct Investments flows. The accession of Romania to EU in 2007 reinforced the dominance of the private sector in the economy of our country, marking the end of the first stage of the transition to the market economy.

From a microeconomic perspective, the private and the newly founded companies best developed during the 1990 decade [8]. Regarding the macroeconomic perspective, most experts argue that the main objective of privatization was not economic efficiency but the separation of politics from economy and the establishment of a functional foundation of the market economy. Even if the amounts collected from the state budget were relatively modest in most CEE countries in 1995 they accounted for less than 2% of the GDP in 9 of the 14 analyzed, the great advantage of the privatization process was to accelerate social reforms and the consolidation of democracy during the transition to the dominance of private property.

2. The Retrocession of Land and Real Estate

Used extensively throughout Central and Eastern Europe, this form of privatization was heavily supported by the public who validated it as legitimate. The popularity of this method of privatization is an important argument that the owner instinct was not annihilated during the communist period and that the collective memory retained the essence of capitalism before the forced establishment of communism.

However, from a practical point of view, the property retrocession encountered many obstacles and generated many conflicts. Most of them because of the inherent difficulties of the property rights reconstruction process of reconstruction. The complexity of this process lies in several factors:

- The action involves the translation of certain relations between society and a historical time of the society. Firstly, this means understanding of those social relations of the past, the "spirit of the law." Not knowing the economic, social and political characteristics of the past and the inadequate preparation of the population in the present could result in a "*transplant failure*." In addition, the international context, as well as the obligations of the country in which the reconstruction process takes place greatly influences the success of the process.

- Structuring the property rights in social terms affects the resource allocation and thus the way the individual's needs are desires are met. As a result, the interest relationships between individuals are affected and the quality of the political environment will make a decisive mark on the reformation of the property.
- The rights are attributed to citizens, groups, organizations or institutions etc. from a certain historical period, but the reconstruction is considering similar entities identified by various procedures for determining the route of succession (certified or implied). There are often disputes that arise between heirs about sharing the property and its related rights.
- The object of property rights is sometimes difficult to identify and especially to assess given period of time between the allocation of rights and the reconstruction. More often than not, moral and conditional depreciation occurs, improvements due to investments for modernization and the economic context of assessment varies from one period to another. In addition, the Second World War, the Communism and other major events destroyed a significant part of the historically documented evidence of property rights that described the characteristics of the property objects.
- The entire society changes starting with assigning the property rights (and the unfair confiscation) and till the reconstruction. People, institutions, political parties and the international context were different at the moment of the reconstitution of property rights.
- The balance of power between political parties, their succession in office and the formation of coalitions, the relationship between politicians and the civil society etc. have had a decisive influence on the reconstitution of property rights and the their social validation and we could state that they still do.

2.1. The Reconstruction of Property Rights on Land

Some of the first attempts to reconstruct the property as founding principles aimed at the agricultural property. In 1991 the Land Law was passed (Law no. 18/1991). The steps to redefine the property rights on land were shy. The main obstacle were the limitations on refunds. Thus, every family entitled could benefit from refunds ranging from 0.5 ha to 10 ha.

Provisions of this kind produced two effects: on the one hand, they created only a partial reconstruction of property rights for certain families, and on the other hand, they led to arbitrary appropriation of families who did not own any agricultural land. There were later attempts to fix these limitations in the reconstruction of property rights by Law No. 1/2000, but it was too late since there were few reserves of land not distributed. Thus, the restorative effects were overcome by new conflicts created between legitimate owners of land and those who were arbitrarily distributed land to, severely undermining the social consensus needed to make the transition to a market economy.

Beyond the errors and abuses of the land retrocession process it is important that this form of privatization contributed decisively to the increase of the share of private ownership in the Romanian economy.

2.2. Private Property Reform and the Restitution of Nationalized Houses

The legislative initiatives designed to regulate the issue of the houses confiscated during the communist regime appeared quite late in the legislative concerns of Romania. Although the Constitution adopted in 1991 guaranteed property rights and ensured its protection regardless of the person, the first major initiative to reinstate the confiscated properties would appear only in 1995 (Law no. 112 for nationalized houses).

Far from providing even a moral reparation on properties confiscated, the institutional arrangements strengthened gradually since the second half of the '90s would significantly distort the significance of property right. The hesitation on the recognition of the essential role of ownership in setting up market relations, led to surrogate measures for the reconstruction of property rights whose main goal was apparently to identify a consensus. The institutional solutions that followed could not solve the problem of retrocession. Instead, they created more confusion both because of the provisions contained, for example Law. 10/2001, and of the many changes that followed the adoption.

Although there could exist only one rightful de facto and de jure owner, the legislation made it possible for both tenants and certain officials to become owners with legal papers and full rights. Some of them took this position automatically, by law, and others by obscure paths opened by certain inconsistencies in the legislation.

That is why there emerged a parallel "market" in which litigious rights were traded by persons with leverage who can influence a favorable settlement. Thus the private ownership right became the subject of some speculation.

Another initiative in this respect was the law on the establishment of the Property Fund, which proposed the repayment in shares of the property confiscated by the communist regime in Romania. This refers to those properties that could no longer be returned in kind as currently they are used with an entirely different purpose than the original, or they are used by the Romanian state. By law, these owners would receive compensation in the form of shares in the Fund, but the European Court of Human Rights (ECHR) warned Romania that these claims are "*inconsistent and disproportionate to the value of the property lost*" [9].

3. Private Property Reform and Entrepreneurial Revival

The essential problem of the Romanian business environment in the post-communist period was the revival of "the entrepreneurship spirit."

The volume, quality and intensity of the entrepreneurial activity, its orientation towards productivity or not, are the consequences of certain favorable economic and social conditions. Therefore, the analysis of the quality of entrepreneurial activity should be correlated with the evolution of institutional arrangements and their implications for the business environment.

3.1. Regulations of the Entrepreneurial Activity

The frequent changes in legislation induce instability in all areas of social life. The legislative instability was marked by frequent changes of laws essential for the regulation (formal) of any entrepreneurial activity. Based on the nature of the institutional framework we can distinguish the following types of entrepreneurial activity [10]: *productive* (incentives guiding entrepreneurs towards activities with social benefits), *evasive* (formal institutions provide incentives for entrepreneurs to ignore and avoid the formal institutional framework). The most common causes that lead to such a behavior of entrepreneurs are the high rates of taxation, regulation and legislative instability. The third type is the *destructive entrepreneurship* that occurs when formal institutions are not stable and are handled, which leads to some incentives for entrepreneurs to exploit formal rules, getting revenue from activities protected by the law, on account of the losses borne by consumers and taxpayers (rent-seeking).

For this reason, the quality and institutional stability can determine the predominant type of entrepreneurial activity and thus the overall economic efficiency. There are a number of factors and conditions that had important consequences. For example, the instability of the tax system is often invoked as a factor that inhibits entrepreneurship. Entrepreneurship is not discouraged just by taxation and the negative effect that it generates on the property value, but also the obstacles against the private initiative as a consequence of economic freedom. In a study of some of the former socialist countries, including Romania, Mole identified this constraint as one of the most severe in the way of entrepreneurship [10]. Frequent changes confuse entrepreneurs and it makes them reassess their options for opening a business.

The tax regime that a middle-sized company in Romania has to put up with is very tough. As shown in a World Bank study conducted to assess the attractiveness of the various business environments in 2007, the developer had to pay directly, withhold or remit a total of 89 taxes, well above the average for countries situated in Europe and Central Asia, which was 48.3. As a result of tax laws, businesses in Romania had lost not only in terms of the value of their property, but also in terms of time resources allocated to preparing the documentation required by the authorities. Thus, in order to fulfill all legal requirements concerning the preparation of documents necessary for the payment of the income tax, the value added tax and the social security contributions, for which there were required 198 hours annually.

Encouraging entrepreneurship is very important for creating new businesses. Beyond this deficiency, Romania and Poland were considered performers in terms of developing new private companies according to a study conducted in 1999.

4. The Contribution of Foreign Direct Investment to Strenghten the Private Property

Most specialized studies show that foreign direct investment (FDI) has a positive impact on economic growth. For this, however, national economies should benefit from certain institutional and economic characteristics: a high degree of political and macroeconomic stability, the institutional system of law rule, the prevalence of the principles and mechanisms of the market economy, a skilled labor force and the openness of the economy to external markets.

In the early 1990s, Romania was perceived by investors as a relatively risky economy. The Romanian economy went progressively from a lack of experience in investing to creating an investment environment more and more efficient and effective.

The analyses conducted by the World Bank and the World Economic Forum shows that in order for the Romanian investment environment to become more efficient some reforms should be prioritized: *improvement of infrastructure; simplification of tax procedures; combating corruption; strengthening financial and capital markets; enhancing the absorption of European funds*.

Until 2003, most foreign investors in Romania were not in the category of the strategic ones, but rather a small or medium economic force mainly interested in trade and services. Since 2000, when the accession negotiations for the EU started, the business credibility of Romania increased significantly, large privatizations were triggered, which significantly increased the attractiveness of the national economy for foreign investors (Figure 2.1).

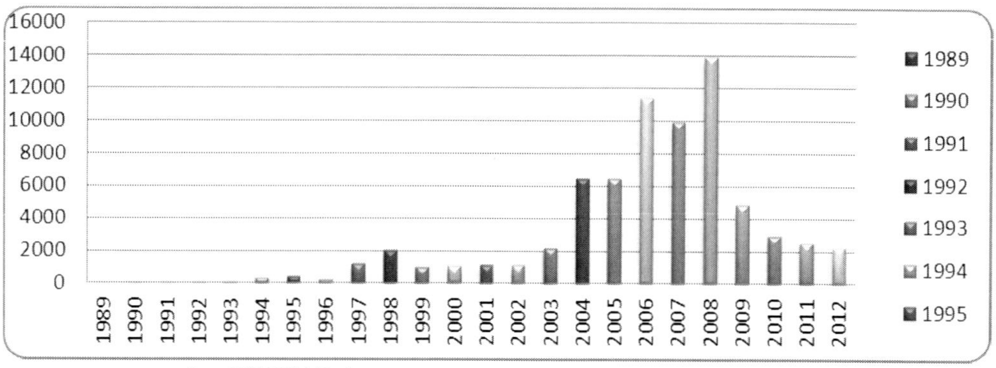

Source: own processing, UNCTAD data.

Figure 2.1. Dynamics of FDI flows in Romania in the period 1990 – 2012.

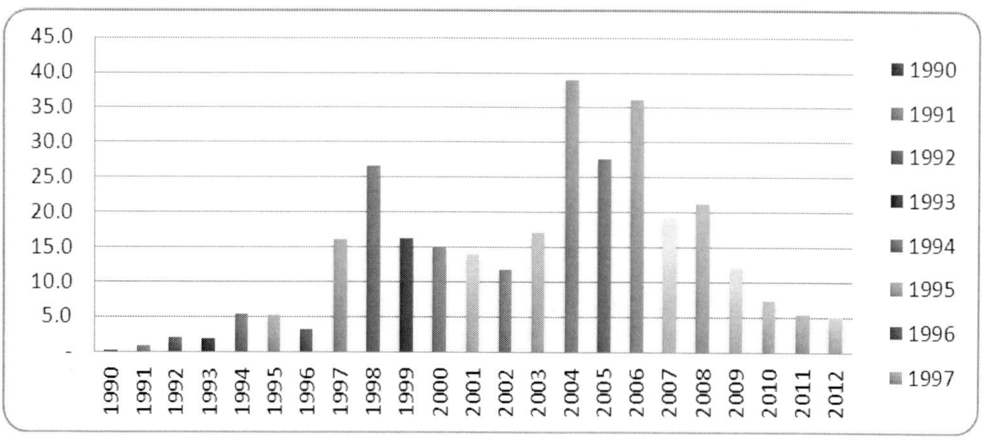

Source: own processing based on UNCTAD.

Figure 2.2. The share of FDI in the gross fixed capital formation of Romania in the period 1991-2012.

However, compared to other Central and Eastern European countries, although the economy could offer quite attractive conditions, the situation was not the best because of some of the following causes: *legislative inconsistency, lack of a clear economic objective and strategy, delaying the privatization of some key sectors, the instability of the institutional framework on foreign investment promotion*.

The global economic crisis that affected Romania beginning with 2009 decreased the FDI flows considerably, the most affected sectors being: metallurgy, foods, beverages, tobacco, wood products, including furniture, computers, communications, textiles, clothing, leather, financial intermediation and agriculture. In the construction and real estate sectors, the strongest decline was recorded in 2010.

Based on the origin, the largest share of foreign investments in Romania (in late 2012) was held by EU countries, namely the Netherlands (22.4%), Austria (18.5%) and Germany (11%).

The Romanian economy remains weak in terms of capital and the FDI had a significant contribution to the gross fixed capital formation (figure 2.2).

The FDI contribution to the capital accumulation in the Romanian economy is highlighted by the leader position of foreign companies in key areas of activity [11]:

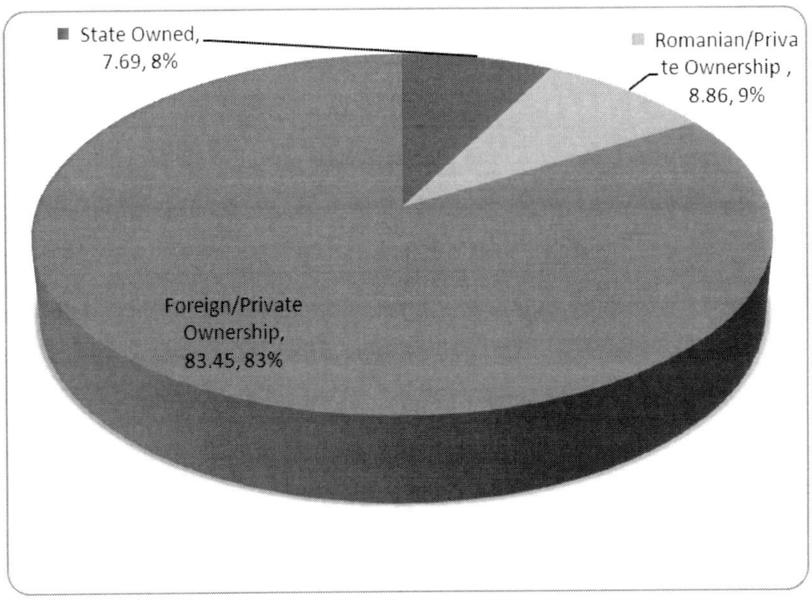

Source: Chart developed by the authors based on data from [11].

Figure 2.3. Percentage share in total turnover (2011) – as ownership majority.

Foreign owned companies are leaders in:

- ✓ the largest extractive industry market - code 06 - oil and natural gas;
- ✓ 22 of the 24 markets in the manufacturing industry (except code 18 - printing and reproduction of recorded media - and Code 33 - repair and installation of machinery and equipment);
- ✓ markets that produce and supply electric and thermal energy, gas, steam and air conditioning (code 35), uptake and distribution of water (code 36), collection and treatment of wastewater (code 37), the collection, treatment and disposal of waste (code 38);
- ✓ all trade activities markets (codes 45, 46, 47);
- ✓ the broadcasting of programs market (code 60);

- ✓ telecommunication markets (code 61) and information technology services (code 62);
- ✓ Legal and accounting markets (code 68);
- ✓ advertising market and market study (code 73)."

The dominance of foreign companies as market leaders is even more obvious in terms of turnover (Figure 2.3)

5. The Effects of Private Property Reform on the Sustainable Development in Romania

The property reform as an essential process to ensure the fundamentals of a market economy (predominantly private property and new, democratic relations between individuals and institutions) requires a profound change in the interest structure of the Romanian society. Given that Romania is forced to undergo a new cycle of an urgent modernization to support the integration in the family of state members of the European Union, the issue of a sustainable development strategy is an imperative of the current historical stage. However, designing and implementing an ambitious strategy for modernization and development of the Romanian society requires a high level of economic and social cohesion based on a balance of interests, supported by property relations consistent with the ethical and moral standards of the developed countries in the EU.

For Romania, as well as for other Central and Eastern Europe countries, the transition to a market economy meant an improvement in the Human Development Index (table 2.4.).

Table 2.4. Dynamics of the Human Development Index for some Central and Eastern Europe countries

Year / Country	1995	2000	2012
Bulgaria	0,722	0,731	0,782
Czech Republic	0,783	0,796	0,873
Poland	0,755	0,788	0,821
Romania	0,703	0,713	0,786
Hungary	0,745	0,780	0,831

Source: HDI Report, 2013 [12].

According to the literature, economic development involves a complex process of transformation of human society marked by the modernization of institutions and public attitudes, the reduction of social inequalities and poverty eradication. The core values of the process of economic development are *sustainability, self-esteem and freedom* [1].

From this perspective, the process of property reform involved the modernization of the legislation and regulation of property rights. Beyond the imperfections and shortcomings of the definition and implementation of property rights it could be seen that there was created the foundation of a market economy in Romania by the predominance of the private sector both as a contribution to the GDP and employment generator. In addition, the adherence to the EU and the adoption of the community acquis also involved institutional modernization and therefore a modernization of the property relations.

Regarding the public attitude, the transition from no one's property (of all people) to regaining ownership and thus respecting the property rights of other citizens, represented a tremendous progress over a short period of time (a generation's timespan) despite the confusion generated by the confusion of defining, understanding and implementing of legal regulations related to the regulation of property. Of course, time and a lot of educational efforts are needed for these attitudinal changes to strengthen at the level of the entire population.

As for the income inequality it is obvious that the reconstruction of property rights, the onerous privatization and its effects caused an increase in the income distribution differences in the Romanian society. Along with the economic crisis the income inequality in Romania skyrocketed above EU's average, but econometric estimates show that the maximum peak of the Gini index on the Kuznets curve was reached, the future growth of the GDP will help to reduce the income inequality.

The transformational crises triggered by the transition to a market economy also led to deterioration in the poverty condition of the population. Privatization also contributed to this process through the liquidation of large state companies, and the fraudulent bankruptcy followed by onerous privatization of some of these. The contribution of these forms and weaknesses of the privatization process to the decrease of the aggregate supply, coupled with the liberalization of prices and the alignment of the energy prices to the EU level aggravated poverty. Thus, Romania comes second after Bulgaria, on the level of poverty in the EU.

However, the increasing in the share of the private sector led to a significant improvement in economic efficiency (especially through the contribution of new companies and FDI) and thus an increase in the population's income. Correlating the increase in income inequality with the poverty level, we notice that there is an emphasis on the state of economic and social polarization that could be dangerous for Romania's development prospects.

In terms of the progress of self-esteem, the new owners began to perceive both the advantages and the difficulties of exercising property rights. This process reinforced a sense of responsibility for the owners, shifted also to their heirs and their employees. If before 1990 the Romanian society was characterized by a general feeling of "escape liability" the citizens that regained their properties with difficulties, learned to be responsible and gained both a certain self-respect and also the respect of others. On the other hand, the dubious privatizations, the abuses in regaining property rights were accompanied by public opprobrium, even if those concerned were suffering from an exacerbation of their own personality assessment. Beyond exaggerations, and bureaucratic abuses, the private property reform represented a revival of the owner's personality and thus a positive revaluation of self and social esteem.

As for the progress in achieving the value of freedom, the simplistic doctrinal approach that the property offers a real basis for the exercise of freedom should be avoided as we notice that the private property reform triggered an exacerbation of individual and group interests. Based on the trend towards democracy, the new owners acquired the courage to express their interests and to fight in order to ensure their satisfaction. In addition, the resources acquired through the private property reform created a support base for the steps related to the full exercise of the property rights.

On the other hand, the evolution of the society contributed to the increase in the number of opportunities for choice so that the people gradually learned to knowingly exploit these opportunities [13].

Despite the justified criticism regarding the cases of the limitation on press freedom, rule of law and the judiciary system, the deficiencies in the manifestation of freedom of opinion and expression, the progress of the Romanian society regarding civil liberties are clear and unequivocal (Table no. 2.5).

Table 2.5. The index of economic freedom for EU Central and Eastern Europe and Baltic countries

Country \ Year	1996	2000	2005	2010	2013
Bulgaria	48,6	47,3	62,3	62,3	65
Czech Republic	68,1	68,6	64,6	69,8	70,9
Estonia	65,4	69,9	75,2	74,7	75,3
Hungary	56,8	64,4	63,5	66,1	67,3
Latvia	55	63,4	66,3	66,2	66,5
Lithuania	49,7	61,9	70,5	70,3	72,1
Poland	57,8	60	59,6	63,2	66
Romania	46,2	52,1	52,1	64,2	65,1
Slovakia	57,6	53,8	66,8	69,7	68,7
Slovenia	50,4	58,3	59,6	64,7	61,7

Source: www.heritage.org/index [14].

The private property reform contributed to a great extent to the democratization of the Romanian society, confirming the trends reported in the literature according to which the privatization and the democracy consolidation processes are positively correlated.

If the progress of economic development is clear, and the contribution of the property reform as an act of social emancipation is undeniable, then the public attitude regarding the natural environment and the resources protection seems to be far away from joining the standards of a sustainable development. Although the privatization and restructuring process of industrial companies meant a massive closing of the polluting sources, it is doubtful to say that this process meant an improvement in the attitude towards the natural environment. Not sure of the irreversibility of the process of reconstruction of property rights (based on a historical negative experience) the new owners were quick to capitalize their usufruct with serious consequences for the natural environment. Massive deforestation, stimulated by the lack of control on the export of timber and wood, seriously affected and affects the ecological balance with negative consequences on the natural environment.

The haste with which the extractive industries were privatized is at least suspect or unclear for the oil industry, which before 1989 produced over 8 million tons of crude oil, and later (1993) produced only 6.717 million tons (because of a continuous increase in the price). The way the exploitation of natural resources was chartered, shows a serious lack of commitment to the legacy of natural resources that the Romanian society will leave for future generations to have. On the other hand, the lack of coordination of the privatization actions and reconstruction of property rights and also the limited horizon of the new owners in the exercise of the usufruct, resulted in an irreversible damage to many valuable natural resources for the Romanian tourism. Thus, unique therapeutic resources in Europe were damaged irreparably by reconstituting the property rights in the areas of sanitary protection, or by uncontrolled agricultural and forest exploitations in contradiction with the ecological operating rules.

Unfortunately, the inter-temporal choices regarding the opportunity for exploitation of natural resources still lays the main emphasis on the present time, ignoring the interests of future generations.

As EU member, Romania adopted the community acquis and become part of the implementation of policies and strategies for its development. As a result, the country is obliged to develop its own policies and development strategies, consistent with those of the European community. The development of the policies and strategies requires a thorough analysis of the factors and the resources of the sustainable development.

As there are certain criteria and conditions, it is necessary to ensure a selective capital inflow, as recommended by N. Iorga: *"open the gates of an honest and active economic competition given by real friends and close for those nations that tend to conquer and rule Romania"* [15]. Although it seems to be totally obsolete this warning from history came back in the present in other forms, given Romania's integration into NATO and the European Union membership, but also because of the military and political tensions in Eastern Europe and the Middle East.

Romania's sustainable development in the context of globalization, its contribution to the "unity in diversity" of the EU means to promote the national identity without chauvinism and hostility towards other countries and in designing Romanian policies and strategies "*it was not about building a Chinese wall, but to achieving a real possession of one's ideals*" [16]. Romania's European integration would be doomed to failure if there were a capitalist society without domestic capitalists or with imported capitalists. The development of a society, whether it is Romanian or not, needs human capital, technology, professionals, labor force, and especially competitive capitalists. By developing entrepreneurship and therefore the creation of new companies, the privatization process can "greatly stimulate the creation of a Romanian bourgeoisie" [17, 18].

5.1. The Broader Image from the Perspective of Regional Stipulations of Romania's Economic Development

To observe clearly how the property reform was needed we turn to the regional-territorial perspective of the economic development of Romania that was affected by two opposite directions: on one hand a natural ambition towards the social and economic cohesion (based on a strong ethno-genetic bond), and on the other hand a range of shocks of fracturing caused by the action of the economic, political and military forces fields exerted by the surrounding empires. In this context, the Second World War suddenly has interrupted the ample process of building the cohesive plan of the Romanian economy and society. With its territory amputated and devastated by the war, Romania has entered the influence zone of Soviet imperialism and also the communist doctrine zone altogether. The new patterns of economic and administrative structures asserted by the Soviet occupier have worsened the gaps between the territorial units of Romania. Moreover, the communist authorities' programs of rationally distributing the production forces on the entire national territory have disrupted even more the clotting of the territorial units in areas of economic and social development.

In the first years of Romania's transition towards the market economy, this important extent of the economic development has been neglected. The issue of the regional development has come up again to the attention of the creators of economic policies at the same time with the Romania's goal to become a member of the European Union. Hence, Romania promised to implement the politics and strategies of the European Union, namely the Regional Policy. Therefore, Romania adopted the national Program entitled "The Green Charter of the Regional Development" in 1997. However this document proved to be insufficient once Romania asked to take benefit of financial and professional support through the pre-adherence funds (PHARE, ISPA and SAPARD). To benefit from the financing of some pre-adherence programs it was necessary (among other things) to adopt the regulation of the EU system of territorial structure – The Schedule of the Territorial Statistic Units. This system is divided in categories – two at local level (STSU 4 and 5) and two at regional level (STSU1, 2 and 3). STSU 2 is of great importance because it represents the entity of implementation of the U.E. regional policy (including that of assigning the conversion financing).

Under pressure, Romania has confined these regions and also the spectrum of the regional development. Through the passage of Law 151 from 1998 – The Law of the Regional Development – there have been established the institutional spectrum, the goals, the jurisdictions and the instruments specific to the politics of regional development in Romania. Hence, there have been set up eight regions of development that have no legal entity and do not represent administrative-territorial units.

This hasty regulation, which has been done by simply "annexation on the map" of many counties and of the regions of developments (STSU 2), has had as a result too big and too inconsistent territorial statistic structures. Compared to other Central and Eastern European countries, Romania has the most reduced number of STSU regions related to population: Bulgaria has six regions for a population which counts less than half the population of Romania, Hungary has seven regions, The Czech Republic has eight and Poland sixteen. Under these circumstances the regions of development of Romania are very inconsistent, the inter-regional gaps being bigger than inter-regional ones. However, besides the malfunctioning confinement of STSU 2 units, the institutional system of regional development in Romania is characterized by certain functional inconsistencies. Hence, at a central level the coordinating body has undergone multiple changes as being the National Agency of Regional Development at first, then a specialized direction appointed towards many ministerial structures, and nowadays the Ministry of Regional Development and Public Administration. On the other hand, at regional level there has never been a consistency in the localization of the main functional unit – The Agency of Regional Development – in some cases, was a medium town, a county seat or other times the biggest town in the STSU 2 region.

These executive and functional deficiencies of the structures of regional development of Romania have not been solved because of the political tensions between the central political forces and the local ones. Hence, the adopting of a law of Romania's territorial administrative readjustment is postponed with serious consequences over the adopting of the new development plans for regions of a STSU 2 type respectively of the new Operational Regional Program. These are instruments without which Romania won't be able to have access to financing from the European Fund of Regional Development. Moreover, due to the contribution of the European Fund of Regional Development to co-finance other operative regional programs, which are specific to the other structural funds and to The Cohesion Fund, an important delay in getting these programs going is possible. Also it is necessary to create a balance between the economical and social development at regional level and the implementation of certain strategies that will trigger the regional competitiveness.

CONCLUSION

The private property reform, as an essential process of the transition to the market economy was achieved with great difficulty, as it was a process marked by the cultural heritage of the socialist society, and by the collective memory of the Romanian capitalist and the persistence of the owner instinct.

The restoring of the property rights was part of the general trend to return to the capitalist society in Romania (a kind of loop in the Romanian society history) [19]. The landmark was perceived as a mirage of the "myth of the golden age" of modern Romania (period 1918-1928), but the legal referential was the "communist nationalization." The historical gap was important because it contained "the Great Depression of 1929 - 1933," marked by the redistribution of property as a result of bankruptcies, World War II that destroyed both properties and owners and led to a new "world order." Moreover, the communist nationalization took place in several stages: 1945, 1947, 1949-1952, being affected by war reparations paid to the Soviets. In these circumstances it is difficult to identify what documents, authority and boundaries the landmark for the reconstruction of property rights is based on. The Romanian society of 1990 found itself in a great state of economic, political and axiological confusion. Regarding the public attitude, the effects of the communist propaganda was felt regarding the hate towards "kulaks and bourgeois" as a rejection of the differentiation of income or envy towards the rich. In addition, blocking the exercise of property rights, and the denial and denigration of private property, created as a reflex the lack of respect for the property relationship (manifested by carelessness and theft of property by the communist state - factory, CAP etc.).

The ambiguities of the property rights legislation and the long period of repeated addition and modification of laws led to a lot of conflicts and undermined the economic and social cohesion. In addition, these weaknesses negatively affected Romania's image around the world, the Romanian state being sanctioned by international courts and obliged to pay substantial damages, but based on the general confusion and political opportunities, those responsible for the errors and abuses were not identified.

Legal rules or laws that stipulated the reconstruction of property rights limited or introduced artificial obstacles in the exercise of property rights (e.g.,: Law 18/1991) *negatively affected the exercise of property rights* and the economic efficiency both at microeconomic and macroeconomic level. An eloquent example is agriculture where restitution limitations led to the persistence for a long period of time of small sized, subsistence farms dominance with an insignificant contribution to the gross value added in this sector. Reconstruction of ownership of the buildings is representative for another "non-closed wound" ethics in the new Romanian society. In addition, the difficulty in finding the successors along with corruption led to numerous cases of wrongful reconstruction of property rights.

Held amid corruption inherited from the communist institutions, the restoration of property rights has turned into a general rush after enrichment, seriously affecting ethical and moral standards of the new Romanian society and enhancing the level of corruption. Numerous abuses and dubious reconstructions have seriously tarnished the prestige of the new Romanian bourgeoisie involved in all sorts of public scandals, resulting in direct economic force weakening relationship between domestic and foreign capital. On the other hand people have seen that there were "disowned" of property rights all people undergoing an important process of differentiation through income and wealth, and sometimes impoverishment as a result of the reconstruction of property rights.

Due to the inconsistency of the political class on the privatization process and the lack of national consensus on the methods and timing of implementation of the relevant legislation, there has been a long delay to reform property [20]. Such delays were confirmed by experts' opinions and that *"The privatization occurs later with greater destruction of physical and human capital"* [8].

Although the literature stresses the importance of privatization for the creation of the functional market economy and supporting democratic reforms, also considering economic efficiency an issue of secondary interest in implementing the methods of privatization policies, the biggest losses and destruction that accompanied the reform of property should not be neglected for a poor country like Romania. These results will still have an effect (at least) in the medium term on the process of nominal and real convergence in the EU [21]. Thus, the lack of heritage winding of former State Owned Agricultural Companies and Cooperatives of Agricultural Production, the policy options for delaying privatization method or another, corruption, duplicitous behavior of trade unions etc. caused the bankruptcy and closure of large industrial capacity which normally would have been viable.

The success of economic and social reform in Romania property could be validated only on the long-term and depends heavily on the social recognition of new property rights.

REFERENCES

[1] Todaro, P. M., Smith, S. C., (2011) *Economic Development,* Prentice Hall, London.

[2] Djankov, S., Murrell, P., (2002) Enterprise Restructuring in Transition: A Quantitative Survey, *Journal of Economic Literature,* vol. XL, September, pp. 739-792.

[3] Estrin, S. (1994) *Privatization in Central and Eastern Europe*, Longman Publishing, London.

[4] Estrin, S. (2002) Competition and Corporate Governance in Transition, *Journal of Economic Perspectives*, 16 (1), pp. 101-124.

[5] *** EBRD, Transition Report - http://www.ebrd.com/news/ publications/transition-report/transition-report-2013.html

[6] Kornai, J. (1990) *The Road to a Free Economy. Shifting from a Socialist System: The Example of Hungary*, W. W. Norton Publishing, New York

[7] *** Romanian Centre for Economic Policies - http://www.cerope.ro/pub/study13ro.htm

[8] Aslund, A., (2010) *Cum s-a construit capitalismul*, TipoMoldova Publishing, Iași.

[9] Manoilescu, M. (1986) *Forţele naţionale productive şi comerţul exterior. Teoria protecţionismului şi a schimbului international*, Ştiinţifică şi Enciclopedică Publishing, Bucharest.
[10] Mole, W, (2001) *The Economics of European Integration. Theory, Practice, Policy,* Ashgate Publishing, London.
[11] Mereuţă, C., Pandelică, I., Pandelică, A. (2013) *Capitalul majoritar străin în companiile-noduri de pe principalele pieţe din România,* Economică Publishing, Bucharest.
[12] *** Human Development Report - http://hdr.undp.org/en
[13] Lewis, W.A. (2003) *The Theory of Economic Growth.* Taylor and Francis Publishing, London.
[14] *** Heritage Foundation - www.heritage.org/index
[15] Iorga, N. (1926) La situation politique de la Roumanie d'apres sa Constitution, *L'Annee francaisse et estrange* II, Paris.
[16] Titulescu, N. (1926) opinion published in *Viitorul*, 16 June 1926.
[17] Madgearu, V. (1924) Doctrina ţărănistă, *Doctrinele partidelor politice. 19 prelegeri publice organizate de Institutul Social Român*, Cultura Naţională Publishing, Bucharest.
[18] Madgearu, V. (1925) Ţărănismul, *Doctrinele partidelor politice. 19 prelegeri publice organizate de Institutul Social Român*, Cultura Naţională Publishing, Bucharest.
[19] Saizu, I. (1981) *Politica economică a României între anii 1922 şi 1928,* Academiei Publishing, Bucharest.
[20] Dinu, M., Brateş, T., (2013) *Răzbunarea trecutului. Capitalismul în cinci luni postdecembriste*, Economică Publishing, Bucharest
[21] Shleifer, A., Vishny, R. (1994) Politicians and Firms, *Quarterly Journal of Economics* vol. 46, pp. 995-1025.

In: What/Who Are We After the Transition? Focus on Romania ISBN: 978-1-63483-947-1
Editors: M. Dinu, D. Ailenei, A. Dachin et al.

Chapter 3

RESTRUCTURING: THE STRUCTURAL ADJUSTMENT

Mariana Iovițu*, PhD, Dumitru-Alexandru Bodislav, PhD, Alina Ștefania Chenic (Crețu) PhD and Cristina Dima, PhD
Bucharest University of Economics Studies, Bucharest, Romania

INTRODUCTION

In comparison with the post-war recovery of countries with industrial economies under development, the restructuring required by transition is different in theory and in practice. The existences of interdependencies between the fundamental components of the reform and the chain coupling steps and the measures' order aimed at transition have a logic that must be respected.

Changing the system, (the centralized economy decline and the transition to market domination) require the combined effort of restructuring and adjustment.

Consequently, the stabilization policies cannot be dissociated from the structural reform, these two processes start and run consecutively. The restructuring elements in Romania came from the new economic structure required by the market and from the specific conditions of the country's technique, mechanisms and tools ready to face restructuring.

The sequential or gradual changes (adjustments), slow or rapid were dependent on the decisional synergy. The decisional oscillation blocked, however, the process of formulating specific objectives of economic growth in Romania, as long as the procedural ensemble for establishing the market economy through privatization and restructuring, which has not been conducted systematically and coherently.

As far as for the adjustment and restructuring process, those could lead to a certain evolution, certified by the economic performance, it could be understood that when it comes to decision and decision makers, the identification cost is supported by society as a whole.

This chapter addresses the structural adjustment from the theoretical point of view as well as a practical and dynamic process that historically deployed and developed in Romania, over

* corresponding author: marianaiovitu@yahoo.com

the course of more than 20 years. The analysis follows the way in which the theoretical foundations are found in the efforts for structuring the Romanian space starting from specific operational adjustment variants.

With a few theoretical amendments and practical constraints, the description of the structural adjustment process highlights a series of economic policy actions undertaken by several governments following the 90's. Important distinctions were raised between the positive effects and limitations recorded as failures or unfulfilled goals as well as the future of an economy structurally adjusted at Europe 2000's horizon.

1. Conceptual Boundaries

Analysing the main stages that have marked the structural adjustment process reveals, in essence, the evolution of the entire Romania's transition process. Treating the adjustment process as if it was a component of transition expresses the bi-univocal relationship between the entire process (as a whole) and a part of it. Objective determining of the adjustment process can only be in the general context of the transition dynamics and changing the system (centralized economy decline and the transition to market dominance) requires the joint effort of the *restructuring and adjustment process*.

In fact, structural adjustment, on the grounds of the restructuring fundamental transforming restructuring process, constitutes the true economic reform. The concrete answer, in this field, to the transition challenges being, from this point of view, the most relevant part, truly creative, from the part of the CEE countries in estimating the path towards the global world. It is, in equal measure, about using the historical experience of the CEE countries to reduce and avoid the possibility of repeating the society transformation experiment from top to bottom.

The complexity of the two processes and the need for their balance within the economic system requires, orderly, conceptual identification and defining the two processes. Economic *restructuring* signifies economy reorganization on modified bases providing a new configuration of the whole system. In return, adjusting is adapting, matching a component (economic branch, business segment, employment content) to the restructured economic assembly functions. It is based on a mechanism specific to the new condition of existence of the economic activity area. The double fundamental moderator mechanism (restructuring-adjustment) determines essentially, a drastic change in the economic system substance.

The distinction between the two processes is, however, essential. Ceteris paribus, the results (effects) of a process depends, largely, on the approach. The micro-macroeconomic effects of the two processes are the consequence of opposite, but not contradictory trends. On the one hand, *restructuring* seeks enrolment, appropriate and relevant, of the old components within the new economic reality.

On the other hand, *the adjustment* may have an uncertainty degree if one of the components is dysfunctional, in relation to the mobile and dynamic economic structural stability. The slow or fast mutations (adjustments) depend on the decisional unity. The restructuring elements in Romania emerged from the new economic structure demanded by the market and from the country's conditions regarding the technique, the mechanisms and the instruments prepared to face restructuring. Supporting market competition is complementary to the process of reducing the monopoly position (reference to Law no. 178/2010 concerning the public-private partnership on holdings and other associations).

Regarding the size order (range and scale) of the two processes contents, the analysis of the content and of the objectives highlights restructuring as the defining process where adjusting elements could be found, subordinated to restructuring.

Process	Content	Objective
Restructuring (and economic development)	-alleviate the imbalances consumption-resources -modifying the configuration and functionality of the national economy -modifying the industrial production structures (re-industrialization) -reengineering -preparing for economic re-launch -resizing the production capacity to ensure sustainable economic growth -managing the economy based on the market economy principles -economic stabilization	-eliminating malfunctions -restructuring some economic sectors through modernization -changing the structure of public investments (in parallel with private investment developments) -computerization as the essential key to reengineering -the differentiation of the profitability degree at a micro/macro level -relocation of the macroeconomic interdependencies within the market economy scheme

Through harmonization and macroeconomic stabilization, restructuring makes the connection with the economic adjustment. The adjustment process is subordinated thus to the restructuring capital objectives that become incentives in an effort to respond to external conditionality's.

Process	Content	Objectives
Structural adjustment (based on internal and external criteria)	-targeting internal and external balances -focusing decision-making on economic efficiency - eliminate losses, arrears, subsidies - Reducing the accumulation rate from 30-35% to 23-24% -Increasing the accumulation efficiency - Romania's international specialization (considering the national interest) -Since 2004, increasing competitiveness and industrial performance under the re-industrialization objective	-resizing some activities as a restructuring result (explains the declining demand of labor force following layoffs) -reducing the adjustment costs -institutional modifications (by taking on the Europeanization criteria)

Restructuring controversies are related to two approaches:

1. On the contents of the process, periodization, the order of the methods, speed imposed by the components urgency (institutional, decisional, proprietary that were to be restructured);
2. Arising from the practical implementation of restructuring to Romania's specific conditions.

As a way of adapting to the new economic reality, the structural adjustment is a process dominated by the partial or total substitutability. The consensual work discipline proves to be effective of the approach is related, complementary and simultaneous.

Work discipline regarding:	Structural adjustment – useful, necessary, mandatory process
Objective	Considered as a dual process, adjustment means continuous adaptation and permanent anticipation of changes in the economic structure Follows the perishable objectives succession in the economic development context
Decisional synergy (solutions and opportunities)	Modifying the economic structure benchmarks Temporary or permanent disappearance of old structures and their replacement with new elements Changing the structural model (by combining the old structural elements with new elements, corresponding to the market economy)
Strategy (as an operational alternative) completed and voluntary aims to promote an economic policy	In accordance with: -Different objectives intensity -The conflict of interests as a consequence of ranking the interests -The ratio population interests/national economic interest Identifies the critical element of adjusting in relation to three criteria: needs, model ,own conception

Source: author's conception.

As a dynamic and progressive organization, structural adjustment is driven from the start by well-defined and specified goals. It is based on material and human resources, as required by a specific orientation in strategic thinking. The lack of coherent concepts based on skills certified by reality and not on constraints imposed by the political factor led to mistakes. Resulted from subjective visions of the governmental bodies, these mistakes were felt during the last 20 years by multiplying at a national level the adverse effects.

The adjustment strategy has a different meaning from the process *tactics*. The difference arises from the potential and dependent connection of the adjustment process with the political area; this dependency widens the interpretation spectrum of the term strategy giving the perception of a certain degree of interference of the political factor in the economic decision-making.

If the structural adjustment would have proved, during the 20 years, to have a clear strategy (without confusion or oscillations regarding the stages, mechanisms, instruments, levers, and not least goals) the economy would have been exempt from failures as it actually happened. These failures occurred in government officials' attitude that has marked discontinuous economic policies. The lack of clarity and rationality defined the structural adjustment; consequently, after the '90s, the conflict between wills and the interests' evolution at the political discourse and also behavior level sharpened. The economic and social control instruments proved insufficient compared to the extensive imbalances due to the radical change of the operating model of the economy and of the society, as a whole.

Every government that followed, during more than 20 years, came up with their own versions regarding the adjustment process. The analysis of the economic and social policy between 1990 - 2012 show different acceptations of the governmental teams on the restructuring-adjustment, acceptations that turned into micro - macroeconomic syncope. The triad liberalization – restructuring – stabilization gained interpretations and different fundamentals, by changing the order of the processes according to moment's imperatives. The delayed nature of reforms, the slow adjustments were due to the governors' unjustified and excessively cautious behavior.

In the restructuring process the adjustment constituted an essential component related to the size of the large, small and medium enterprises.

Descriptive components of the structural adjustment	What was, in fact, the goal of the structural adjustment ?
Speed	-Speed of formulating the adjustment measures in relation to the urgency expressed by the main branches and economic activity sectors (concrete, in industry) -Influences the eco-social stability, taking risks and priorities based on time (short-medium-long time)
Priorities	-Increasing profitability for the sectors with accumulated losses, in time -Encouraging competition between businesses in order to increase efficiency
Types	-Priority analysis and performance assessment of businesses determines a certain form of adjustment: -radical, -on components, -partial, -sequential
Methods	-Reorganization, redefinition, resize, dividing (preserving the homogeneity character)
Beneficiaries	-Micro-macro environment (intern) -European Economic Area (after integration in the EU) -The global economy by connecting Romanian economy, global economic flows

Source: author's conception.

2. Structural Adjustment in Retrospect

Economic system transformation in Central and Eastern Europe constituted a challenge, but also an explanatory effort and virtually without precedent in the Europe's economic history. Belonging to OECD, the Centre for Cooperation with European economies in transition, held in September and November 1990, January and September 1991 a number of conferences and meetings with the theme: the complexity of the economic reforms, the economic, social, political difficulties characteristic to every country in transition.

On this occasion, macroeconomic and structural problems have received opinions and contributions of R. Dornbush, J. Sachs, S. Fischer, A. Gelb, M. Tardos and D. K. Rosati (1992), who formulated definitions, recommendations and personal points of view regarding the controversial and divergent aspects of the transition. The main concerns focused on two determinants: the sequencing and order of the macroeconomic-restructuring-liberalization economic stabilization processes and the pace of transition progress. The conclusion showed the relationship between domestic politics on sequencing, dimensions and proportions of economic - institutional reforms and the transition's pace.

Soon after 1989, Romanian economic politics manifested primarily two drawbacks: first, it referred to the competitive environment characteristics (European-global) which imposed a very different vision and approach of the economic politics, viewed also as a mechanism with levers; the second, insufficient support and priority promotion of the national interest.

Moreover, the Romanian politics perpetuated and maintained a state of conflictual tensions between the economic ideas and opinions embraced by the new political elite' and the Romanian economic practice. In addition, there was the Romanian politics oscillation between the decision to apply the principles of economic liberalism of the market, and promoting and supporting the current interventionist.

According to some authors, subject to the new type of management imposed by privatization and also to the pressure created by the interest system, newly emerged, this way a corporate technocracy gained shape. The following analysis presents in brief the period between 1990 - 2012 in the due course of the mandate of the 8 governmental cabinets, of which only 3 have completed their 4 years' terms of office.

For relevance purposes, the analysis is not limited to fixed 4 years periods (the electoral cycle), but it comprises also the 2 and 1 year stages, shorter periods of time due to resignations or censure motions of the governmental groups. The evolution map of the restructuring and structural adjustment process comprises the characteristics, achievements, errors and shortcomings resulted from the governmental programs carried on during a period of transition and reform.

In Romania the first stage˙ (the first document dealing with the transition in Romania is „Draft regarding the strategy for accomplishing the market economy in Romania" and it represented the foundation for the governance program of the first cabinet since 1989) of the economic reform, aiming to make the transition to market economy, starting with the 1990's, was characterized by:

a. establishing the practical/actual transition trajectory in Romania (the transition from hyper-centralization to the liberalized structure operative on the market economy principles):
b. formulating some specific programs for the branch in the transition process (the 28 ministries operated on the main economy branches, particularly the industrial ones):
c. conception coagulation according to 3 directions: making all activities profitable, efficient use of resources, implementing technologies applied worldwide.

In short, the transition strategy aimed, actually, the economic activity capitalization. A key feature of this first stage is the conception of covering the transition costs at the same time that these costs emerged (costs have been accepted but the consequences, anyway unforeseeable, were considered less important, at the time).

Having a strong populist character, the measures adopted during this period (decree-Law no. 83 February 1990 on the return of the shares submitted by employees in the share capital account of the companies) were meant to satisfy the population's desire to consume anything other than what was imposed during the previous system. Despite these efforts, aiming exclusively, the support of the population for the country's new political management structure, the adopted measures led to the emergence of some macroeconomic imbalances accompanied by inflationist signals, increasingly persistent (in 1991 the inflation rate was 170,2%, 1992 of 201,14%, 1993 of 256,1%, 1994 of 136,7%).

Characteristics and accomplishments of the adjustment measures	1990 The transition strategy consists of capitalizing the economic activity. A key feature of this first stage: covering the transition costs at the same time that these costs (covering the social cost is contingent on the capitalization –reengineering of each activity sector) The golden rule for an operating market economy is cost-efficiency and then profitability. An important feature: the concept of cost reduction inherent to transition, the idea and the consensus idea concerning the economic, social and political transformations. The state's role should have been reconsidered Decentralization of the economic activity parallel with production de-monopolization were opening measures for the economy's functionality: - macroeconomic stabilization by eliminating subside subsidies - bankruptcy legal grounding Refining the measures in accordance to the national specific. Applying the businesses restructuring methods prepared the framework for economic stabilization. The policy makers' decision to put the social needs first instead of the economical ones. Privatization before institutional reform. A gradual transition was chosen, fast-paced, in the shortest time possible, but the speed and the extent of the measures, not being prepared in advance, the conditions for implementing the measures have led to huge costs, with negative side effects for the population (price liberalization, ungrounded privatization, monetary convertibility).
Errors and /or omissions	During this stage the economy showed signs of collapse as a consequence to the effects regarding the segmentation of the activity sectors according to the efficiency principle. Structural adjustments had more of a guidance character, through operational plans for short periods of time (branches, sectors or regional), then long term forecasts. The adjustment process was based on the economy status prior to privatizations with guidance formulations without direct involvement of the economic agents.
Deficiencies	Transition phasing was ignored and the oscillation between the transition models applied by other countries (with or without proven success) within the East-European zone slowed down economy's evolution/ The lack of an adjustment model that takes into account: - the rapid and irreversible mutations towards private property - the depression of an unprepared market for the transformation impact - failures on fluctuating interest rates have contributed to decision making process regarding the closure and transition to the inefficient category of entire sectors of activity.

They believed that covering the social cost is contingent on the capitalization – reengineering of each activity sector. In other words, capitalization must induce a cost-efficient operating economy and only then its profitability.

Characteristics and accomplishments of the adjustment measures	1992 -A new stage of transition outlined new targets concerning structural changes corresponding to new institutions and mechanisms of the market economy. Dramatic decrease of industrial and agricultural production required resorting to imports. -The structural reforms continued, with the risk of maintaining very high the transition costs. Harmonizing the economic stabilization measures merged with the structural adjustment (adjustment of the intensive-energy and large consumers of raw materials branches) affected the performance of the entire economy. -Structural adjustments (short and medium term) called for expenditures and for state's direct involvement in investments. Thus, not a gradual and systematic withdrawal of the state, by displaying private capital, but continuing its investment potential through financial levers. Re-technologize objectives and economic activity re-launch are supported by the state-owner through assets and state shares. -Insufficient generalization of the market economy mechanisms and the lack of a consolidated market were arguments in favor of maintaining the state as an economic priority in defining position (interventionist economic policy exceeding, sometimes, Keynesian doctrine) -Fear that increasing efficiency, especially of the industrial branches (primarily) will result in job loss led to the initiation of public investment programs that offer jobs to the layoff workers. -The Copenhagen criteria, which Romania had to fulfil with the perspective of joining the European community, provided the structural adjustment with perspective advantages but with high immediate costs. -Slow transition with minimal negative effects in terms of population endurance
Errors and /or omissions	-Political measures marked by oscillations decisional have imposed a low speed of the reforms. -It doesn't appear clear the orientation towards free initiative and private sector development. -The speed of the reforms was timid, insufficient and unsupported manifesting fears in regards to the courage for introducing free initiative.
Deficiencies	Left wing measures were reluctant showing total lack of experience. Reluctant behavior towards foreign capital with direct impact on the economic restructuring. Providing people with energy was supplemented by imports. Harmonization of macroeconomic stabilization measures with structural adjustment measures

Characteristics and accomplishments of the adjustment measures	1993-1996 - As a result of structural adjustment measures were formulated particular social protection programs -Gradual passing to the sectorial structural adjustment assumed the formulation of short/medium term measures (comparative advantages) specific to Romanian economy. - Funding structural adjustment was made by direct participation of the state to investment projects. - Through "The global restructuring program and economic development" were pursued measures to modify the industrial structures and re-technologization. - Mitigation of imbalances generated by transition through measures that cover t he primary requirements of the economy.
Errors and /or omissions	-The packages of measures did not correlate to the different sectors and fields of activity. -Economic flows were disturbed. -Substantial reduction in industrial production (by 23%) and agricultural (by up to 60%). Consequently emerged the population supply crisis with domestic basic food products.

Deficiencies	Positive effects of the past structural reform didn't came through in the real economy. Crisis effects were emphasized. Speeding up the removal of old structures has not been compensated with the new market-specific institutions. The state supported the state-owned units (through direct participation). The state withdrew gradually, slowly by increasing the share of private sector and NOT by extensive privatizations and liquidation of state units.

Characteristics and accomplishments of the adjustment measures	1996-1998 -Macro-stabilization program included: • restructuring policies (especially industrial and energy) • policies for competition support • privatization policies, etc. New elements: there were formulated policies for reforming the public administration(separating the local from the central one). - Efficient use of resources as a prerequisite for structural adjustment meant the composition of a system for markets integration (following the creation of the proper framework for the functioning of free market mechanisms).
Errors and /or omissions	From a direct interventionism, the state limited only to: • Regulating the operational framework of economic activities • Failure to correct a poorly functioning market (Labor market registered a record unemployment of 11%). • Redistribution of income. The lessening the state' role in economy was compensated by triggering the privatization and restructuring in sectors of strategic importance
Deficiencies	The doctrine was obviously liberal, with severe accent of the state's withdrawal from economy. It manifested high preference for restructuring prevailing over privatization

Characteristics and accomplishments of the adjustment measures	1998 Emphasizing the concerns for reform. De Delimitation of situations requiring state intervention: when should the state intervene to correct market failures ? delays recovery, accelerating structural adjustment as a goal, achieving economic stability. Do - The liberal doctrine supports the state's role only for correcting failures and macro stabilization - The economy restructuring policies correlate only with the public administration reform. -The formulated measure aimed at: reform businesses through adjustment and privatization (quantitative accelerated privatization included the selection of units after the qualitative component), strengthening competition, the regional development, small - medium enterprises segment, characteristic for this period was the order of the two privatization and restructuring processes, privatization priority was claimed before the restructuring. Both processes were based on reducing the state's role in economy.
Errors and omissions	It's supported the state's role only for correcting failures and macro stabilization. Governments have turned their attention, in particular, to supporting rapid structural adjustments disregarding the alarming social costs.
Deficiencies	Specific objectives for economic growth were not formulated, because the procedures for the establishment of the market economy have not ended. The doctrine of center-right-wing oriented the economic policy o r reducing the role of the state and speed up privatization.

State's intervention was accepted only to correct market's failure. Concerned about recovery delay, accelerating the structural adjustment, attaining economic stability, the governments were not cautious about the alarming social costs increase.

Economy's restructuring policies were linked to public administration reform policies and the measures specified the businesses' reform through adjustment and privatization. There was, in this context, the motivation for choosing the *quantitative-qualitative coexistence of the privatization.* In other words, the privatization consistency was in the number of privatized units and the demonstrated economic efficiency of these units that deserved to be privatized before adjustment. Strengthening the compulsory competition within the market economy, the efforts for the regional development and focusing on small and medium enterprises segment, appear as persistent targets, within the complexity of economic policy of transition, in this stage.

If, during the period prior to 1998 the option has been restructuring then privatization, in the next stage the order of processes has changed: privatization before restructuring. Although in both cases, the two processes were based on reducing the state's role in economy, the processes order represented the vulnerability of the decision from a governmental program to another.

Characteristics and accomplishments of the adjustment measures	2000-2004 It was the stage of a series of innovative solutions based on the E.U. recommendations, the IMF and the World Bank. - Government attention focused on balancing the requirements of market economy and social protection (has been expressed a left-side orientation, with clear interventionist shades). Economic re-launch was subject to: the business environment performances subject to structural adjustment, encouraging the small-medium sector, attractiveness of foreign investment capital. Structural reform continued to give hassle to the macro-stabilization process through: boost production, quantitative and qualitative privatization acceleration (regarded as efficiency). Supporting market competition became complementary to the process of reduction of monopolies' position
Errors and /or omissions	Were NOT established the structural adjustment criteria. Restructuring was characterized by: • lack of order and discipline, • lack of a default pace, • discretionary nature, • economic and social impact zones were not taken into consideration, • selection of industrial sectors to be privatized. It was noted the decision oscillating continuation between adjustment priority and privatization, decisional oscillation which marked the previous stage (1998-2000). It was assessed the target failure. Has been maintained the state's fundamental role in economy through an Keynesian interventionist orientation supported by market liberalization policies.
Deficiencies	National interest WASN'T conditioned economically but politically (by harmonizing the political forces of that stage) It was regarded as fundamental in assessing the efforts and results undertaken for the proper functioning of the market mechanisms.

Characteristics and accomplishments of the adjustment measures	*2004-2008* - *A new focus, by* returning to the right sided economic policy provide elaboration more judicious, more scientific objectives of reform. -The objectives materialization regarding the industrial policy were subordinated to competitiveness increase on the European and global external market (as a consequence to implementing the knowledge economy objectives of the Lisbon Agenda 2000); national unemployment decreased to 4%. *This objective was formulated as a requirement of compliance with the national interest entirely subordinated to Romania's objective of integration in the EU it emerges for the first time the reindustrialization objective correlated to a new energetic program.* -The problem of disparities compared to the European standard became priority (economic and social strengthening was targeted since it was mandatory for fulfilling the European standards) *Characteristics*: 1.- liberal orientation of the political decision that hovered over the economic programs of improvement of the business environment, 2.- the issue regarding state's role was resumed by gradual reduction of state intervention, maintaining only its functions in regards to the legality character for enforcing the economic functionality normative acts.
Errors and /or omissions	*State's controversial position was explained by*: *On the one side*, reducing the state's role in economy simultaneously with the reduction of some economic branches that supported the public demand represented the gradual reduction of the state's assistance function. *On the other hand,* the state was forced to support rescuing some branches condemned to extinction. Interventionism was temperate and helped maintain the aggregate supply market.
Deficiencies	*Restructuring and privatization have not shown emergencies in building a market economy*

Characteristics and accomplishments of the adjustment measures	2008-2009-2012 1.-Governors attention focused on the economic crisis effects. The emergence of the critical symptoms of the crisis led to: - decrease in production with consequences on labor force(workplaces were restructured and the wages degreased) - the governments had difficulties regarding: respecting the commitments made to MIF and the World Bank and European funds absorption 2.-Measures to resume economic growth were subordinated to public sector reform in parallel with increasing its efficiency. 3.-The international context triggered implementation of domestic economic policy having a pressure effect on population in terms of the capacity to pay wages and pensions (which decreased) and also on the public spending capacity in terms of investments. 4.-In 2010 compared to 2009, the turnover rose insufficiently from 772,7 billion to 779 billions(with 0.83) the industry branch increasing by 6.74% (steel industry in Romania doesn't produce high value added)
Errors and /or omissions	The existence of controversial situations: fighting the crisis through austerity measures consecutively with supporting measures of the global demand by increasing public spending. -from the IMF and European commission recommendations passed to reducing public spending. -decisions inconsistency and a contradictory policy that proved the wrong perception of reality, Romanian society had to endure at the same time the crisis effects and the high costs of economic policy mistakes employment decrease below 60% of the active population. Privatization process reduced the turnover from exclusively state owned companies by about 4 times from 23.4% to 5.9% in 2009; Profitability rate became positive over the economic boom, but during the recession that began in 2008 state owned companies reported losses compared to 2003
Deficiencies	The financial crisis generated a series of maximum austerity measures that exacerbated and maintained social discontent. Slowing, blameworthy, of the EU structural funds absorption.

Complementary groups of reforming policies, applied sequentially, whose details take into account the condition and in transition country's economic performance represented viewpoints and support from many economists˙. Fisher-Gelb's conception expresses the possibility that some studies, opinions, points of view represent pragmatic guidelines governing economic programs. These guidelines maintaining or assuming, may remain trapped in the form imposed by the politic. *The sequencing issue* has been widely debated over the years of reform. Application of methods restructuring of enterprises prepared the framework for economic stabilization. In Romania, gradualism was a minimum risk strategy.

Therefore, the belief that the events would be under control has been deceived by reality. The time of the reformation worked against gradualism. The danger of overrating the abilities regarding timing of changes, led to rethinking and reassessing the gradualism's advantages. According to Dornbusch, a sequence of the reform can be carried out over seven days as follows: the first day, establishing an economic model, in the next day, creating appropriate institutions, on the third day, achieving the macroeconomic balance, on the fourth day, privatization, on the fifth day, the introduction of trade liberalization and achievement of convertibility, on the sixth day, integration into the global economy through trade and not through economic, financial aids, on the seventh day, refreshing of finances internally.

Following the analysis of governmental programs, gradualism has not shown convincing valences for the Romanian economy. During the 20 years of transition, the qualities of the structural reform overshadowed and disputed the success of the reform agenda.

2.1. Adjustment Policies in Reorganizing, Redefining and Resizing Old Businesses

Economic disintegration of old forms of existence of businesses because of the structural adjustment, which was aiming for the efficiency criterion and involved the following:

Type of company	Type of Adjustment
Small businesses, economically weak	Immediate closure Capital goods will be sold quickly
Small businesses, economically strong	Immediate privatization Capital goods sold (totally / partially) to employees The state provides funding for sale
Large businesses without economic potential	Extensive Restructuring Switching to the private sector Total Transformation
Large businesses with economic potential	Represents the key of privatization Partial adjustment but rapid progress The emergence of the first state holdings along the way, were to be privatized

Source: author's contribution.

Following these resizing, the structural adjustment pursued the following objectives: reducing the accumulation rate from 35% to 24% to attract foreign capital in order to increase economic activity efficiency, revamping changes of investments diversion public (the occurrence of new objectives), encouraging private investment (following of privatization).

Adjustment transforms referred to agriculture and the intensification of computerization (the latter showing one of the major gaps in Romania). In this last direction was proposed requesting foreign loans as well as retrieval mechanisms of high performance technologies. Complementary and associative, auction sales of state units went along with previous resizing of large units that showed monopolistic behavior and monopoly functionality.

Privatization limitations (or exceptions) in this stage occurred as a result of the two types of privatizations. Two groups of examples illustrate the difficulty of the process. Minimal form of privatization was provided on full or majority state control. Were excluded some units in the strategic sectors (energy, mining, forestry and farms, transport, telecommunications, education, health infrastructure and social protection).

The a priori attitude strategically tinted led to some for the moment satisfactory decisions. Verification over time showed, however, that alternatives selected were not based on procedural rationality beneficial to transition economy.

The adoption in 1990, of the Land Law aimed settling the private property issue in agriculture as a form of procedural justice in favor of the Romanian peasant. Subsequently, the Land Law (No. 18/1991, republished in 1998 and later amended in 2011) drew (by its content on farm fragmentation) negative results. Thus, excessive fragmentation, especially the emergence of the 2,135,319 tiny owners having less than 1 ha is the result of how the transition from the vast socialist household production to the agriculture based on individual property was conceived.

A historic mistake was made in a moment of excitement generated by a populist political class, without social-economic and political necessary knowledge. The effects were immediate: the worsening of the economic and social situation of the rural population as well as the quantitatively and qualitatively backwardness of the agricultural production.

Asymmetric information, without fair and real foundation, unvarnished and commanded by the central decision-making structures of the socialist economy provided.

The adjustment process began considering the state of the economy prior to privatization, having a guiding character without direct implication from the economic agents. The adjustments were formulated through operational plans on a short-term period, on branches, sectors and regions, then through long-term forecasts.

The policy makers' decisions to put first the social needs before the economic ones, for example the option to cover transition's costs as they occur, constituted errors with different degrees of complexity that affected also the content and quality of the institutional system reform. In our opinion transition in Romania was flagged by the subjective load of the "triplet" mentality-attitude-behavior whose difficulty to change blocked (or delayed) economic reasoning.

The transition staging was ignored, more or less knowingly, and the oscillation between the transition models applied (with or without demonstrated immediate success) by other countries within the East Europe, slowed down the economy's progress. It has been proven that the mimicry regarding the models of the market economies in East European countries and those with a long tradition (confirmed by the economic mechanism functionality subordinated to the market bylaws) has no promising prospects if they deviate from the national specific. Not the dissolution of the historic support, of the characteristics and national traditions into one of the transition models referred to as success and not building a hybrid model with strong Romanian economic and social resonance constituted the path to follow.

2.2. The Dynamics and the Purpose of the Structural Adjustment

Regarding the speed of adjustment, the restructuring process required a longer time, with a nonlinear progress.

Compared with the post-war recovery period of countries with emerging industrial economies, restructuring demanded by transition differed in theory and practice. There is interdependence between the fundamental components of the reform, the chain phases and the order of measures targeting transition. In conclusion, stabilization policies cannot be dissociated from the structural reform and these two processes must be initiated and carried out consecutively.

Starting with 1992, a new phase of transition came with other objectives, concerning structural changes corresponding to the new institutions and mechanisms of the market economy. Dramatic declines of the industrial and agricultural production called for imports; finally, the structural reforms continued with an excess of transition costs.

Harmonization of the economic stabilization measures combined with structural adjustment (in particular the adjustment of energy intensive industries consuming large amounts of raw materials) affected the functioning of the economy as a whole. Being about structural adjustments (short and medium-term) that require expenditures, direct state participation to investments appears as a means to support state-owned units.

Thus, not the withdrawal of the state from the economy, gradually and systematically by allowing a field for privatization manifestation, but further manifestation through financial levers of the overwhelming investment potential. It does not appear conspicuous the orientation towards free initiative and the private sector development.

Following the structural adjustment, supporting reengineering and economic activity re-launch, was made using the community property state's funds, assets and stocks. The lack of a consolidated market and insufficient generalization of the market-specific mechanisms were arguments for maintaining the state as a priority and defining economic agent; interventionist economic policy exceeded, at times, the Keynesian doctrine.

The speed of the reforms was timid, insufficient and unsupported, manifesting fears in regards to the courage for introducing free initiative. Hesitant and oscillating have also been the measures that fall under the leftist ideology, that showed total lack of experience (i.e., increases and then cuts in the financial rights of the public sector employees as a result of fiscal measures; supporting programs which pursued the child protection with particular media impact, but which remained at the theoretical stage; developing a new remuneration system for civil servants and for the contractual staff, which also remained at the planning stage).

To all these, it adds up the reluctant behavior towards foreign capital with impact on economic restructuring. The fear that increasing the efficiency, especially of the industrial branches (priority), will result job loss that also determined the initiation (in advance) of programs for public investments that will provide employment to those that were to be laid off.

The Copenhagen criteria, which Romania had to fulfill with the perspective of joining the European community, provided the structural adjustment with perspective advantages but with high immediate costs.

The years 1996-1999 marked the transition to a new Christian-democratic-liberal political doctrine that impregnated the set of measures regarding economic restructuring.

Characteristics of this stage can be found in the macro-stabilization program. This program included restructuring policies (especially, industrial and energetic) policies for supporting competition, privatization, etc. A new element appeared in the formulation of reforming policies of the public administration (separating the local administration from the central one).

3. Externalities of the Adjustment – Restructuring

The massive and continuous loss of jobs due to the complex and conjugate effect of economy's restructuring and structural adjustment during the transition was a natural result, or at least an easily predictable one, from the beginning of this long period. Matter of fact, not being the only ex-socialist state from Eastern Europe faced with the unemployment-galloping phenomenon, the effects were felt in Romania more acutely than in most other states.

Noteworthy is the fact that the economic restructuring leads directly to a quantitative unemployment by abolishing a great number of jobs existing skills. At the same time structural adjustment imposed by restructuring implies new skills, modern, usually not or only partially covered by an appropriate level of competence, which leads to unemployment qualitatively due to impossibility, occupancy, jobs available.

It does not mean however, that the assembly restructuring-structural adjustment represents automatically an evolutionary regression within the transition of human societies to a market economy. Restructuring could support economic and social progress, but only if structural changes are anticipated correctly, if affected businesses could take corrective action and could quickly and efficiently manage the necessary change and whether the public authorities should help create favorable conditions.

Restructuring is not a new phenomenon, it has always been a part of the normal economic cycle, as businesses are forced to adapt in order to remain competitive. Restructuring is regarded often as an inconvenient phenomenon, with serious effects on employment and working conditions, as well as on local and regional economy. Nevertheless, when the restructuring process is managed efficiently and effectively, it can maintain the professional insertion capacity of workers and assist their transition to another workplace of equivalent quality in case they do not preserve their initial workplace.

Within the emblematic initiative "An industrial policy for the globalization era," part of the Europe 2020 strategy, it is mentioned that the European Commission will: *strives to promote the restructuring of sectors in difficulty for their orientation towards future activities, including through quick redeployment of skills to sectors and markets with rapid growth rate"* and Member States will have to *"work closely with stakeholders from various sectors in order to identify bottlenecks and develop a joint analysis on how to maintain a strong industrial and knowledge base."*

Both the Commission and the member states could be supported by the European Restructuring Monitor (ERM), which is, currently, the only source of information in terms of restructuring, at the EU level, providing general data and information on national public support and legal regulations in restructuring.

Despite the many restructuring implications on employment, prior to the ERM setup, few systematic attempts were undertaken to asses the nature and extent of the restructuring activities and their effects in the European Union.

In a context where there are no comprehensive surveys across Europe regarding businesses restructuring, ERM is considered a viable alternative and, until now, the only and best solution to cover gaps. Although ERM is mostly an guiding tool than a representative one in terms of the restructuring size and effects on labor force, it identifies the general trends and provides numerous information for subsequent qualitative analysis.

Similarly, there are compiled examples of national instruments of support for the businesses and workers within the restructuring processes that could provide a general overview on the different possibilities and to encourage the exchange of ideas. Despite its obvious limitations and because of the relationships between restructuring and employment, ERM represents a valuable source of information for the policy decision-makers at European level in an attempt to measure the extent of the businesses restructuring across Europe.

For Romania, during the transition from centralized economy to market economy, the unemployment official evolution (unemployed reported and registered at the NEA) was fluctuating, corresponding to distinct periods of internal and external development.

As shown in the following chart, the unemployment rates evolution followed 3 stages, somewhat similar, corresponding to the following time intervals: 1991-1996; 1997-2006; and 2007-2013. Although at a first glance it seems that during the crisis period 2007-2013 the unemployment rates were, on average, inferior to the other two periods, the reality experienced by the society as a whole is a very different one. That is because after the emergence of the global economic and financial crisis, unreported unemployment took a large extent manifested through the intensification of population migration outside country's borders, working on the black market and, not least, through a massive wave of layoffs with no compensation rights, to which early or medical retirement in the absence of other survival alternatives adds up. Moreover, the emergence and introduction on a large scale of the part-time contracts and of seasonal employment contracts led to a quantitative decrease in the unemployment rate with a massive reduction of the average actual time of work/person/year.

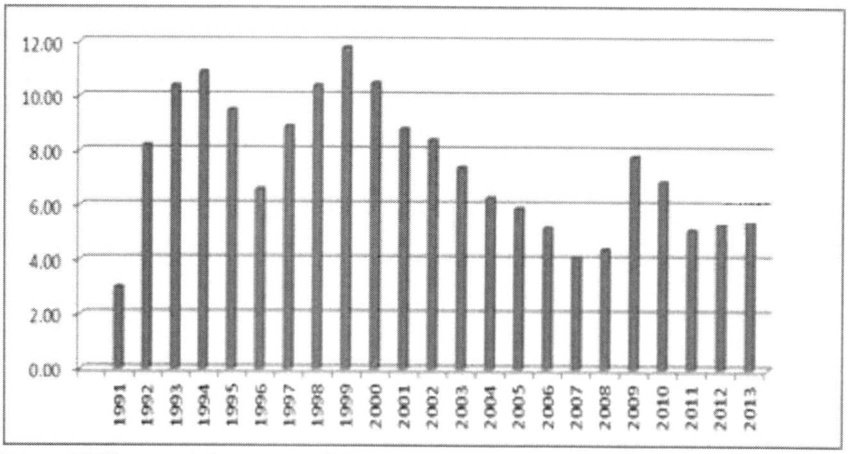

Source NEA and NIS- copyright processed data.

Figure 3.1. Evolution of unemployment rate in Romania stated during the transition to a market economy 1991-2013.

The use, under normal conditions of the labor force, from an employed population in a proportion of 95-98% means 2-5% vacancy. Between the number of people able to carry out an activity - potentially - and the actual number of jobs, there is not, practically, equality. Occupancy rate takes into account:

a) its own organization system having available- at one time- a limited number of jobs. Over-sizing the "threshold" is not impossible, but it will be completed with an increasingly higher cost, requiring fundamental justifications;
b) the level of social stratification regarding: income heterogeneity, influencing negatively and in a defining manner the occupancy degree;
c) information transparency, economic rationality, workforce mobility;
d) factors defining directly (often disproportionately) the unemployment extent: increase in the population number, technical progress and education.

Due to the inability to use the available workforce, one works with the non-used workforce notion. Incomplete occupancy (underemployment) is characteristic to situations where the supply exceeds the demand on the declared labor market. In terms of the effects of structural adjustment, losing the workplace is assessed at two levels: macroeconomic and microeconomic level.

The fear of losing employment affects all components of the individual's life: concentration, relationship with family, health, relationship with the social environment, etc.

Underemployment analysis, because of macroeconomic restructuring is multidimensional. Regarded as quantitative and qualitative indicator, underemployment illustrates the inability of the economy to provide jobs under the terms of a modest, inconclusive and inefficient industrialization. Economic organizations reduce prices to meet consumer partial insolvency, operates layoffs and wage cuts. The pace of the economic degradation triggers strong bottlenecks in the demand for workforce.

The multitude and severity of the economic and social effects caused by chronic underemployment of the workforce is exacerbated by the current crisis and economic recession.

Political and institutional imbalances, the budgetary system difficulties generates an inability to absorb the labor force in the private sector. Consequently, the innovative solutions concerning employment at a national and European level (access of workforce to jobs in other countries) are controversial and disputable.

Paradoxically the loss of jobs due to restructuring - adjustment can also have some positive effects. Increasing labor discipline and punctuality, increase of employee productivity, increased interest for the job, increase the competitiveness of existing workers, of the concerns for continuous improvement, setting up reserves of people willing to work to cover possible demands for workforce, are all beneficial effects for a restructured economy.

The crisis caused and continues to cause effects within various branches of the economy, of the most acute resonance on the economic system, we find the job loss due to lack of funds that will compensate lay-offs. Unemployment skyrocketed, America and Europe facing extremely high vacancy rates; Spain, Portugal, that based their economies on real estate development, reports record unemployment rates (around 20%) due to real estate market collapse (construction).

Following the severe global economic issues, the crisis spread rapidly in all areas. Currently, many strong companies, and not only, were forced to limit their activities, as an adapting measure to the market turbulences, which leads to lay-offs and often to wage cut-offs. According to recently published studies, Romania, along with Turkey and Lebanon are among the most vulnerable countries to effects of the crisis.

The global economic crisis caused massive lay-offs in Romania, and impacted heavily on the Romanian industrial giants, the most affected areas being metallurgy, textile and chemical, urging them to rethink their cost and personnel structure. Increasingly tougher crediting conditions as well as the decrease in the living standard turned into a vicious circle: people have drastically decreased consumption due to lower revenues, and companies' production decreased significantly. The relocation process of some big businesses greatly contributed to disrupting the ratio between demand – supply of labor force.

In order to avoid bankruptcy, the economic agents have cut costs, including salaries through layoffs. Lay-offs determined an increase in unemployment increasing thus the pressure exerted on the state budget and on the employees that failed to keep their job.

In an effort to compensate the social assistance, spending has increased; this decision has led to an increase in the budgetary deficit, given that the budgetary revenues have not increased.

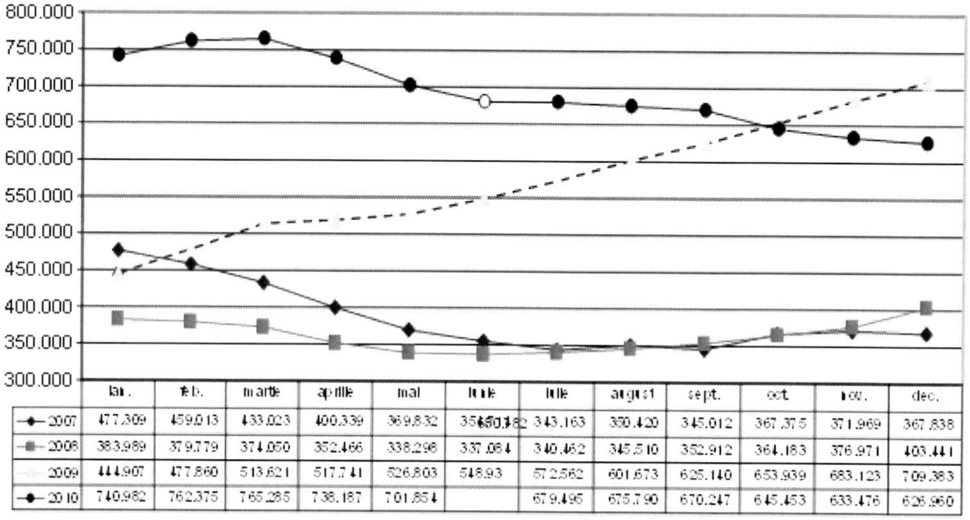

	ian.	feb.	martie	aprilie	mai	iunie	iulie	august	sept.	oct.	nov.	dec.
2007	477.309	459.013	433.023	400.339	369.832	[illegible]	343.163	350.420	345.012	367.375	371.969	367.838
2008	383.989	379.779	374.050	352.466	338.298	337.084	340.462	345.510	352.912	364.183	376.971	403.441
2009	444.907	477.860	513.621	517.741	526.803	548.93	572.562	601.673	625.140	653.939	683.123	709.383
2010	740.982	762.375	765.285	738.187	701.854		679.495	675.790	670.247	645.453	633.476	626.960

Source: NEA, statistical operative unemployment recorded statement December 31, 2010.

Figure 3.2. The evolution of unemployment in Romania following the economic crisis 2007-2010.

The year 2009 brought a sharp decrease of employment, below 60% of the total number of active population. At the microeconomic level, the labor market dynamics in Romania demonstrates the effect of businesses' restructuring process, of employment opportunities by delaying privatization. The economic downfall led to industrial production decrease, failure of the macroeconomic policies arrested attracting FDI's. Short recession period ('97- '99) led to a record high unemployment rate of about 11% nationwide. In the following period, along with the economic recovery, the unemployment rate fell, reaching in 2007, 4%.

In the near future, it is expected for the emigrant domestic labor force to return home, which may create additional pressure on the labor market, succeeding, largely, to eliminate the positions held by stable employees. Employers may prefer the re-migrated potential workers. Explanation: they posses superior skills and can contribute with a higher economic added value than the current employees.

Economic and social effects of job loss		
Effect type	Negative impact	Positive impact
a. Extension of part-time employment, acceptance on the part of employees, of the concomitant decrease (usually proportional) of working hours and wage levels	1. At the micro level: basically, it doesn't exist especially since the measure is proportional to a decrease in turnover due to decrease in demand or increase in the inter-firm trade payments dues 2.At the macro level: lowering the amount of work carried out, with a direct impact on lowering GDP respectively on decreasing the tax base thus increasing the negative balance of the consolidated public budget;	1. At the micro level: it is avoided the permanent loss employees, thus their recovery costs, when the economic activity will resume at the initial parameters or at improved parameters compared to the current situation; 2. At the macro level: maintaining a low unemployment rate, by the fact that for 8 hours of activity are employed more than one person; furthermore, the phenomenon is beneficial for the labor market as it encourages competition in occupying a job.
b. Accepting " sacrifice curves " by the employed personnel, accepting wage decrease without affecting the number of employees or working hours	1. At the micro level: possible disincentive concerning work quality and productivity at work 2. At the macro level: lower incomes (impacting on the decrease in the GDP and in the domestic demand - according to the average marginal propensity to consume - as well as on the corresponding decline in indirect tax revenue); simultaneously the decrease of direct tax revenue, due to lower direct tax base	1. At the micro level: it is avoided the permanent loss employees, thus their recovery costs, when the economic activity will resume at the initial parameters or at improved parameters compared to the current situation; 2. At the macro level: the employment level is maintained, exempting the consolidated public budget from a series of expenditures on the labor market
c. Restructuring of employment: requalification, redeployment of employed personnel at the non-financial business level without reducing the workload	1.At the micro level: disrupting the activity with a possible "U" curve, in the short term, of the level, quality and productivity; 2. At the macro level: aggregate negative effects	1. At the micro level: maintaining the employed workforce using professional "ventilation in order to increase the output of the microeconomic production function; 2. At the macro level: preservation or even optimization, microeconomic, of the workforce professional structure
d. Restructuring of the business environment: change or anticipating structure change and intensity of demand (internal and external) for the domestic output	1. Exiting the market- the dissolution of non-financial business having as direct consequences the cancellation or reduction of existing jobs. 2 major difficulties of adaptation / readapting of the existing workforce to new working conditions imposed by the reorientation of production / services of restructured companies.	1. These restructuring of the business environment can have a positive quantitative –qualitative impact (of the structure and employment) 2 Chance for young university graduates in the fields of communications, computer technology and language skills.

4. Prospects for Integrated Industries in the Context of Globalization

The EU adoption (October 2010) of the main action directions regarding the future of the integrated industrial policies ("An integrated industrial policy for the globalization era") prompted the European Commission to develop a specific European industrial policy, subordinated to Europe 2020 strategy. According to this strategy in the coming years, the industry's role should increase at the same time with the branch's contribution to the EU GDP: from 15.6% in 2012 to 20% in 2020.

The European Commission adopted in 2012 two important documents on industrial policy:

a) development of Member States in the current context, and
b) the report for assessing the countries competitiveness in Europe.

Comparison fields	EU objectives expected for 2020
1 Investments in innovation(6 domains)	Ecologic and advanced production technologies, Essential generic technologies, Markets based on bio production Sustainable industrial policy, Construction and raw materials, vehicles and non-polluting ships Intelligent networks
2 Improving the market conditions	Improvement in the domestic market functioning by increasing the domestic trade (from 21%-currently to 25% by 2020), Boosting the digital single market (DSM) small businesses carrying out electronic commerce should reach the 33% target by 2015) Protection of the intellectual property rights Spreading the SME within EU from about 13% to 25%.
3 Access to fund and capitals	Increasing the efficiency of resource channeling with direct impact on the real economy financing improvement.
4 Human capital and competencies	Promoting cooperation between employers, employees and specialized bodies by creating so-called alliances or skill councils.

Source: author's contribution based on the European Commission submitted data, 2012.

Figure 3.3. Key areas for the analysis and comparability of the European industrial policies.

4.1. Trends and Asymmetry of the Performance Indicators

According to the four domains, each member state of the E.U. performance evaluation was based on the following indicators:

1. *Labor productivity in manufacturing industry.* While the relevance of he manufacturing sector in the total value added in industry increased, the industrial production as a percentage from the value added of the output decreased in 2011 compared to 2006, at the EU27 level (Appendix 1)

In Romania, the evolution is different than the EU average since within the EU the share of the industrial production is reduced from 20.1% to 19.3% while the share of the manufacturing sector increases from 83.5% to 84%. Industrial sector achieves a slight increase in our country (from 27.9% to 28.5%) while the manufacturing sector records a slight decrease in the period under review from 84.8 to 83.9%. In Romania, the share of manufactured goods from the total manufacturing value added in the E.U. is quite low (about 0.8%), a value close to that of Hungary and about 3 times higher than that of Bulgaria.

Labor productivity from the manufacturing sector is very high in developed countries such as Belgium, Denmark, Germany, Sweden, Ireland; their production is based on modern technologies and specific intensive production process oriented towards knowledge. Ireland's high productivity is due to the activities of foreign multinational companies outside the country especially those operating in the chemical and pharmaceutical sectors, as well as to the research and development and marketing companies that carry out their activities outside Ireland or due to transfer pricing. Italy has an important manufacturing sector and labor productivity reaches a level near the EU average, due intensively technologically equipped sectors, least oriented towards innovation. Companies are small and show no attraction for structural reforms.

2. *Education and skills.* Countries with the highest level of employed workforce in science and technology are France, Germany, Denmark, and Netherlands. Here are highlighted the highest values of labor productivity from the manufacturing sector (Appendix 2- 3). The lowest level recorded in Portugal reflects the image of low professionally qualified workforce and of industries with reduced added value. In terms of employment in these areas, Romania is positioned below the E.U. average without an important evolution over the period 2008-2011. Romania produces mainly in sectors with low value added labor productivity. It is also one of the largest energy consumers within the EU, especially in the production.
3. *Exports of goods and services as a percentage of total EU exports.* Germany records the best performance in the line of exports (23% in 2006 and 25% in 2012) while France, Spain and Italy have lower orientation on exports (about 25% in 2006 and 22% in 2012) recording at the same time a decrease in their share in the period under review (Appendix 4).

Romania's exports are below 1% of the total EU exports. Maintaining this number, relatively constant, during the period under review, shows a lack of interest for the competitive export increase objective. Efforts in recent years have shown a structural improvement of Romanian exports, but with insignificant percentage and a low value added.

4. *The degree of innovation* is estimated at the EU level using a composite index (that includes values between 0 and 1) calculated based on a series of indicators. Depending on the degree of fulfilment of the criteria contained in the composite indicator are identified three groups of countries (Appendix 5) in which Romania is well below the EU level (0.22 compared to 0.55). failure to comply with the criteria is due to workers lacking in workforce skills and due to low research and development investments. These are in fact warning signs regarding the orientation of investments policy.
5. *Business environment.* Lack of transparency predominance in decision making, insufficient cooperation a significant phenomenon of "red tape of excessive regulations" contribute to the fragility and inconsistency shown by the Romanian business environment. By comparison, the UK is the country with the highest business index (Appendix 6) and Hungary is in a similar situation as Romania showing a changing legal environment that limits the confidence of potential investors.
6. *Access to finance.* Due to the banks aversion to risk, there has been a substantial decrease in the access to finance, in several EU countries, small companies suffering

from these restrictions. EU follows the development of the access to finance using several indicators, among which a composite index of two sub-indicators: access to credit and access to risk capital (Appendix 7)

Denmark had the most consistent access to funding in 2010, right after, in 2008, the best position belonged to the Baltic countries. Romania and Bulgaria who had a finance index above the E.U. average in 2008 (111,68 points respectively 107.82) significantly reduced this indicator in 2010. The high value of the indicator in 2008 can be explained by the delayed manifestation of the crisis.

Although, the EU countries have made progress in domains like public administration reform and industry sustainability through technologization, the convergence from an innovative point of view decreased in recent years, just as the access to finance has. Particular to each country, the legislative character and preferential state support for certain sectors of activity has a special resonance on the business environment.

Sustained merger of the internal efforts and external cooperation with the purpose to build a performing industry in a favorable business environment for the complex European market represents the key to success for a sustainable economy with an increasingly larger offer of employment.

4.2. The Industrial Policy Requirements in Romania, under the Aegis of the Europe 2020 Strategy

The recent financial crisis has demonstrated the fragility of an economy based on speculation. Romania needs an industrial policy because it gave up its own trade policy by joining the E.U. and is preparing to renounce to the currency and monetary lever, by joining the Eurozone.

Romania's reindustrialization (expressed as an objective since 2004 - 2008) becomes current again to change the previous growth model, built on consumption from imports. The Romanian industry has further on, difficulties in terms of competiveness, lack of complementarity between services and industry, granting mostly consumption credits and not investment credits.

From the supply perspective, Romania's economy benefits from foreign investments but the differentiated access of producers to the production factors, the infrastructure quality, population's education and mentality continue to represent impediments in achieving favorable performance. Although the Romanian market is significant in size, the demand has a low degree of diversification and modernization, which determines low orientation incentives to customers.

Competition between companies is based more on price, companies not being motivated to invest in research-development as long as the collective demand is limited to unpretentious products.

The deindustrialization in Romania was not only achieved at the expense of relocation and replacement with the tertiary sector as how it has happened in developed countries, but it represents itself the effect of a dysfunctional system as a whole. Bankruptcy or sale of companies did not improve the situation in the industry. Justifying the need for reindustrialization of Romanian economy is based on the industry share in GDP indicator. Comparison with the E.U.'s average shows the bigger picture of Romania's position.

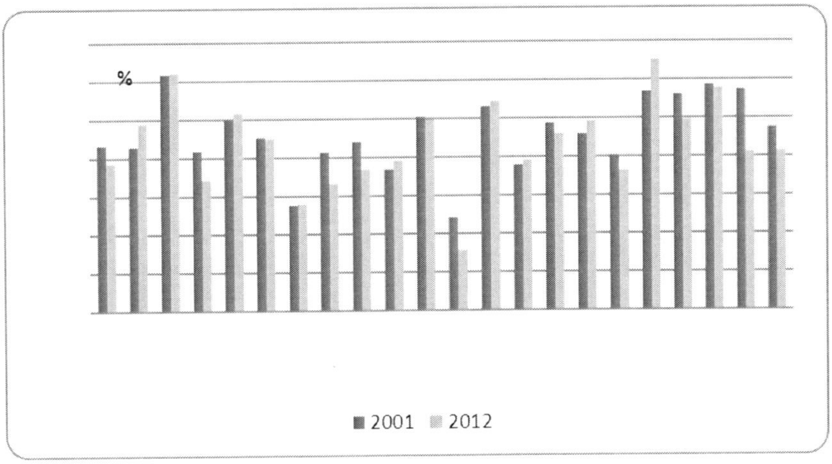

Source: Eurostat.

Figure 3.4. Gross value added in industry of the total gross value added in the economy (except construction).

It can be seen that the share of industry of the total value added of the economy grew between 2001 and 2012, from 28% to 32%, currently Romania owning the largest share of the industrial sector of total value added (figure 3.4). The motivation is that in other countries the service sector is better developed, sector that has a low potential in Romania.

Another indicator that expresses the need for reindustrialization is the specialization degree, measured as a percentage of an industrial branch of an economy total value added.

Romania is the most specialized country in the E.U. for the extraction of crude oil and natural gas, leather and recycling. It also ranks second in the fur industry and other transport equipment and third in mining. All these are part of the industrial sector and represent the possibility of developing a competitive advantage in these industries, which also represent viable arguments in supporting Romanian industry's revival.

The reason why restructuring and adjustment processes failed to assess, in real time, the possibilities and the importance of national economic competitiveness, represents a general deficiency related to government team performances. Only the external conditionalities were able to modify somewhat, and focus Romania's efforts and national performance, towards connecting to the growth rates and European and global social - economic progress.

Conclusion

Adapted to the transition process, *restructuring* has acquired specific accents in Romania. Determined by subjectivity, "the triplet" mind-set - behavior - attitude was the hardest changeable element in the absence of a coherent concept based on competence certified by reality rather than on compulsions from the political factor. Errors occurred following the faulty interpretation of the different meanings regarding the strategy and tactics of the structural adjustment process. Moreover, Romanian politics manifested and maintained a state of conflicting tensions between economic ideas and opinions supported by the newly political elites and the Romanian economic practice. To this was added the decision oscillation, of Romanian politics, between supporting and implementing the market's economic liberalism principles and promoting and supporting the interventionist current. With a few theoretical amendments and practical constraints, the description of the structural adjustment process highlights a series of economic policy actions undertaken by several governments following the 90's. Important distinctions were raised between the positive effects and limitations recorded as failures or unreached goals as well as the future of an economy structurally adjusted at Europe 2000's horizon.

APPENDIX 1.

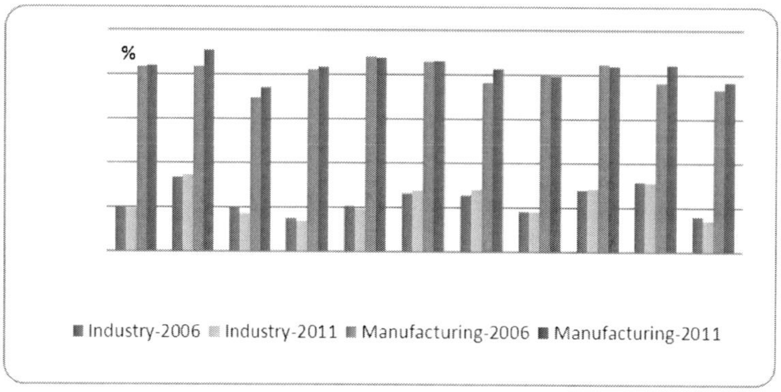

Source: own calculations based on Eurostat data: http://appsso.eurostat.ec .europa.eu/nui /setupModifyTableLayout.do. Data on Bulgaria is missing.

Figure 3.5. Share of industry in total activities and share of manufacturing in total industry, 2006-2011.

APPENDIX 2.

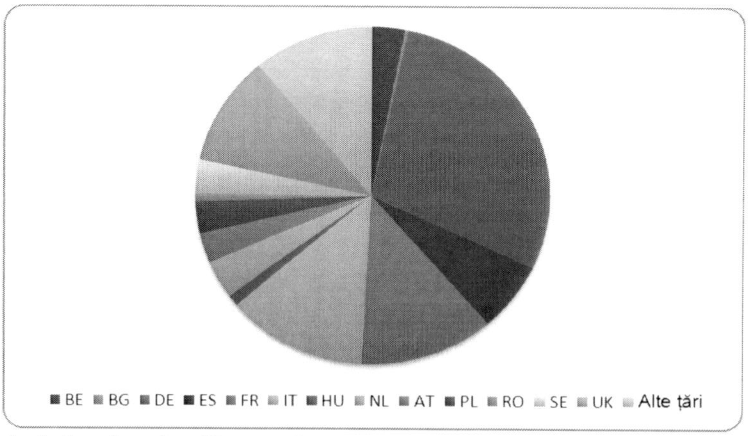

Source: own calculations based on Eurostat data.

Figure 3.6. Value added at factor cost of manufacturing in each country from the total value added of manufacturing in EU – 2010 - %.

APPENDIX 3.

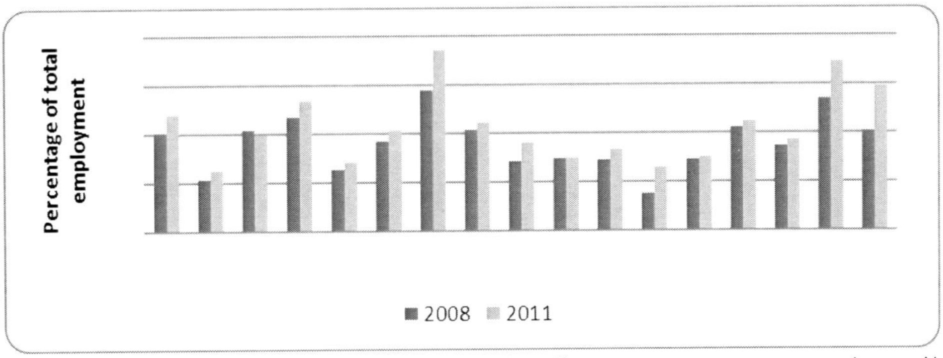

Source: own computations based on http://appsso.eurostat.ec.europa.eu/ nui/setup ModifyTableLayout.do.

Figure 3.7. Human resources employed in manufacturing (from Science and Technology) in total employment.

APPENDIX 4.

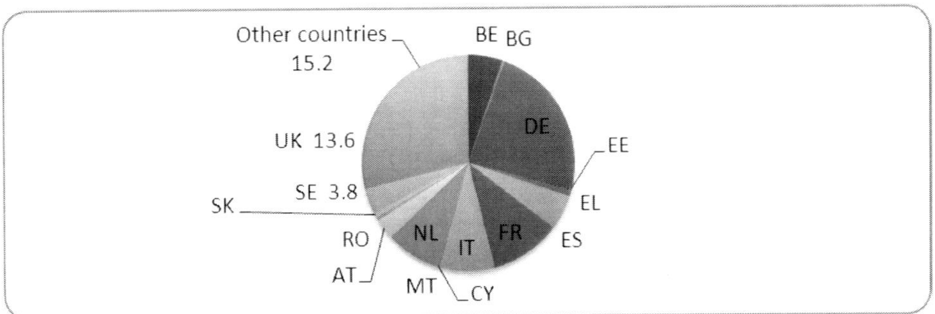

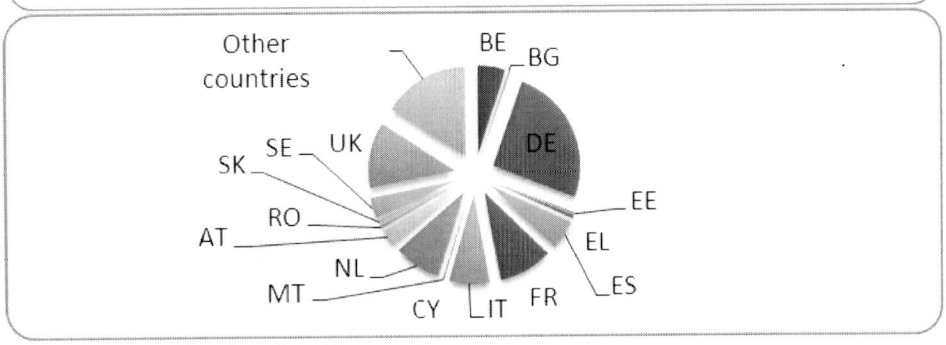

Source: own computations based on Eurostat data.

Figure 3.8. Exports of goods and services as percentage of the total EU exports (2006 vs. 2012).

APPENDIX 5.

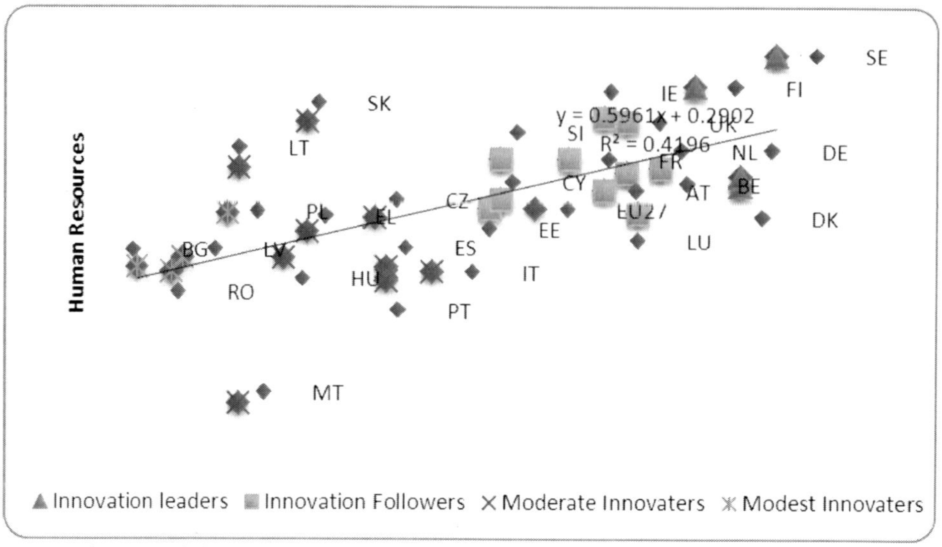

Source: graph created in Excel 2010 based on data from http://ec.europa.eu/enterprise/archives /ius2013/IUS 2013.html.

Figure 3.9. Innovation index in 2012.

APPENDIX 6.

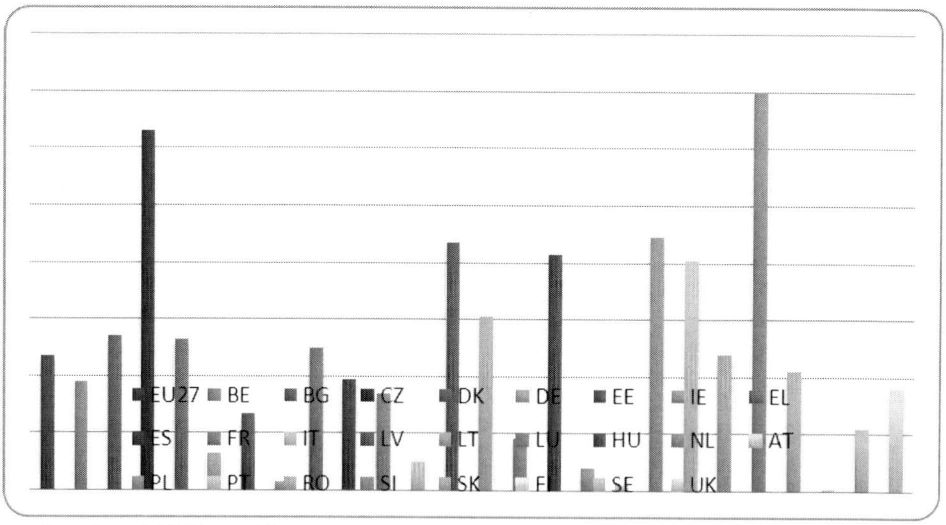

Source: Scoreboard 2012, pg. 15.

Figure 3.10. Business environment improvement 2006-2011.

APPENDIX 7.

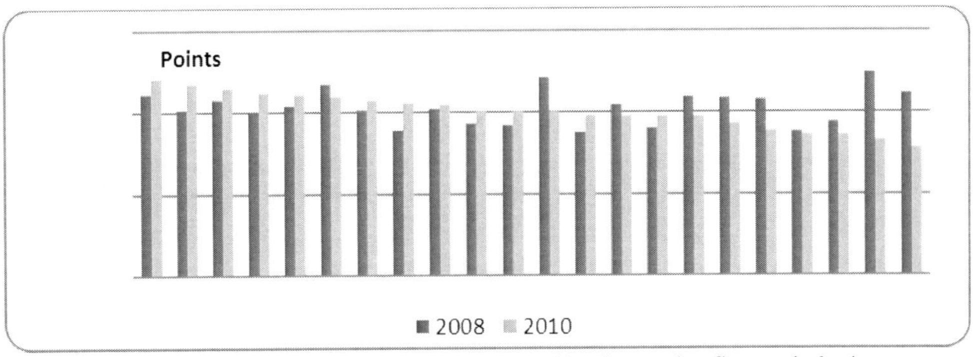

Source: http://ec.europa.eu/enterprise/policies/finance/data/enterprise-finance-index/sme-access-to-finance-index/index_en.htm.

Figure 3.11. SME Access to Finance Index (SMAF Index).

REFERENCES

[1] Amuedo-Dorantes, C., Serrano-Padial, R. (2010) *Labor market flexibility and poverty dynamic,* Labor Economics 17, pages 632-642.

[2] Perugini, C., Signorelli, M. (2010) *Youth labor market performance in European regions, Economic Change and Restructuring* 43, pg. 151-1852.

[3] [3] Constantinescu, N. N. (1992) *Transition to the market economy dilemmas*, Ager Publishing House –Economist, Bucharest.

[4] Iovițu, M. (1998) *Transition to market economy. Contemporary ideas confrontations,* TEMPER Collection, Economic Publishing House, Bucharest.

[5] Dogan, M., Pelassy, D. *Mixt economy half capitalist, half socialist,* Alternative Publishing House, Bucharest.

[6] Allais, M. (1994) *Traité d'économie pure*, Clément Juglar Publishing, Paris.

[7] Angelescu, C., Chenic (Cretu), A. Ș. (2011) *Implications of economic crisis on the labor market in Romania* , Economic Magazine No. 2 (55) /2011,pp. 39-47.

[8] Campolieti, M. (2010) *Labor Market Outcomes and Skill Acquisition of High-School Dropouts,* Journal of Labor Research 31, pp. 39-52, http://www.springer.com/ economics /journal/12122.

[9] Kregel, J., Matzner, E., Grabher, G. (1993) *Market shock*, Economic Publishing House, Bucharest.

[10] *** (1991) *The Transition to a market economy-La transition vers une economie de marche*, vol.1, The broad issues-les grands problemes O.C.D.E, Paris.

[11] Dobrescu, E., Postolache, T. (1990) *Economic records*, Romanian Academy Publishing House, Bucharest.

[12] Cărămidariu, D. A. (2012) *Economic thinking, governance programs and interventionism in Romania after 1989*, SOLNESS Publishing House, Timișoara.

[13] Cretu, A. S. (2010) *Labor Market Flexibilisation*, ASE Publishing House, Economics Collection, Bucharest.

[14] Giarini O., Liedtkre, P. (2002) *Employment dilemma and labor future*, Bucharest, All Beck Publishing House, Iaşi.
[15] Blanchard, O., Dornbusch, R., Krugman, P, Summers, L., (1991) *Reform in Eastern Europe*, MIT Press, Cambridge, Massachusetts.
[16] Isachsen,A., Hamilton, C., Gylfason, T. (1992) *Let's understand market economy,* European Free trade Association, Oscar Print, Geneva.
[17] *** Executive Unit of the National Council of Vocational Qualifications and Training of Adults (2011) European project "Development of an operational system of qualifications in higher education in Romania-DOCIS" study "of recent graduates of higher education and their integration into the labor market."
[18] ***European Committee (2014) Proposal for a Decision of the European Parliament and of the Council on establishing a European platform for enhancing cooperation related to the prevention and discouraging of undeclared work, Brussels.
[19] *** Foundation Focus, Issue 8, June 2010, How are you? Quality of life in Europe www.eurofound.europa.eu/publications/focusform.htm.
[20] *** Institute for Innovation and Development Project – IPID (2010), Coordinator: Maliţa, M., Georgescu, C., Romania after the crisis. Re-professionalization, Publishing Company.
[21] *** National Institute of Statistics (2014) – Employment and unemployment in 2013 underemployment and potential additional labor – PRESS RELEASE No. 96.
[22] *** National Institute of Statistics (2007-2010), Statistical Yearbook, Bucharest, Romania.
[23] *** International Labor Organization (ILO) (2006). Global Employment Trends for Youth. ILO, Geneva.
[24] *** International Monetary Fund (IMF) (2009), From recession to recovery: how soon and how strong? Chapter 3 in IMF (2009). World Economic Outlook (WEO) Crisis and Recovery, April2009. IMF, Washington, D.C.
[25] *** European Commission, Access to Finance, 2010, http://ec.europa.eu/ enterprise/policies/finance/data/enterprise-finance-index/sme-access-to-finance-index/index_en .htm], accessed on 24.04.2013.
[26] *** European Commission, Industrial Performance Scoreboard, 2012, [http://ec.europa.eu/enterprise/policies/industrial-competitiveness/monitoring-member-states/files/scoreboard2012_en.pdf], accessed la 28.04.2013.
[27] *** European Commission, Industrial revolution brings industry back to Europe, Press Release, 10 October 2012, Brussels, [http://europa.eu/rapid/press-release_IP-12-1085_en.htm], accessed on 24.04.2013.
[28] *** European Commission, Innovation Union Scoreboard, 2013, [http://ec.europa.eu/ enterprise/archives/ius2013/IUS2013.html], accessed on 27.04.2013.
[29] *** European Commission, Member States' Competitiveness. Performance and Policies. Industrial Performance Scoreboard, 2012 Edition, [http://ec.europa.eu/ enterprise/policies/industrial-competitiveness/monitoring-member-states/files/ms_comp_report_2012_en.pdf], accessed on 10.05.2013.
[30] *** Group of Applied Economics, Romania's reindustrialization. Policies and strategies, the Association for Studies and Social- Economic Forecasting, June 2010, [http://www.gea.org.ro/documente /ro/studii/studiu_reindustrializarea_ro_bostina_ok.pdf], accessed on 15.05.2013.

[31] *** http://appsso.eurostat.ec.europa.eu/nui/setupModifyTableLayout. do. www.wall-street.ro 360 INSIGHTS, The evolution of Romanian perception on the financial crisis Bucharest 2012

[32] www.whyfiles.org -The psychological price of job loss-2011-http://whyfiles.org/2011/the-psychological-price-of-job-loss/

In: What/Who Are We After the Transition? Focus on Romania ISBN: 978-1-63483-947-1
Editors: M. Dinu, D. Ailenei, A. Dachin et al.

Chapter 4

Agitation Around Budgets

Marius Corneliu Marinaş*, PhD, Alexandra Adam, PhD, Mina Fanea-Ivanovici, PhD, Ioana Gavril (Moldovan), PhD, Cristian Ionescu, PhD candidate and George Ştefan, PhD candidate

Bucharest University of Economics Studies, Bucharest, Romania

Economic theory argues that fiscal policy should reduce the intensity of turbulences that generate macroeconomic imbalances by distancing economies away from the sustainable growth path. Romania's post-1989 experience suggests that the fiscal measures that have been taken have been effective neither in reducing economic fluctuations, nor in boosting the potential output. In general, fiscal policy has been developed for a short period of time, in response to the requirements of the transition process, at the requests of international financial organizations and to certain pressures induced by the electoral cycle, thus sacrificing economic growth and structural reforms. Under these circumstances, the budgets that the economy functioned with became only a reporting tool of the financial administration. The lack of medium-term and long-term fiscal vision, the inconsistency, the hesitations, the poor predictability of fiscal policy options and the weak management of collecting and using budgetary resources have disrupted the economy with the intensity which is explained by the pendulum effect.

Accordingly, Romanian economy has entered in a vicious spiral in which fiscal policy makers have been blamed for both during recovery periods and during crises and economic downturn periods. As we are going to explain in this chapter, Romanian fiscal policy during the transition period seems to have lost its role of stabilizing economic fluctuations and fostering economic growth. This process was obvious in the first decade of transition, as well as at the beginning of the economic and financial crisis. The measures that were taken by the government between 1990 and 2013 were evaluated both from the perspective of their impact on the annual budget execution, and of their impact on the business environment.

---

* corresponding author: mariusmarinas@gmail.com

1. Budget Construction between 1990 and 2013

The diagnostic analysis of the fiscal policy measures taken in the last 24 years was divided in three sections, in accordance with the assumed budgetary objectives, with the constraints that were specific to budget construction and with the processes that occurred in the real economy. Fiscal policy management in the first decade of transition (1990-1999) was influenced by the government's efforts to balance the imperative of structural reforms and the necessity to mitigate their effect on the economy. The application of certain reform measures (such as price liberalization) in an economic environment which did not create market economy specific institutions led to a widespread financial blockage, which governments tried to diminish. However, the adopted decisions had only temporary effects that increased the economy's decline when it started to face the transformational recession between 1997 and 1999.

The second section analyzes the stage of economic growth in Romania (2000-2008), marked by the country's accession to the European Union. In this interval, fiscal policy was rather procyclical, contributing to fiscal consolidation until 2005 and to economy overheating between 2006 and 2008. The current economic crisis and the new European Union institutional arrangements radically transformed the role of fiscal policy, which shifted from fighting against the effects of the economic crisis to ensuring financial stability, by promoting austerity measures. Therefore, between 2009 and 2013, fiscal policy became restrictive, aiming to consolidate the public finances that had been deteriorated by the economic recession and by the inadequate measures promoted during the preceding economic growth period.

1.1. The Shock of Transition

The transition to a market economy has implied the reforming of the fiscal system and of the public expenditure policy, with a view to achieving macroeconomic stabilization. The new tax system created in Romania should have been simple, transparent and entrepreneurship-stimulating, while the Government should have allocated the collected resources in order to finance the economy and to minimize the economic and social costs of transition. The main measures of reform of the tax system were adopted in the first decade of transition and they involved the replacement of income tax charges to public companies, from the taxes on movement of goods and labor taxes to the tax forms specific to a market economy - income and profit progressive taxes, value added tax and other indirect taxes, thus:

- in 1991 the profit tax was implemented and it replaced the public firms' profit payments, canceled in 1990. Initially, a progressive tax was established, with over 50 installments between 0 and 70%, their number being reduced in 1992 to two - 30 and 45%. Between 1996 and 2000 the income tax was 38%, the highest tax rate among Central and Eastern Europe economies. The corporate tax system has been simplified since 2000, and most temporary tax deferrals practiced in the 1990s have been abolished.

- the tax on movement of goods was replaced by value added tax in 1993, its standard rate being 18%. Starting with 1994, a reduced rate of 9% was added for three categories of goods, which increased in 1998 to 11% when the standard rate increased to 22%. Poor tax collection caused by administrative difficulties in tax collection and refund, value add tax exemption for some companies and increasing categories of goods (to 19 in 1998) with low rate, led to the introduction in 2000 of a flat tax of 19%.
- progressive payroll tax replaced the gross salary tax. In 1992 a complicated scheme was implemented, with 13 installments between 6% and 45%, the threshold being increased to 60% in 1993. Between 1997 and 2000, the highest rate was reduced to 40%, the spread between the highest and lower rate (from 35 to 22 percentage points) being thus reduced; the number of tax thresholds was also reduced, but the efficiency of tax collection was affected by the addition of new exemptions.
- social insurance contributions were increased in 1990 and 1991, being maintained at 35% of gross salary until 1997. The accumulated arrears to the pension fund and the introduction of health insurance contributions increased the contribution share to 43% in 1998 and to 60% in 1999, increasing the labor costs by 25% in just two years. In the early 2000's Romania recorded the highest level of social contributions, twice higher than the European average and at least 10 percentage points higher than the rates of other Central and Eastern European economies.

The institutional implant of the new fiscal system was performed with difficulty and did not have the anticipated effects on the real economy and on budget revenues, for the following reasons:

- decreasing production during the first years of transition has led to the erosion of the tax base for the new forms of taxes;
- there was no culture of interaction with the tax authorities, which hindered both the collection of taxes and their administration;
- there was a resistance of most economic agents (that were facing financial difficulties) to accept the role that taxes have in the market economy, which was reflected in the accumulation of arrears in the consolidated budget.

The budget construction was influenced not only by the low efficiency of tax collection, but also by the low capacity to adapt to the real economy during the transition processes. The government aimed to support the economic restructuring, but financial difficulties of the economic environment altered the government's strategy, transforming it into a *stop and go* one, marked by failures and unreliable measures. Liberalization of prices, lower domestic demand and external demand, following the dissolution of the Council for Mutual Economic Assistance, generated financial difficulties for the public enterprises, in the context of the disappearance of weak budget constraints that were specific to a planned economy. In fact, the competitiveness of these companies was affected even before 1990 due to a decision to lower investments in order to increase the budget savings required by the payment of Romania's external debt.

The government tried to mitigate the impact of transition on public enterprises and agriculture, through subsidies and tax breaks, in order to reduce financial blockage and stop the economic decline, but the positive effects were visible only on the short term. In order for the restructuring process to be effective, the weak budget constraints imposed on firms during the planned economy period (automatic access to investment resources, financing, ceiling prices on energy and raw materials etc.) should have been replaced with stronger constraints specific to flows that occur within a market economy. Unfortunately, fiscal and financial facilities were not accompanied by conditionality on business restructuring and modernization of economic activity, which led to the appearance of financial blockade as a result of the accumulation of intra-firms arrears, as well as arrears towards the government and towards the banking sector.

Therefore, the restructuring process lost its credibility, being hampered by the threat of financial destabilization as a result of the deepening structural reforms. Consequently, government strategy generated high intensity adverse effects, dynamiting the increase of production during 1993-1996. Fiscal policy objectives changed starting with 1997, aiming to decrease quasi-fiscal subsidies, arrears and dampen inflationary pressures. However, fiscal consolidation efforts were hampered by the recapitalization of banks that faced financial problems and by the poor capacity of refinancing public debt.

One of the channels through which arrears were accumulated were the losses of large energy intensive firms. The government did not fully implement the policy of ceasing energy to customers with large losses and of subsidizing those with social impact, so that arrears increased, which negatively affected the budget revenues and the ability to pay for government guaranteed loans. Under these circumstances, not only public utility companies, but also public banks were transformed into relief valves in order to remove the financial deadlock in the economy. In the context of the persistence of low budget constraints for state-owned firms, economic agents that were acting as buffers began to be weaker once the currency crisis and the liberalization of interest rates started in 1997, which increased the budget pressure. Thus, the share of nonperforming loans reached 90% for the largest state-owned bank, and its debts were taken over by the government. Due to fiscal and quasi-fiscal deficits during the early years of transition, public debt increased rapidly from 10% of GDP in 1991 to 27% of GDP in 1996, which increased the share of interest expenses in total budget expenditures from 4% in 1995 to 11.2% in 1997 and 15.3% in 1999.

Between 1990 and 1999 annual budget execution results were comparable to those of Poland, and superior to those of Hungary, although the macroeconomic performance was relatively lower compared to these economies. Thus, the Romanian economy was characterized by a double transformational recession, while in Poland and Hungary the domestic production has not decreased anymore after 1993. However, relatively low levels of consolidated budget deficits hiding quasi-fiscal deficits persisted, being characteristic for Romania's transition. From the brief analysis of the construction budget of the first ten years of transition, we reached the conclusion that there were three subperiods, consistent with the electoral cycles (table 1).

The decrease of the GDP by 25% in 1992 compared to 1989 was not immediately reflected in the consolidated budget balance, due to a delayed triggering of fiscal reform measures and due to dependence of the volume and structure of budgetary expenditures to the previous form of economic organization. Budget revenues were quickly adjusted in comparison to those of 1989, their share in GDP being reduced by 15% in 1992, while the proportion of budget spending remained relatively constant between 1989 and 1992. The distinctive feature of this period was the government policy of increasing the expenditure subsidies by 6 percentage points, especially for agriculture, in the context of financial deadlock within the economy. In order to solve the problem of arrears accelerated growth, that reached 81% of the GDP at the end of 1991, the Government implemented a global compensation scheme of central bank's credit losses, after currency issue. Arrears were reduced in 1992 to 35% of the GDP as a result of the decision of taking over bad loans and losses of state-owned enterprises by the government and public banks. The cost of these measures was twofold, postponing the state-owned industry restructuring and deteriorating the quality of the assets held by the commercial banks. The effect of adopting such a program was the appearance of the moral hazard behavior within the companies with losses, which led to increasing arrears.

Table 1. Implementation of the general consolidated budget (1990-1999)

(% of GDP)	1990	1991	1992	1993	1994	1995	1996	1997	1998	1999
1.Balance of consolidated budget	1	3.2	-4.6	-0.4	-1.9	-2.6	-3.9	-3.5	-3.6	-1.8
2. Budgetary revenues	38.7	41.2	36.8	33.4	31.5	32.1	30	30.4	31.5	32.8
2.2. Tax revenues	35.5	33.2	33.5	31.3	28.2	28.9	26.9	26.5	27.8	30.1
2.2.1. Direct taxes	22.7	23.7	25	21.6	20.1	19.6	17.9	17.5	17	18.5
2.2.1.1. Corporate income tax	7.1	5.1	5.3	3.8	3.8	3.9	3.3	4.3	3	3.1
2.2.1.2. Income tax	6.8	7.6	7.6	6.6	6.5	6.4	6.1	5.5	5	5.2
2.2.1.3. Contributions to social insurance	7.9	10	10.3	9.3	8	7.9	7.5	6.6	7.9	8.7
2.2.2. Indirect taxes	12.8	9.5	8.5	9.7	8.1	9.3	9	9	10.8	11.6
2.2.2.1. Excise, VAT	11.8	8.3	6.9	7.3	6.1	6.7	6.3	6.3	8.3	8.9
2.3. Non-tax revenues	2.9	5	2.5	1.9	3.1	2.5	2	1.8	1.5	1.6
2.4. Income from capital	0.3	3	0.8	0.2	0.2	0.7	1.1	2.1	2.2	1.1
3. Budgetary expenditures	37.7	38	41.4	33.8	33.4	34.7	33.9	33.9	35.1	34.6
3.1. Staff costs	6.8	7.6	7.4	6.6	6.5	6.5	6	4.9	5	4.9
3.2. Material expenses	4.5	5.5	6.2	5	5.4	6.1	5.8	5.7	6.4	6.6
3.3. Interest expense	0	0.1	0.3	0.9	1.4	1.4	1.7	3.8	4.7	5.3
3.4. Subsidies	7	9.1	13	6.8	3.8	4.1	4.3	2.5	1.7	1.6
3.5. Transfers	11.6	9.9	9.4	9.5	10.5	10.8	10.4	11.5	13.1	13.4
3.6. Capital expenditure	7.9	6	4.1	4.2	5.5	5.3	5.2	4.8	3.6	2.8

Source: Ministry of Finance.

Starting with 1993 much progress was made in terms of adapting the tax and budgetary system to the mechanisms of market economy, the deepening of tax system reform and reducing budgetary subsidies by about 9% of the GDP compared to 1992. Several social protection measures were also adopted in order to alleviate the costs of the restructuring process and of the inflationary phenomenon.

The share of public spending in the GDP was relatively constant between 1993 and 1996, but its structure was modified (the share of social transfers, material costs, interest and investment increased by 2 percentage points). Consolidated budget revenues were influenced by the adopted tax reform and by low budgetary constraints on tax collection.

Consequently, there was a continuous deterioration of the budget execution caused by the reduction of the share of budgetary revenues from 36.8% of GDP in 1992 to 33.4% in 1993 and 30% of GDP in 1996 (table 1). The cause was a decrease in the level of taxation, measured by the ratio of tax revenue to GDP, despite a cumulative growth of 17% from 1993 to 1996, compared to 1992. The evolution of the fiscal revenue was affected by the restriction of direct taxes (7% of GDP) as a result of decreasing budgetary resources collected from profit tax (by 2% of GDP), from income tax (by 1.5% of GDP) and from social contributions (3% of GDP). The evolution of the last two components was influenced by the reduction by 900,000 of the number of workers (i.e., 14%) in 1996 compared to 1992 and also by the perpetuation of the losses of state-owned enterprises, which increased the arrears of the general consolidated budget.

Table 2. Execution of the consolidated budget (2000-2008)

	2000	2001	2002	2003	2004	2005	2006	2007	2008
1. Balance of the consolidated budget	-4	-3.3	-2.5	-2.3	-1.3	-0.6	-1.3	-3.1	-4.8
2. Budgetary revenues	31.2	30.1	29.6	30	31.1	31.4	32.3	32.3	32.2
2.2. Tax revenues	29.2	28	27.6	27.9	27.0	27.3	28.1	27.8	27.9
2.2.1. Direct taxes	17.9	16.9	16.4	15.7	15.0	14.6	15.1	15.8	15.9
2.2.1.1. Corporate income tax	2.5	1.9	2	2.3	2.6	2.3	2.3	2.5	2.5
2.2.1.2. Income tax	3.4	3.2	2.8	2.8	2.9	2.4	2.8	3.5	3.6
2.2.1.3. Contributions to social insurance	10.8	10.7	10.7	9.6	9.1	9.5	9.6	9.5	9.5
2.2.2. Indirect taxes	11.3	11.1	11.2	12.2	11.9	12.8	13.0	12.0	11.9
2.2.2.1. Excises, VAT	8.6	8.6	9.1	10.4	9.9	10.9	11.1	10.5	10.6
2.3. Non-fiscal revenues *	1.9	2.1	1.9	1.9	3.3	3.2	3.3	3.4	3.1
2.4. Capital income	0.1	0	0.1	0.2	0.2	0.3	0.3	0.2	0.2
3. Budgetary expenditures	35.2	33.4	32.1	32.3	32.4	32.0	33.6	35.4	37.0
3.1. Staff costs*	5.5	5.0	4.8	4.8	7.1	7.4	8.0	8.1	8.9
3.2. Material expenses *	7.0	7.0	7.0	7.6	5.8	6.3	6.2	6.1	6.4
3.3. Interest expenses	4.9	3.8	3.0	2.1	1.3	1.2	0.8	0.7	0.7
3.4. Subsidies	2.2	1.6	1.6	2.3	2.2	2.2	2.2	1.7	1.5
3.5. Transfers	12.2	12.7	12.4	11.8	12.4	11.9	12.2	14.1	14.5
3.6. Capital expenditure	3.1	3.1	3.2	3.5	3.5	3.0	4.3	4.7	5.0

Note: *) since 2004 there have been some methodological changes that have influenced the structure of revenues and expenditures relative to 2003 but not their level.

Source: Ministry of Finance.

The economic and financial tensions accumulated between 1990 and 1996 exploded starting with 1997 as a result of the full liberalization of the exchange rate and interest rates, due to the accumulation of losses in the banking system and due to the increase of the cost of refinancing debt (as a result of the triggering of the regional financial crisis' global impact). Budget execution ended with deficits of 3.5% in 1997 and 1998, caused by the economic decline of 12% between 1997 and 1999 compared to 1996, and by the spending increase of 1.5% of GDP compared to 1996. The Government assumed the deepening of the restructuring process of state-owned enterprises in order to improve fiscal discipline and to reduce financial blockage. The government also implemented a program of fiscal consolidation by reducing subsidies and personnel expenses, which allowed a savings increase by 4% of the GDP in 1997. These measures should have mitigated the budgetary impact of increased interest expense on debt.

The Government failed to meet both objectives, due to the resistance to restructuring and due to the phenomena of debt rescheduling, direct tax revenue reduction and losses of the banking sector. In this context, a set of restrictive fiscal measures was adopted, such as tax and social security contributions increase, despite the recession that was installed when the GDP decreased by 6.9% in 1997. Revenues from VAT and excise duties were raised by 2.5% of the GDP in 1999 compared to 1997, providing a higher impact on the collection of indirect taxes in total revenues from 29% to 34%, while the share in the GDP of the contribution collections increased by 2% of the GDP in the same period.

The deficit reduction was not accompanied by streamlining government spending, but rather by adopting decisions contrary to sense, such as social transfers increase by 2% of the GDP between 1997 and 1999. The opportunity cost of fiscal consolidation increased the tax burden on economic agents that were good payers, while increasing the share of the unofficial economy. Therefore, a vicious circle of budget construction was created, where the solutions adopted in order to compensate for the effects of previous decisions created new imbalances in the real economy, which reduced the tax base and induced unexpected increases in future taxes.

1.2. The Economic Growth Stage

Between 2000 and 2008 Romania recovered the production losses compared to 1999 (in 2002) and 1989 (in 2003), and decreased the income gap by 20 percentage points compared to the European Union average, reaching 44% of GDP per capita at purchasing power parity. Fiscal policy objectives changed as compared to the previous period, aiming to stimulate and strengthen economic growth, to reduce unemployment and inflation, in order to limit the trade deficit. However, the problems of budget construction in Romania, specific to the first decade of transition (fiscal unpredictability, low tax collection, low share of tax revenues, the companies' arrears to the public budget etc.) were persistent, but more easily managed once the economy entered a cycle of nine years of economic growth in the context of preparation for and actual accession to the European Union.

One of the imperfections of the tax system was its reduced ability to collect taxes, regardless of the direction of taxation changes. Unfortunately, the tax reduction measures, which created a temporary empty budget, only temporarily increased the tax base, despite a higher real GDP by 62% in 2008 compared to 2000. The main episodes of fiscal loosening consisted of:

- reduction of corporate tax from 38% to 25% in 2000 and to 16% in 2005, when the unique income tax principle was introduced;
- decrease in social contributions by 12 percentage points in 2007 compared to 2001;
- replacing progressive income tax rate (from 18% to 40%) with an unique rate of 16% in 2005;
- decrease of VAT from 22% to 19% in 2000 and setting a supplementary rate of 9% starting with 2004.

In general, tax reduction led to a decrease in budget revenues over a larger period of time than it would have been natural in an economy that responds to incentives. Thus, the social contributions revenue, expressed as a percentage of the GDP, decreased from 10.8% in 2000 to 9.5% in 2008, the profit tax revenue had not exceeded 2.5% of GDP, while the VAT revenues declined between 2003 and 2006. Therefore, tax revenues were capped at 28% of GDP, at a lower level by about two percentage points compared to 1999, significantly influencing the evolution of total budget revenues (table 2). Moreover, Romania was characterized by the lowest level of taxation in the European Union, the EU average being of 40-41%. Among Central and Eastern Europe countries, Hungary and the Czech Republic were closer to the average, while the economies that had implemented a flat tax system (the Baltic countries and Slovakia) were more similar to the Romanian economy.

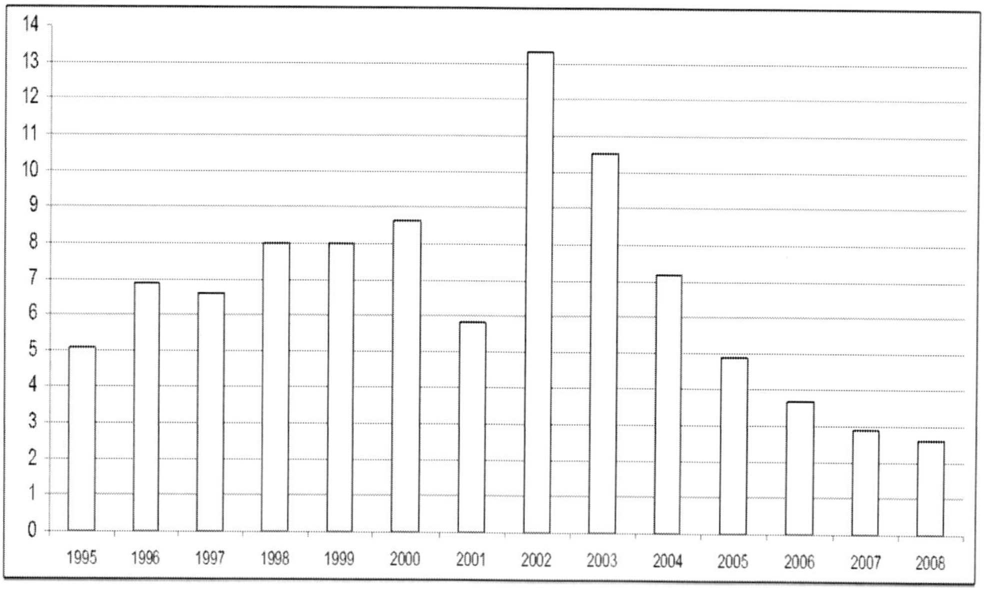

Source: IMF (2004), Romania: Selected Issues and Statistical Appendix, IMF Country Report No. 04/220; Elena Pelinescu (2013), Mechanisms of arrears in Romania; Ghizdeanu and Ristea (2010), Evolution and structure of arrears.

Figure 1. Evolution of the consolidated general government arrears.

Another problem of the construction of the budget, manifested in the planned economy, but amplified by the shock of transition, was given by the persistence of firms' arrears to the consolidated budget, which adversely affected the collection of budget revenues. Progress regarding the reduction of arrears was relatively limited until 2003, when stricter budgetary constraints prevented only temporary accumulation of new arrears. Governments tolerated not only the state-owned firms' arrears (with full capital or majoritary capital), but also those of private companies, whose arrears increased from 0.5% of the GDP in 1995 (10% of total) to 5.3% of the GDP in 2002 (40% of total).

Therefore, solutions to reduce arrears (taking over the losses, staggering debt, turning them into shares etc.) for state-owned firms that were to be privatized seemed meaningless as long as the private sector itself increasingly accumulated arrears. The reduction of arrears as a percentage of the GDP was due to the frequent measures of erasing debt, by taking over the debt and by improving the economic performance of firms in the context of economic growth between 2004 and 2008 (figure 1). Similarly, total arrears registered by the domestic economic agents (to suppliers, state, banks and other creditors) fell from 37% of GDP in 2002 to 14% of GDP in 2008 (Ghizdeanu and Ristea, 2010).

Regarding government spending, the prudent policy adopted until 2005 was designed to support the consolidation of public finance. The public spending to GDP declined by 3.2 percentage points in 2003 relative to 2000 and was due to reduced spending for interest on public loans, from 4.9% to 1.2% (Table 2). In contrast, government consumption (consisting of material costs, personnel and capital) increased from 15% in 2002 to 16, 4% in 2005.

Since 2006 a series of budgetary pressures accumulated and led to increased expenditure from 32% to 37% of the GDP in 2008:

- an increase in the number of public employees, justified, in particular, by a better absorption of post-accession EU funds, along with wage increases for public employees, measures that determined an increase of personnel spending by 1.5% of the GDP;
- an increase in pensions by approximately 150% in real terms, due to both social and political considerations, which led to an increase of pensions expenditure by 2% of the GDP;
- an increase in the capital spending by 2% of the GDP in order to compensate for the deficit and quality of Romanian infrastructure (roads, education, health etc.).

All this additional expenditure was made in the context of overestimating the budget revenues by 5% of the GDP within the budget construction. In addition, the prospect of sustainable growth in the future enhanced the government propensity to consumption, and the growth of current expenditure was hoped to be financed from budget revenues that were expected to be higher in the coming years.

1.3. THE Economic and Financial Crisis

The economic growth model between 2005 and 2008, based on lending for consumption and unproductive investment, proved unsustainable in the context of the global financial crisis and weakened external demand. The contraction of the private sector since 2009 was caused by both external adverse conditions and vulnerabilities induced by overheating in 2007 and 2008. Therefore, the economy faced the third recession in the last 24 years, real GDP suffering a cumulative reduction of 8% in 2009 and 2010 relative to 2008. Economic recovery was slow, relying on increasing exports and industry, agriculture respectively, in years with favorable natural conditions. Thus, domestic production is still 1.6% below the 2008 level, despite a growth rate of about 3.5% in 2013.

The first impulse of the fiscal authorities was to establish a set of measures for economic recovery. Private demand reduction was to be replaced by additional government demand, in order to restore the confidence of investors and consumers. This program would have generated an additional budget deficit caused by the revenue decrease as a response to the contraction of economic activity. Therefore, in 2009, a status quo of the construction budget was maintained, motivated both by fiscal space exhaustion before the crisis and by electoral considerations. However, the economic downturn led to an increasing government deficit from 4.8% in 2008 to 7.3% of GDP in 2009.

Fiscal policy strategy changed dramatically since 2010, along with the advent of European second-round effects of the economic crisis - weak capacity for financing current deficits and public debt. Therefore, the risk of economies with unsustainable public finances (including Romania) got higher, which increased interest rates associated with debt refinancing. In order to regain the trust of international lenders, Romania was forced to adopt fiscal consolidation programs that would lead to deficit reduction. Therefore, the role of fiscal policy was radically transformed - from combating economic crisis to financial stability, by promoting austerity measures. The opportunity cost of fiscal consolidation was a weaker economic recovery capacity and the main adjustment measures consisted of:

- increasing VAT from 19% to 24%, which raised revenue by 6.8% of the GDP in 2009 to 8.6% of the GDP in 2011;
- increasing excises, in several rounds, their share in the GDP growing by 0.4 percentage points;
- raising social contributions (since 2009) by 4 percentage points, which led to a revenue decline of 1% of the GDP relative to 2008;
- lowering public sector wages by 25% and reducing the number of state employees by 10%, which determined savings of 2.4% of the GDP in 2012 compared to 2009;
- taxing above average pensions and limiting access to various forms of social assistance, which led to a decrease in social spending by 1.5% of the GDP in 2009-2012;
- capping material costs;
- lowering capital expenditures in the context of access to European funds.

The decrease of the budget deficit by 4.8% of the GDP in 2012 compared to 2009 was largely achieved due to a spending decrease by 4.1% of the GDP (Table 3). Budget revenues were capped at 32-33% of the GDP, while the proportion of tax revenue was high only temporarily. The increased taxes adopted during the recession enhanced tax evasion, the stock of arrears to the state budget and negatively affected consumption and investment. Therefore, the arrears from the economy increased in just two years by 10% of the GDP, reaching 31% of the GDP in 2010. In addition, budget arrears to private and public sector increased, which reduced the quality of public services and negatively affected the financial position of firms. Both arguments for fiscal consolidation and compatibility solutions to the economic growth process will be detailed in Section 4.3.

The analysis in this chapter reveals the real economy`s tendency to decouple from the fiscal measures taken in the last 24 years. The shock of transition, inappropriate and circumstantial fiscal decisions, but also the three periods of economic recession Romanian economy had to struggle with contributed to entrench arrears (including to the state budget) and to the low level of tax revenue collection, with the complicity of government authorities. In an economy with altered incentives, not even fiscal relaxation measures had natural effects on output, employment and tax evasion. In this context, the level of taxation was reduced from 31.3% in 1993 to 27.2% of the GDP in 2013, and Romania recorded the lowest share of tax revenues in the EU, while the total budget expenditure was, on average, about 10% lower than the EU average.

Table 3. Consolidated budget execution (2009-2013)

	2009	2010	2011	2012	2013*
1. Balance of the consolidated budget	-7.3	-6.4	-4.3	-2.5	-2.5
2. Budgetary revenues	31.4	32.2	32.7	32.9	32
2.2. Tax revenues	27.1	26.4	27.8	28.1	27.2
2.2.1. Direct taxes	15.9	14.3	14.5	14.4	14.3
2.2.1.1. Corporate income tax	2.7	2.1	2.0	2.0	1.7
2.2.1.2. Income tax	3.7	3.4	3.4	3.6	3.6
2.2.1.3. Contributions to social insurance	9.6	8.7	9.1	8.8	8.7
2.2.2. Indirect taxes	11.2	12.2	13.3	13.8	12.9
2.2.2.1. Excises, VAT	10.0	10.8	12.0	12.0	11.7
2.3. Non-fiscal revenues	3.1	3.8	3.3	3.1	2.7
2.4. Capital income	0.1	0.1	0.1	0.1	0.1
3. Budgetary expenditures	38.6	38.6	37.0	35.4	34.5
3.1. Staff costs	9.3	8.2	6.9	6.9	7.4
3.2. Material expenses	5.7	5.6	5.7	5.9	6.2
3.3. Interest expenses	1.2	1.4	1.6	1.8	1.7
3.4. Subsidies	1.4	1.3	1.2	1.0	0.8
3.5. Transfers	16.7	18.2	17.3	16.3	15.6
3.6. Capital expenditure	4.4	3.7	4.1	3.3	2.9

Note: *) estimated values.
Source: Ministry of Finance.

1.4. The Effects of IMF Financial Assistance

After 1990, the International Monetary Fund has supported the political authorities in Romania in implementing the market economy and achieving macroeconomic stabilization, by granting the country a total of ten stand-by loan agreements, three of which, i.e., the 2004 loan, the 2011 loan, and the last one, granted in 2013, were merely precautionary loans, meaning that the Romanian authorities do not intend to make drawings. The need for the first post-revolution IMF agreements arose at a point in which the country's foreign exchange reserves were depleting rapidly in the first half of 1990.

The agreement allowed the country to avoid cessation of its external payments and prevent the negative effect thereof, namely the loss of the country's international creditworthiness. The following post-revolution loan agreements were called forth by the fact that the transformation of the centralized communist economy into a market economy – and in particular the process of privatization – implied the existence of funds and technical expertise that post-communist governments lacked. The assumption that stood at the basis of these agreements was that the access to capital resources would fundamentally change the economic coordinates of the country. According to the IMF practice, loan conditioning is a primary rule, a real guiding principle. Thus, loan conditioning increased in time and became more personalized with every new loan granted. The initial paradigm underlying the first agreements consisted of a set of constraints: reduce state intervention, liberalize prices, privatize, deregulate domestic markets, eliminate negative real interest rates, decrease inflation, adjust taxes to income, devaluate the exchange rate, introduce a floating exchange rate etc.

To be able to repay the money borrowed, Romania was required, according to the IMF, to ensure macroeconomic stability, a condition that could not be attained without constant real economy stabilization, decreased inflation rate, budget balance, strategic privatizations and support of currency stability. The achievement of these goals, mainly in recent years, presupposed eliminating salary increases in the state budget-based system and maintaining pensions at a constant level, coupled with reducing social benefits and the pace of the administrative reform, the privatization in strategic industries, the stimulation of inward foreign direct investments, tax adjustment and, in general, a very rigorous fiscal discipline, a much stricter monetary policy and the boosting of structural reforms, particularly in industries such as energy, transport and public enterprises.

These tough constraints, which were hard to bear both by the economic system, and by the Romanian population, were nevertheless implemented, except for the criterion on decreasing the arrears to the state budget level, where Romania failed by a very little margin. At present, the focus switched to constraints dealing with structural adjustment and economic recovery, as well as to deregulation of the electricity and gas market, which the IMF included among the structural performance criteria, along with integration of the accounting reporting system with the Treasury payment system and the elaboration of comprehensive amendments to healthcare legislation. IMF experts consider that progress in terms of structural reforms, and in particular in the privatization of state enterprises, continues to be slow. The structural benchmark criterion regarding the organization of initial public offerings (IPO) for shares owned by *Hidroelectrica* and *Romgaz* was delayed and eventually partially met in the case of *Romgaz* – the sale of a 15% stake – on November 12, 2013, and in the case of *Nuclearelectrica*, between 9 to 13 September 2013 – by selling a stake of newly issued shares under a 10% share capital increase. But, in other cases, the fulfillment of this benchmark was re-phased – in the case of *Electrica, Oltenia* Energy Complex, *Hidroelectrica,* at the end of June 2014, with a stake increase from 10% to 15%, waiving the capital increase that had been previously envisaged.

Delays were recorded in recruiting private managers for loss-making companies and in drawing up a shortlist of proposals for management positions in state companies where private management is to be introduced. Corporate governance was introduced in the case of *Hidroelectrica, Romgaz, Transgaz* and *Nucleareletrica*, the companies subordinated to the Ministry of Transport, *CFR Calatori, CFR SA, Tarom, Aeroporturi Bucureşti, Administraţia*

Porturilor Maritime Constanța and *Administrația Canalelor Navigabile*, but the process is costly and its outcome uncertain because many managers quickly gave up their positions, as they could not stand the pressure.

Currently, many of the sophisticated constraints described in *The Washington Consensus II* manifest themselves to a significant extent: corporate governance; anti-corruption; flexible labor markets; WTO agreements; financial codes and standards; prudent capital account opening; non-intermediate exchange rate regimes; independent central banks/inflation targeting; social safety nets; targeted poverty reduction. As an EU Member State, Romania must comply with the convergence criteria set by the EU. These are largely similar to the requirements imposed by the IMF and deal with: price stability, sound public finance proven by the absence of excessive government budget deficit and a government-debt-to-GDP ratio of less than 60%, currency fluctuations within the normal limits established for the EMS exchange rate mechanism, long-term average nominal interest rate not higher than 2 two percentage points than that in the first three EU countries with the lowest HICP inflation, evolution of the current balance of payments, evolution of the unit labor costs.

The last agreement with the IMF is of recent date: on 27 September 2013 the Romanian authorities requested and obtained a 24-month precautionary standby agreement with a proposed access of SDR 1,751.34 million - about 2 billion Euro - 170 percentage of quota, while also requesting assistance from the European Union - Euro 2 billion (Letter of Intent, 2013). The argument invoked to justify this new agreement was that Romania could not regain the confidence of the foreign markets and that a safety belt like that was needed to boost investors' confidence in the country. Conditionalities of this program cover the continuation of the gradual fiscal adjustment – the budget was prepared to match a main deficit target of 2.2% of the GDP in terms of cash – and the taking of short-term actions designed to sustain domestic demand. Structural reforms continue what has been achieved so far under the previous program, with a focus on reducing arrears.

2. The Impact of Fiscal Policy on the Real Economy

2.1. Fiscal Relaxation vs. Tax Burden

Theoretically, tax facilities lead to lower distortions in resource allocation within a market economy, generating an immediate positive impact both on aggregate supply and aggregate demand, in the short term, but also on the productive potential of the economy. These were the arguments for decreasing taxation in Romania by introducing the flat tax on January 1, 2005.

In reality, the obtained effects were divergent from those anticipated, because it was assumed that reducing taxes will automatically generate increasing payment compliance from taxpayers thus enlarging the tax base, so that the budget would not be affected in the medium and long run. In the absence of additional measures, such as reducing bureaucracy, lowering tax burden, increasing the efficiency of the administration sector, or reducing waste of public money, the business environment did not register a significant attractiveness gain, which was reflected in the increase of tax evasion and undeclared work. An attractive business environment is a fundamental condition both for the development of entrepreneurial capacity and the manifestation of free enterprise, and also for improving labor market flexibility, with positive effects on the ability to neutralize economic shocks and reduce structural unemployment.

Romania faces the following paradox about taxation – some of the major taxes (income and profit) are relatively lower than the European average and the ones in CEE economies, but tax burden is perceived as extremely high. According to the data collected by the World Bank in Doing Business reports, in those economies where it is difficult and costly to pay taxes, economic activity ends up in the informal sector. In order to reflect the paradoxical situation of the tax system in Romania, we performed a comparative analysis of the level and dynamics of some relevant indicators regarding the degree of fiscal pressure.

Thus, regarding the number of tax payments made by firms in one year, Romania exhibits a more favorable environment, with the introduction of the flat tax relaxation (Table 4). Generally, developed economies have stable tax systems, characterized by a reduced interaction with the state, and the trend was for CEE countries to adapt to this reality. The exception was Romania, where bureaucracy increased in the period 2008-2011, and decreased in 2012. Currently, in Romania, the number of tax payments is over two times higher than in any CEE economy included in the table below. Moreover, the number of para-fiscal taxes rose between 2005 and 2009, reaching 558, and then decreased to about 280 in 2012; however, the number of such taxes is double as compared to economies in the same region, which negatively affects the competitiveness of the economy in terms of attracting FDI.

Table 4. Tax payments by businesses

	2005	2006	2007	2008	2009	2010	2011	2012
Romania	108	108	108	113	113	113	113	41
Bulgaria	29	29	15	15	15	15	15	15
Czech Republic	27	12	12	12	12	12	8	8
Hungary	13	13	14	14	14	14	13	12
Poland	40	40	40	40	40	29	29	18
Slovakia	32	31	31	31	31	31	31	20
Slovenia	22	22	22	22	22	22	22	11
Germany	12	12	12	12	12	12	12	9
France	19	19	19	7	7	7	7	7
Italy	15	15	15	15	15	15	15	15
United Kingdom	8	8	8	8	8	8	8	8

Source: World Bank, Doing Business Reports 2005-2013.

In addition to the relatively large number of para-fiscal taxes or tax payments, Romania is characterized by high fiscal requirements for labor, despite the transmitted signal of introducing a wage tax of 16%. Thus, the share of labor taxes in total wage bill was above the EU average throughout the period 2000-2011 (Table 5), where the European Union was characterized by an average wage tax of about 25%. The explanation lies in the higher amount of social security contributions for employers and employees covered by the economic agents in Romania, given the relatively low tax base, a large number of beneficiaries and evasion in collecting contributions. The flat tax did not generate a significant impact on the tax burden for employees, the tax wedge decreasing by only 0.5% in

2005 relative to 2004. Moreover, the increased budget deficit due to the economic crisis led to the growth of this indicator, contrary to the situation in other economies included in the table below. Additional fiscal pressure generated both increasing production costs and reducing disposable income, negatively affecting the capacity of economic recovery. Moreover, companies were forced to resort to passing a great number of employees to the underground economy. The Fiscal Council (2013) estimated that tax evasion generated by undeclared work did not diminish following the fiscal relaxation of 2005, which is evidence for the ineffectiveness of that measure. Thus, undeclared work remained at a total level of 1.7-1.8% of the GDP in 2005-2008. Along with the economic crisis, this phenomenon became a way of survival for firms, rising to around 3.2% of the GDP in 2012 and representing approximately 25% of tax evasion in the economy (Figure 2).

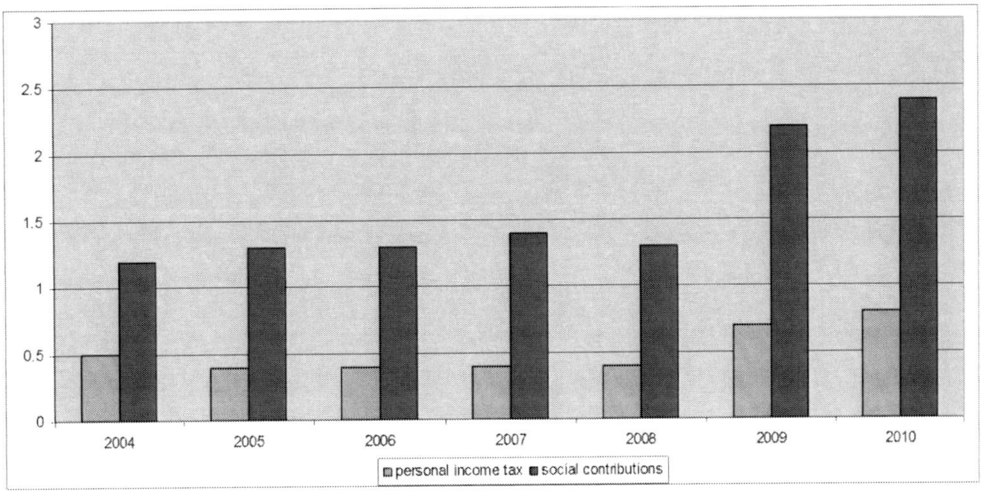

Figure 2. Tax evasion from undeclared work (% of GDP).

The situation shown in the figure above is generated by a 45% increase in the number of workers illegally employed in 2012 compared to 2008, their share exceeding 23% of the total number of employees in Romania (Fiscal Council, 2013). The number of unregistered workers was only marginally influenced by the fiscal easing in 2005, so that between 2005 and 2008 this number was at least 25% higher than the one in the period 2000-2003 (Figure 3.).

Table 5. Tax burden on labor income

	2000	2001	2002	2003	2004	2005	2006	2007	2008	2009	2010	2011
EU (27 countries)	41.3	40.7	40.8	41	40	39.9	40	39.9	39.5	39.3	39.3	39.3
Bulgaria	40	36.9	36.2	36	35.8	36.3	31.5	32.3	35.1	33.9	32.5	32.5
Czech Republic	41.3	41.3	41.5	42	41.9	42	40	40.5	40.1	38.7	38.9	39.5
Hungary	51.4	50.9	48.2	45	44.8	43.1	43.3	46	46.7	46.2	43.6	45.2
Poland	37	36.8	36.7	37	37.2	37.5	37.8	37.1	33.6	33.2	33.4	33.4
Romania	44.7	45.2	44.6	43	42.9	42.4	42.2	41.8	40.9	43.1	43.1	43.1
Slovenia	42.6	43.5	43.5	44	43.6	41.8	41.3	40.9	40.3	39.7	38.5	38.5
Slovakia	40.6	41.2	40.6	41	39.2	34.8	35.2	35.5	36	34.4	34.5	36.1

Source: Eurostat.

Table 6. The share of public investment (% of the GDP)

	European Union (28 countries)	Bulgaria	Czech Republic	Hungary	Poland	Romania	Slovenia	Slovakia
2000	-	4.0	4.1	3.6	-	3.9	3.7	3.6
2001	-	3.8	3.8	3.9	-	3.1	4.0	4.1
2002	-	3.5	3.7	5.2	-	3.3	3.8	4.2
2003	-	3.4	7.1	3.8	-	3.6	3.7	3.2
2004	-	3.5	4.5	3.8	-	2.8	3.9	3.1
2005	-	3.7	4.9	4.2	-	2.8	3.8	3.6
2006	3.2	4.3	4.9	5.2	-	5.2	4.3	3.7
2007	3.2	5.5	4.5	4.2	-	6.4	4.6	3.3
2008	3.4	5.7	4.9	3.2	-	6.8	4.8	3.5
2009	3.7	5.1	5.6	3.4	-	6.0	5.1	3.8
2010	3.5	4.8	4.7	3.7	5.7	5.7	4.9	3.6
2011	3.3	3.6	4.2	3.4	6.0	5.5	4.1	3.7
2012	3.1	3.6	3.9	3.7	4.8	4.9	3.9	3.0
2013	3.0	4.2	3.5	4.4	4.1	4.6	4.3	3.1

Source: Eurostat.

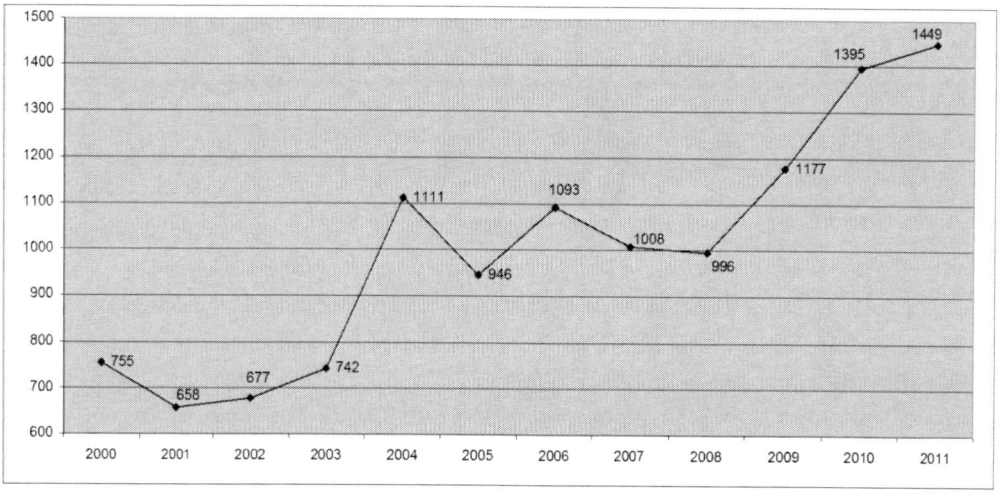

Source: Fiscal Council, 2013.

Figure 3. Number of workers employed without legal forms.

2.2. The Impact of Public Investment

From a theoretical perspective, public investment has a strong multiplier effect on the aggregate demand in the short run and a multiplier effect on the aggregate supply in the long run, especially when determining the reduction in transaction costs. However, there are other conditions that can influence the impact of these costs on the economy, without which the public investment multiplier will be insignificant.

First of all, the government should ensure that there are sufficient financial resources for the achievement of the established investment projects. Any interruption/ lock of the budgetary funded projects will generate only temporary effects on the output and the long-term multiplier will tend to zero or will even become negative. Therefore, the economies characterized by a lack of a multi-annual programming of investment spending or by a radical change of the public funds destination based on the election cycle will register a limited multiplier effect and private economic agents will perceive the state investment as a waste. They will not want to increase the tax contribution for future projects and any decision to increase the tax would generate tax evasion.

Secondly, the public investment projects must be transparent about the expenditure and should not be affected by the corruption specter. Its' perception will lead to the loss of domestic support in the achievement of any state project, and it will also prevent the implementation of effective public-private partnerships for major projects.

Romania was characterized by a paradoxical situation in terms of public investment, in the sense that it had the highest share of the EU 27 in this area between 2006 and 2011, but registered a weak performance of the infrastructure (transport, education, health), according to the Global Competitiveness Index. Thus, the share of capital expenditure in the GDP increased from 2.8% in 2004 to 6.8% in 2008, compared with a European average of 3.4%, in 2008. Generally, the emerging EU countries (including Romania) are characterized by a greater volatility of the public investment rate compared to developed economies because the emerging economies have lower financing capacity, especially during periods characterized by high budget deficits. Only the countries with more prudent fiscal policies during economic expansion (such as Poland and Slovakia) benefited from sufficient fiscal space to increase the investment rate in the interval 2009-2011 as compared to previous years (Table 6).

In Romania, the public investment spending had a pro-cyclical role, increasing during periods of expansion and contracting during recession, in the context of the public finance consolidation process.

The weak efficiency of public investment in Romania is also visible if we analyze the capital expenditure effects on the road infrastructure. Thus, since 2006, at least 2% of the GDP has been allocated for the investment projects in this area, but about 1% has been allocated for the maintenance costs of the existing road infrastructure. According to OECD, Romania is the first country of the EU in terms of these expenses, given that there is an important gap regarding the road infrastructure between Romania and the developed economies of the EU, or the other Central European countries. However, the quality of the existing infrastructure in Romania is perceived as the lowest in the European Union, according to the "Quality of roads" sub-index from the Global Competitiveness Index. According to the data from the table below, one can conclude that the increase of used public resources did not generate the improvement of the infrastructure quality, the appropriate index persisting at a level close to 2.

The main reasons for the low efficiency of public investment in the case of Romania are the following:

- lack of a multi-annual budget planning that prevents the achievement of large projects or continuing existing projects;
- dependence of project objectives on the electoral cycle, which generates "another" investment prioritization;

- lack of multiplication effects in the medium and long run in the real economy;
- lack of transparency in public spending, which results in a budget allocation higher than actual expenses for the projects;

Table 7. Investment in road infrastructure and the quality of infrastructure

	The quality of infrastructure	The share of investment expenses in road infrastructure (% of GDP)
2005	2.05	1.67%
2006	1.99	1.99%
2007	1.91	2.25%
2008	1.97	2.78%
2009	2.11	2.63%
2010	2.09	2.29%
2011	1.94	2.50%

Source: Global Competitiveness Index, 2013.

3. Fiscal Consolidation Constraints

Discretionary fiscal policy tends to take a new dimension with fiscal consolidation programs because the government intervention is not directly aimed at economic activity, but at the change of the budget balance, with a view to increasing public finance sustainability. At a first glance, diminishing the fiscal space for maneuver in economic boom represented the main constraint of the fiscal policy makers in Romania when the primary objective became fiscal consolidation. Therefore, the pro-cyclical fiscal measures promoted in 2006-2008 had a boomerang effect on the economy starting with 2009, when we witnessed the contraction of the private sector at the same time with increased taxation and public spending cuts.

Beyond this obvious conclusion, we believe that the current situation is only a result of the action of factors disturbing the entire economic system, analyzed in the previous chapters, factors such as the fiscal policy dependence of the electoral cycle, the lack of multi-annual programming investment, the increase of tax burden applied to the private sector in the context of encouraging wasteful budgetary resources and tax evasion, the persistence of arrears etc.

3.1. Budgetary Vulnerabilities

In the period prior to the economic crisis, the government behavior was similar to the one of the private sector, promoting expenditure increase on the assumption of growing long term income. Despite strong economic growth between 2006 and 2008, there was not an expressed concern about reducing budget deficits and creating budgetary reserves for the recession periods. Although the apparent economic prosperity was an enhancer of the fiscal discipline, the requirements regarding tax evasion reduction and the increase of the efficiency regarding resource collection and use were neglected. The fiscal policy became pro-cyclical, increasing pressures on inflation and external deficit, as it follows from the analysis of the structural budget balance dynamics (Figure 4.).

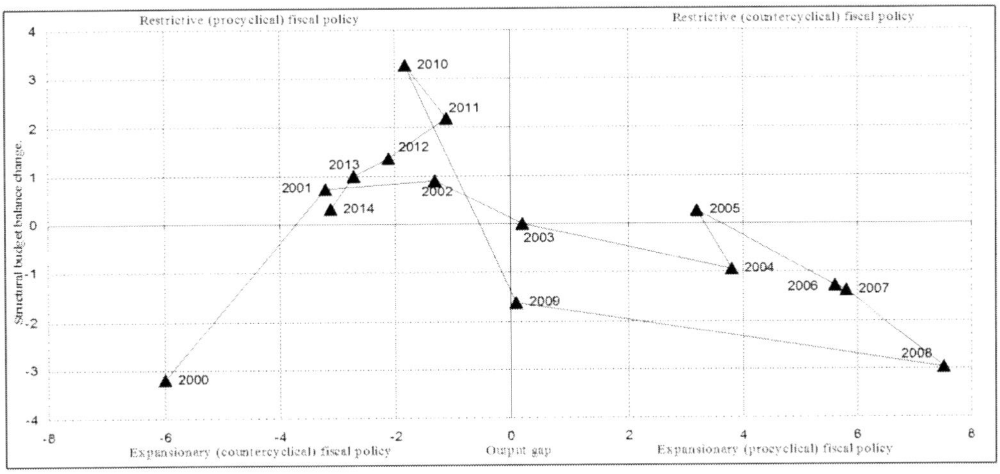

Source of data: European Commission, 2013.

Figure 4. Fiscal policy stance in Romania (2000-2014).

The budget balance registered in an economy does not rigorously reflect the impact of fiscal measures adopted by the government because it also captures the automatic response of the government revenue and expenditure to the evolution of the economic activity. For example, promoting an expansionary fiscal policy leads in the short run to an increase of the budget deficit. However, increasing deficit may be caused not only by the state intervention, but also by the economic downturn, which has automatic effects in terms of budgetary revenues decline. Consequently, the budget balance evolution is both the result of discretionary fiscal policy reflected in the structural balance change and the result of automatic stabilizers action captured with the help of the cyclical budget balance.

In the figure below we represented the fiscal policy stance from Romania (as evidenced by the change of the structural budget balance), depending on the output gap phases in the interval 2000-2014, based on the European Commission data (2013). According to the analysis carried out, only in two years (2000, respectively 2005) the fiscal policy was counter-cyclical, so it corresponded to the stabilizing role of the Government in an economy. Under these circumstances, Romanian economy entered the vicious circle of pro-cyclicality and expansionist measures contributed to the overheating of the economy, whose potential growth was approximately 5.5% in 2006-2008. In this context, only an incidental increase of governmental revenues was registered, which was determined by an increased consumption supported by foreign capital inflows and by loose banks' lending policy.

In Romania, the period of rapid economic growth prior to the financial crisis (2006-2008) was characterized by a positive fiscal impulse, contributing to overheating and thereby strengthening the accumulated imbalances in the economy. In addition, the pro-cyclicality of the fiscal policy has exhausted the fiscal space needed to stimulate the economy during recession, inducing the need to reduce the budget deficit in the context of additional fiscal constraints. If before 2009 the structural budget deficits increased by about 2% every year of economic expansion, starting with 2010, the government resorted to the correction of previous fiscal imbalances in a short period of time, which corresponded to a significant effort of fiscal consolidation.

According to the European Commission estimates, the fiscal policy in Romania was to be restrictive between 2013 and 2014, which was to reduce the likelihood of promoting substantial fiscal measures for economic recovery.

Automatic stabilizers acquire a greater relevance for monetary integration and economic crisis because they can significantly affect the budget balance in the context of relatively neutral discretionary fiscal policy. The size of automatic stabilizers is influenced by the degree of government's intervention in the economy, by the structure of budgetary revenues depending on the contribution of different forms of taxation, but also on the progressive income tax. Unlike fiscal stabilizers, discretionary fiscal policy has a number of disadvantages related to the period of time required for the implementation and enforcement of certain measures. Moreover, the government spending decisions are transmitted with a certain lag in the economy, and it is possible for the restrictive measures implemented with a view to reducing the effects of prolonged expansion to reach the economy when it is going through a period of economic recession.

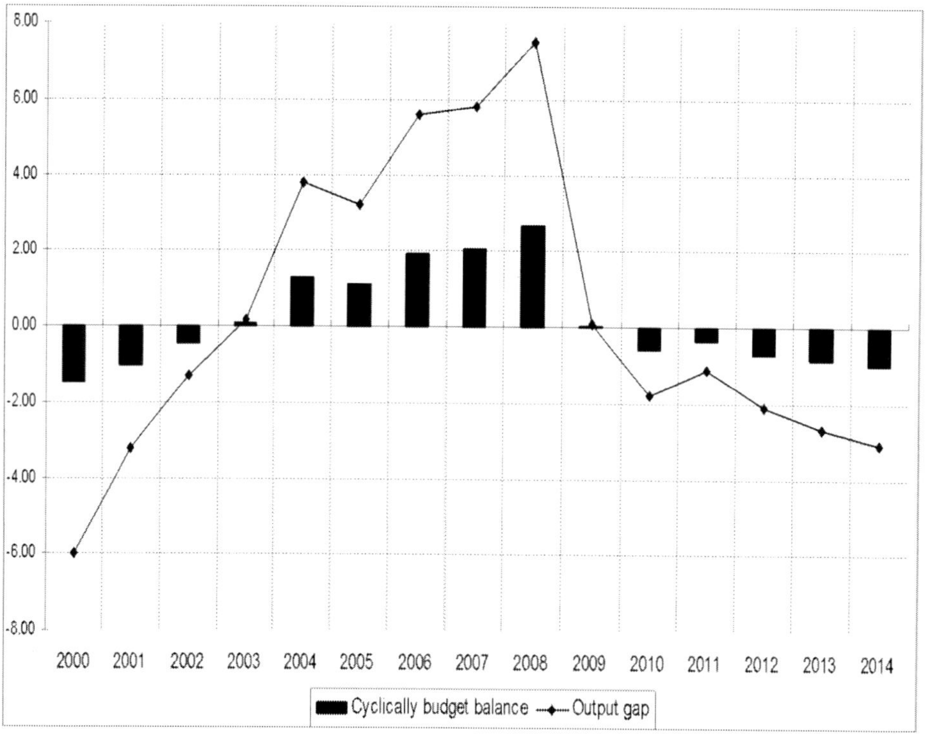

Figure 5. The impact of automatic stabilizers.

Throughout the period 2000-2014, an output gap of 1% of the GDP entails a cyclical budget balance of about 0.33% of the GDP, corresponding to a relatively reduced level of automatic stabilizers in the Romanian economy, while the average of OECD economies or the one of the EU economies is of 0.48 percentage points of the GDP. As we can see in figure 5, emphasizing output gaps (negative/positive) led to a higher cyclical budget balance (in absolute terms), which improved the public finance during periods of economic expansion, but also worsened it in years of economic recession. However, the size of cyclical budget deficit in the interval 2010-2014 was lower than the one of cyclical budget surpluses between 2004 and 2008, in the context of less intense recessionary gaps.

A low level of automatic stabilizers is a drawback for an expansionary economy but an advantage for an economy in recession, as the economic decline will have a relatively smaller impact on the cyclical budget balance.

3.2. Public Debt Dynamics

Although the level of public debt in Romania (38% of the GDP at the end of 2012) is inferior to the level set by the Maastricht Treaty (60% of the GDP), its growth rate in the interval 2009-2011 generated high costs of refinancing. The public debt increased 2.6 times only in 3 years, due to pro-cyclical fiscal policies pursued in the years preceding the economic crisis, but also because of the economic downturn that has reduced budgetary revenue (Figure 6).

At a time of global uncertainty, marked by the sovereign debt crisis, Romania had to demonstrate that it was able to stabilize the public debt. Thus, the debt growth rate has slowed significantly since 2011, anticipating that the level of public debt will not exceed 40% over the next five years.

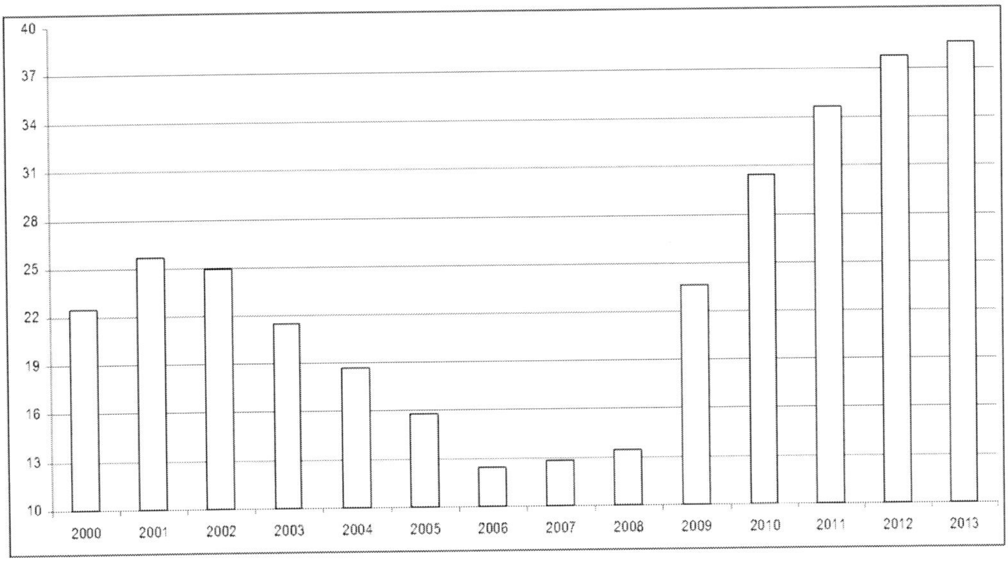

Source: Eurostat.

Figure 6. The stock of public debt in Romania (% of GDP).

Even if the level of public debt does not seem to be a concern, this service has increased significantly, putting additional pressure on the management of public debt financing. In just two years (2007-2009) the debt service increased 4.6 times, respectively by 9% of the GDP, after which it stabilized at about 10.7% of the GDP in 2011-2013. The financial crisis created additional debt in Romania and because of unfavorable external and internal conditions its financing was contracted at high interest and on short term. In the context of economic downturn, the Government had only one option, namely refinancing maturing debt, operation that led to the increase of interest expense to 1.8% of the GDP in 2012-2013, compared to 0.7% of the GDP before the economic crisis.

Thus, the Government was trying to gain time and postpone debt payment due in a few years' time, when it hoped that the economy could generate primary budget surpluses. But if public debt roll over is in the short (or medium) run, there will be a rapid increase in interest expenses. Apart from financing budget deficits that will occur in the coming years, the Government must find the resources to pay the outstanding capital ratios corresponding to the previously accumulated debt.

As the data in the table below shows, the significant decrease of the current budget deficit since 2012 has not generated reduction of pressures regarding the public debt service, given that about 25% of the previous public debt must be refinanced every year. Under these circumstances, the average monthly financing needs exceeded 1.2 billion Euros, which creates a strong crowding out effect of the private sector. The loans contracted in 2013 financed the primary budget deficit at a rate of 0.8% of the GDP, the interest expenses related to debt at a rate of 1.8% and the capital ratios due in that year at a rate of 8.1% of GDP.

Table 8. Gross financing need in Romania

	2007	2008	2009	2010	2011	2012	2013
Primary deficit (% of GDP)	2.2	5	7.5	5.3	3.9	1.1	0.8
Gross financing need (bn lei)	10.4	14.3	56.9	46.1	59.5	64.3	66.7
Gross financing need (% of the GDP)	2.5	2.8	11.4	8.8	10.7	10.9	10.7

Source: Eurostat.

In order to reduce the public debt service, the government has only one viable option - improving the management of public debt refinancing by contracting loans on longer terms (at least 5 years) and at relatively lower interest rates. The decreasing risk at global level, due to measures adopted by the European Commission and ECB amid sovereign debt crisis favored reducing the Romania risk premium by about 200-250 basis points and cheaper government borrowing costs. The same trend was supported by the success of the fiscal consolidation process assumed by Romania within recent agreements with the IMF and by the decrease in domestic inflation without any significant adverse shocks on the supply side.

Thus, the average interest rate on prior government debt fell about 2 percentage points in the interval 2010-2013, reaching a minimum rate of 5%. The downward trend of the interest rate started in 2000 and was stopped in 2009, when the financial problems of the Romanian government worsened, Romania paying for the strategic mistakes made in the pre-crisis period. Reducing debt refinancing rate alongside decreasing primary deficits slowed the growth of interest expenditure share in the GDP. However, this expenditure represented approximately 5% of the total budgetary expenditure in 2013, similarly with 2003 (Figure 7). In this context, the expected reduction of government expenditure will lead to cutting other categories of expenditure, such as social expenditure, acquisition of goods and services or investment.

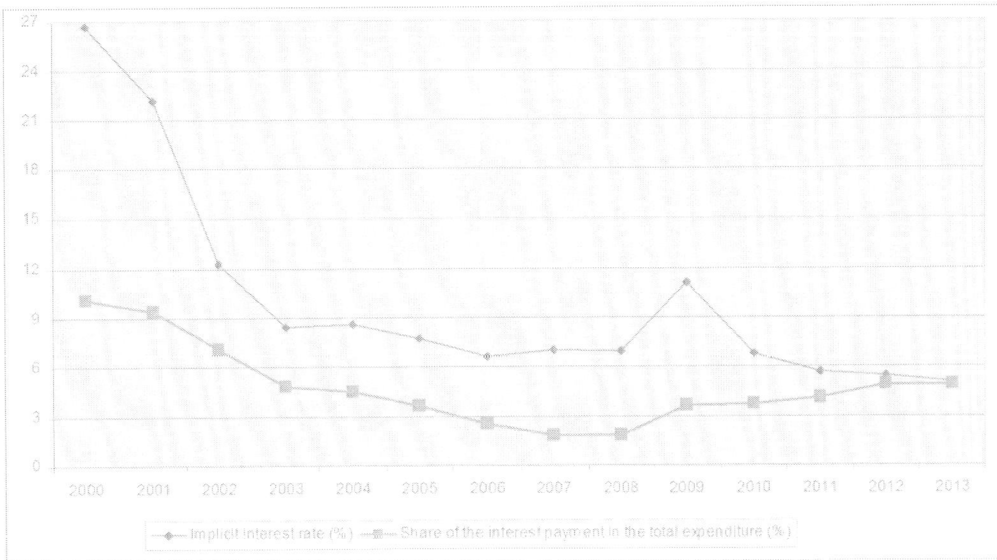

Source: Eurostat.

Figure 7. Interest rate on public debt in Romania.

3.3. Analysis of the Fiscal Consolidation Measures in CEE Countries

Generally, before the economic crisis of 2008, Central and Eastern European countries were not facing fiscal problems, thus in 2007 the region had a fiscal surplus of 1.5% of the GDP. However, Romania and Hungary represented the exception in the region, exhibiting fiscal deficits despite strong growth. After the emergence of the crisis and the recession, CEE states started to accumulate fiscal deficits, and some of them, such as Romania and Hungary, needed financial assistance from the IMF and the European Commission in order to reduce financial instability. Subsequently, imbalances were amplified by the international crisis that reached the region in the second half of 2008.

The global crisis affected CEE countries asymmetrically and often resulted in even higher public deficits and increases in the share of public debt in the GDP, as the governments needed to respond through discretionary fiscal-budgetary measures to limit the negative effects of the financial crisis – either to stimulate economic recovery by supporting aggregate demand or by supporting the banking sector.

As a reaction to the fiscal problems that occurred during the economic crisis, a number of reforms were adopted globally both in the area of expenditure and revenue. Similarly, some reforms were implemented at institutional level to improve oversight and fiscal discipline of the national economies.

Thus, in the CEE region reforms on the expenditure side were mainly oriented towards reducing or freezing the public sector wages and controlling the size of civil service, towards changes in the public pension system, towards reducing the expenditure with health and other social benefits, or towards diminishing the government investment expenditure.

Regarding pension systems, Hungary and Poland nationalized completely and, respectively, partially the assets held by the private pension pillar, and some states considered the gradual raising of the retirement age. At the same time, in countries such as Hungary, Latvia, Lithuania, Poland and Romania reforms were adopted to reduce spending on social protection and health, in order to improve the situation of public finance. In general, it is recognized that the reduction of capital expenditure has stronger negative effects on economic growth than with the reduction of the wages of public employees and the expenditure with goods and services, with direct impact on domestic demand.

The expenditure categories with the lowest impact on growth are social benefits and subsidies. The impact of the measures taken on the budgetary expenditure is detailed in the table below.

Table 9. Change in expenditure items in selected CEE countries, 2009-2012 (% of potential GDP)

	Total expenditure	Interest expenditure	Compensation of employees	Capital expenditure	Social and other benefits
Romania	-4.88	0.58	-3.64	0.97	-2.79
Lithuania	-4.26	0.66	-2.35	0.73	-3.32
Slovakia	-3.79	0.28	-1.14	-2.53	-0.39
Hungary	-2.04	-0.43	-1.27	1.16	-1.50
Slovenia	-1.32	0.94	-1.12	-1.08	-0.06
Czech Republic	-1.12	0.18	-0.37	-0.54	-0.39
Poland	-1.09	0.26	-0.53	0.26	-1.08
Bulgaria	-0.19	0.17	-0.50	-0.53	0.67

Source: IMF Database.

On the revenue side, some measures were oriented to raise taxes on personal income, on corporate income and on capital gains. Similarly, other measures were aimed at increasing social security contribution rates, the VAT rate, the level of excises and property taxes. Among these changes, the variables with the lowest distortion effects on the economy are property taxes and VAT. The most distorting effects are those of the income taxes (personal/corporate) and social contributions. Therefore, EU countries tried to shift the fiscal pressure from labor (an important factor for the competitiveness of the region) to consumption or the environment. Changes in VAT were a handy tool for many European states that aimed to increase fiscal revenue, either by increasing the VAT rate, or by broadening the tax base on which it applies (by giving up to certain categories of goods that previously had a reduced VAT rate). Apart from Bulgaria, who has maintained the standard rate of VAT at 20% from 2008 to the present, all other CEE countries have changed this rate with values between 1 percentage point (the cases of Slovakia and Poland) to 7 percentage points (the case of Hungary).

At EU level, the average standard VAT rate increased from 19.49% in 2008 to 21.31% in 2013. Moreover, some countries have increased the level of property taxes (Latvia, Lithuania) or the tax base on which the taxes apply. The following table synthesizes the key fiscal measures taken in CEE countries amid crisis.

The effects of the measures taken in CEE selected countries (expressed as GDP share of budget revenue in the interval 2009-2012) are detailed in the table below. It seems that during this period, the countries that increased indirect taxes, and the standard VAT rate respectively, obtained extra fiscal revenue, while Bulgaria, which maintained the VAT rate, was the only country whose fiscal revenue from indirect taxes decreased. This shows that, in terms of fiscal consolidation, the use of indirect taxes was an appropriate instrument.

Table 10. Tax Measures in Selected Countries, 2010–2013

Country	Personal Income Taxation		Corporate Income Taxation		Value-Added Tax		Social Security Contributions		Excises		Property	
	Tax Rate	Taxation Base	Tax Rate	Taxation Base	Tax Rate	Taxation Base	Tax Rate	Taxation Base	Tax Rate	Taxation Base	Tax Rate	Taxation Base
Czech Rep.	⇧	⇧		⇧	⇧		⇩	⇩	⇧			
Slovakia	⇧	⇧	⇧		⇧		⇧	⇧	⇧			
Slovenia	⇧		⇩						⇧			
Bulgaria					⇧	⇧	⇧		⇧			
Estonia									⇧	⇧	⇧	
Hungary	⇩	⇩	⇩		⇧		⇧		⇧			
Latvia	⇩	⇩		⇩	⇧	⇧	⇧		⇧	⇧	⇧	⇧
Lithuania	⇩		⇩	⇩		⇩		⇧	⇧		⇧	⇧
Poland					⇧	⇧	⇧		⇧	⇧		
Romania					⇧				⇧			

Source: IMF Database.

Table 11. Change in revenue items in selected CEE countries, 2009-2012 (% of GDP)

	Total revenue	Interest revenue	Direct taxes	Indirect taxes	Other
Poland	2.64	0.00	-0.20	1.06	1.78
Czech Republic	1.17	-0.03	0.34	1.44	-0.58
Romania	1.07	-0.13	-1.18	1.72	0.65
Slovenia	1.02	0.06	-0.69	0.55	1.10
Lithuania	-0.79	-0.05	0.72	1.76	-3.21
Bulgaria	-0.86	-0.06	-0.69	-0.72	0.62
Hungary	-1.11	0.02	-3.22	1.26	0.84
Slovakia	-1.59	0.03	0.62	0.57	-2.82

Source: IMF Database.

3.4. The Intensity of Public Finance Adjustment Process

In general, it is considered that the reduction of budgetary imbalances is advisable only when the economy has fully recovered from a recession, not to put extra pressure on the business environment faced with an economic downturn.

An argument in favor of the postponement of this adjustment is that an economy is more vulnerable to the deepening recession when growth is low (Nalewaik, 2011; Sheets, 2011). Another argument is that an increase in taxes which reduces the disposable income of households is more painful when there is already some decrease of the disposable income due to other reasons. The effect of this adjustment process on the unemployment is based on the same principle – a future growth of the unemployment is more distressing when unemployment is already very high.

Similarly, the quality of the adjustment can be increased if the process pace is very slow, to avoid an aggressive cutting of public expenditure or a significant increase of taxes (Bakker and Christiansen, 2012). The main reason these authors put forth is that the reduction of production and income, alongside a weak financial system, implies a bigger dependence of the consumption on the current income than the future income, in the same measure as the investment is more dependent on current profits than on the future profits.

When considering fiscal consolidation, there is a whole debate about the size of fiscal multipliers, as they capture the reaction of the economy to restrictive fiscal measures. Blanchard and Leigh (2013) note that fiscal multipliers were underestimated for some economies (particularly for advanced countries) and the link between fiscal consolidation and economic growth was stronger than forecasts showed. Economic reality suggested that the reduction of budget spending generated a bigger than expected negative impact on production, while tax increases had an impact close to that previously estimated (Blanchard and Leigh, 2013).

Recommendations based on the literature have been neglected in the CEE economies (including Romania) due to difficulties in refinancing deepening debt at low interest rates. Emerging European economies have a higher country risk and are more exposed to capital outflows that will directly influence their financial sector and indirectly affect the public sector. The process of fiscal consolidation has occurred even in the context of an economic downturn (the case of Romania, Latvia, Hungary, etc.) in order to gain external credibility, a prerequisite if these countries were to prevent reducing exposure of foreign banks in their countries and to avoid the rising cost of state borrowing. It was considered that delaying this process could be beneficial in the short run for an economy in recession, but the persistence of budgetary problems will send a signal of distrust and uncertainty, canceling the (potential) temporary gains.

In addition, fiscal consolidation is required by the Treaty on Stability, Coordination and Governance in Economic and Monetary Union. The treaty includes a component called Fiscal Compact that aims to strengthen fiscal discipline in the UE, introducing more automatical sanctions and enhanced fiscal surveillance of Member States. The Compact had two main modules: a balanced budget including an automatic correction mechanism and the strengthening of the Excessive Deficit Procedure. In other words, fiscal balance should be close to zero „over the economic cycle," because high levels of deficit and debt represent a threat for fiscal stability.

Under the first module, the contracting parts (member states) should adopt in their national legislation and implement a fiscal rule involving government budget balance or surplus. In fact, this implies a structural deficit of 0.5% of the GDP and 1% of the GDP for countries with a public debt significantly below 60% of the GDP and reduced long-term risks on fiscal stability. The balanced budget rule should include a correction mechanism which is automatically triggered if there are significant deviations from the MTO or the adjustment path. The mechanism is designed to correct deviations, including the cumulative impact on government debt dynamics and it should also apply to temporary deviations justified by exceptional circumstances. These refer to unusual events outside the control of a country, with financial impact on the consolidated budget, or extensive periods of severe economic downturn for the Euro zone or the whole European Union.

The second module aims at strengthening the Excessive Deficit Procedure, in particular by increasing the automatism if a Euro-zone country violates the deficit criteria. Moreover, countries that are subject to the procedure should provide an economic and budgetary partnership program, including a detailed description of structural reforms, to enable an effective and sustainable correction of the excessive deficit. In addition, the fiscal compact imposes a legal obligation on states with high government debt and some risks to debt financing, to correct the excess of government debt above 60% of the GDP.

To explain the influence of these constraints decided at EU level on the national fiscal policies of CEE countries, we made a comparison between the values of structural budget balance under medium-term fiscal objectives and its actual values in 2012. The lower these values are as compared to targets, the more intense the fiscal consolidation will be in the respective economies. Furthermore, if the medium term objective is superior to that established under the rule of Fiscal Compact, the necessary consolidation will be stronger. In the table below we additionally included the stock of public debt in 2012 because depending on the level of public debt the target for structural budget deficit can increase to 1% of the GDP.

Table 12. Fiscal Medium Term Objectives in CEE countries

	Structural fiscal balance in 2012 (% of the GDP)	Medium Term Objective (% of the GDP)	Public debt in 2012 (% of the GDP)
Bulgaria	-0.4	-0.5	18.5
Czech Republic	-1.7	-1.0	45.8
Estonia	0.2	0.0	10.1
Latvia	-0.3	-0.5	40.7
Lithuania	-3.2	0.5	40.7
Hungary	-0.7	-1.5	79.2
Poland	-3.8	-1.0	55.6
Romania	-2.7	-1.0	37.8
Slovenia	-2.7	0.0	54.1
Slovakia	-4.1	-0.5	52.1

Source: European Commission, 2013.

As we can see in Table 13, it appears that the adoption of Fiscal Compact will lead to the adjustment to medium-term objectives for countries such as Hungary, Poland and Romania, which will lead to a higher intensity of public finance adjustment. In 2012, Bulgaria, Estonia and Latvia recorded values of the structural balance lower than new fiscal rule and also values of public debt below 60% of the GDP, so they have some fiscal space for discretionary measures in the coming years. The largest fiscal consolidation efforts should be done in the next period by Slovakia (a structural balance adjustment by 3.6% of the GDP) and Lithuania (3.7% of the GDP). The latter established the most ambitious medium term objective among all CEE states – a structural balance surplus of 0.5% of the GDP. The disadvantage of the new EU fiscal rules is the fact that the fiscal space available to stimulate the economy during recession periods is very low.

To avoid any deterioration of public finance, Romania appealed to foreign institutions' aid, signing a stand-by agreement for the 2009-2011 interval with the IMF (for 12.95 billion Euro). Additionally, Romania received an aggregate amount of 7 billion Euro from the

European Union, the World Bank and the European Bank for Reconstruction and Development. Loans helped to maintain the stability of the financial sector and national currency alongside the improvement of confidence in the economic prospects of Romania. Because the risk of an unexpected deterioration in the financial-economic situation of Romania was not removed, authorities called a precautionary financial assistance arrangement, for about 3,6 billion Euro from the IMF in the interval 2012-2014, in addition to two other preventive arrangements for 1.4 billion and 0.4 billion Euro with the European Commission and the World Bank.

In the context of widening public deficit and amid pressures from international organizations, in 2010 Romania started an ambitious fiscal consolidation process, which involved reducing public spending - especially by reducing the wages and number of employees in the public sector, reducing public pensions - and increasing fiscal revenue by raising the VAT and the social security contributions. As a result of these restrictive fiscal measures, structural budget deficit fell from 9.1% to 3% of the GDP between 2009 and 2011, the pace of adjustment of 2 percentage points per year being very alert. The adjustment was made mostly on the expenditure side, by structural reforms promoted especially on public sector wages, public pension system reform and budgetary planning.

The aggregate fiscal adjustment estimated for the 2009-2012 interval is the second most ambitious in the EU, its size being proportional to the initial structural fiscal deficit in 2008. As a result of these measures, the pace of public debt growth rate slowed from 10.2% of the GDP between 2008 and 2009, to about 2% of the GDP in 2013 as compared to 2012. Fiscal adjustment measures reached their quantitative objective, and fiscal deficit started to fall, which increased Romania's credibility on external markets, and was reflected in the decreasing spread risk premium for government loans from over 8% at the beginning of 2009 to less than 2% in 2013.

CONCLUSION

On the one hand, fiscal consolidation based on expenditure cuts is most effective if it is accompanied by reforms aimed to improve the efficiency of public services. On the other hand, increasing taxes indicates a weak commitment to structural reforms. Moreover, measures that reduce long-term costs send encouraging signals to financial markets regarding the long-term sustainability of public finance. Improving fiscal institutions, medium-term budgetary planning and better expenditure control represents a strong base for the long-term consolidation of public finance. Even if the Romanian public debt is still within acceptable limits, long-term fiscal solvency is jeopardized by the public pension system funding costs, given the aging population and the fact that the fiscal system in Romania is one of the least efficient in the EU, as Romania has the lowest level of taxation.

Therefore, the fiscal consolidation process will continue even if the economy will come out from the recession. At a first glance, fiscal policy will not be used to stimulate the economy, as expansionary measures must be offset by other restrictive measures with higher intensity to reduce the structural deficit and to keep it at a level close to the fiscal medium-term objective (as explained in Section 4.3.4.). However, there are some solutions that can alleviate the trade-off between fiscal consolidation and economic growth for Romania:

- improving the quality of public expenditure by reducing the budgetary waste and spending resources in a more efficient manner, following programs with the World Bank, such as prioritization of investments;
- increasing the budget revenue, not by increasing taxation, but by increasing the tax base as a result of measures to reduce bureaucracy and tax evasion;
- increasing taxes with less distorting effects on resource allocation in the economy and use parts of extra revenue to stimulate investment in high added value sectors;
- privatizing state companies that accumulate significant arrears to the state budget, covered by state subsidies;
- adopting structural reforms in sectors such as: pensions, education, health, to increase the sustainability of security budgets and workforce flexibility in order to diminish the long-term effects of some structural problems, such as aging, poor health and low employment rate;
- improving EU funds' absorption, which provides financing for the potential output growth and increase budgetary revenue; for each Euro Romania receives from the EU structural and cohesion funds, about 0.3 Euro represents revenue for the state budget;
- creating fiscal space during periods of economic expansion and using it to stimulate economic recovery, on condition it will comply with the Fiscal Pact requirements;
- implementing tax incentives to reinvested profit and attracting some productive foreign investment, which will lead to increasing economic activity and budget revenue.

In general, quantitative fiscal consolidation (reducing expenditure and raising taxes) is achieved in the short term and cannot be avoided, as it is often used as a signal for external creditors. If the purely quantitative beginning is unavoidable, further consolidation must involve a mix of qualitative and quantitative measures, but the share of the former should exceed the latter, as a country surpasses initial financial pressures.

REFERENCES

Bakker, B., Christiansen, L. (2012). Crisis and Consolidation-Fiscal Challenges in Emerging Europe, *IMF workshop* no 17.

Blanchard, O., Leigh, D. (2013). Growth Forecast Errors and Fiscal Multipliers, *IMF working paper* 13/1.

Elena Pelinescu (2013), The Mechanisms of Arrears in Romania, *Romanian Journal of Economic Forecasting*, 16(2).

*** Fiscal Council (2013), 2012 Annual Report. Romania.

Ghizdeanu and Ristea (2010), Evolution and structure of arrears, *Public finance and accounting Review*, No.3, March 2010.

IMF (2004), Romania: Selected Issues and Statistical Appendix, *IMF Country Report* No. 04/220.

Nalewaik,J. (2011). Forecasting Recessions Using Stall Speed, *Finance and Economics Discussion Series, Federal Reserve Board,* 2011-24.

Sheets.N. (2011). Is the US Economy Approaching 'Stall Speed'?, Citi Empirical and Thematic Perspectives, 11 November.

World Bank (2013), Doing Business Reports 2005-2013.

World Economic Forum (2013), Global Competitiveness Index, 2013.

*** Eurostat database.

*** European Commission data (2013).

*** IMF database.

*** Ministry of Finance database.

In: What/Who Are We After the Transition? Focus on Romania ISBN: 978-1-63483-947-1
Editors: M. Dinu, D. Ailenei, A. Dachin et al.

Chapter 5

THE DEMOGRAPHIC CRISIS

Christina-Marta Suciu*, PhD, Mirela Ionela Aceleanu, PhD, Mihaela Hrisanta Mosora, PhD and Marilena Chiva Papuc, PhD
Bucharest University of Economics Studies, Bucharest, Romania

INTRODUCTION

This chapter provides a diagnostic analysis that highlights the current state of the demographic crisis in Romania and some of its trends. As the authors of the chapter have highlighted in previous published reports [1, 2], demographic trends are not optimistic for Europe and Romania is not an exception. The chapter includes some of the most relevant issues considered to be relevant from the perspective of the whole book.

1. DEMOGRAPHIC TRANSITION. DYNAMICS OF POPULATION

Romania entered the demographic transition later than other European countries as a result of a relatively late economic, social and political development [3]. According to specialized studies, in Romania, the demographic transition and its correlation with the stages of change in the age structure of the population has followed three main stages (figure 5.1.):

- *the first stage* was manifested by reduction in mortality (especially infants) and decreasing birth rates. The youth population has grown faster than the working population.
- *the second* stage was the result of increasing youth population in the first stage and reaching working-age. There has been a faster increase in the working-age population as compared to the one in its total population. However, there has been a decline in the working-age population, mainly as a result of falling birth rates.

* corresponding author: suciu31@gmail.com

- *the third stage* is characterized by an increase in the elderly population (aged 60 and over), due to falling birth rates; it has resulted in a decline of the working-age population.

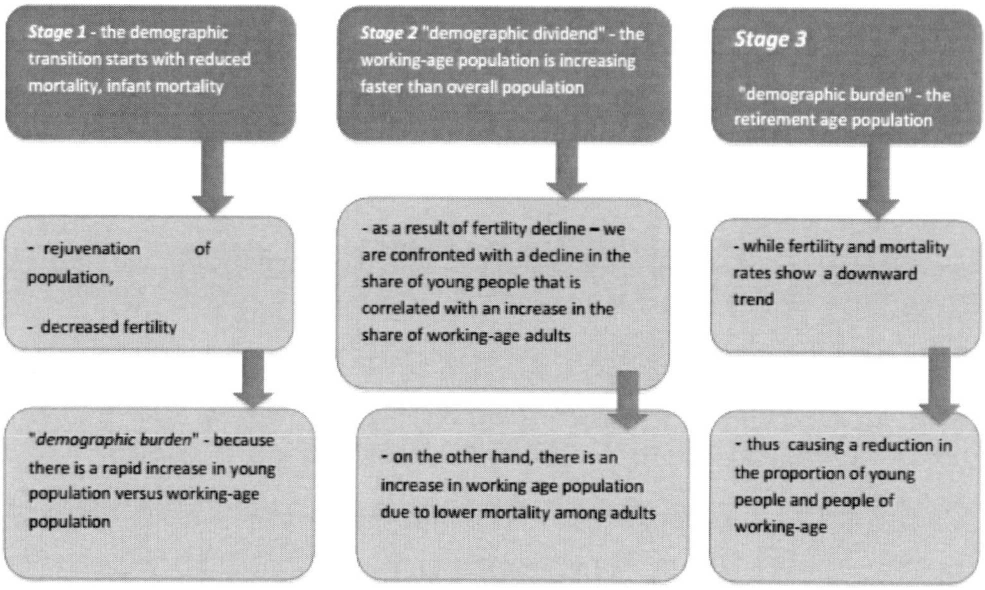

Source: synthetic scheme based on literature analysis.

Figure 5.1. Stages of demographic transition in Romania.

The main factors that have influenced the demographic transition in Romania are:

- a downward trend in mortality rates in general. Reduced number of pandemics as a result of scientific discoveries in medicine and improved living conditions;
- reduced birth rates, due to changing lifestyle and particularly women's empowerment and their increasing participation in the economic and social life;
- other factors such as culture, education, legislation, technical progress, economic and social factors.

We hereby summarize the developments characterizing the demographic transition in Romania. It should essentially be noted that if during 1930 to1991 the Romanian population dynamics enrolled on an upward trend, since 1992, year after year, there has been a more obvious demographic decline.

- *Between 1930 and 1966* there were important historical events (war of 1941 to 1945 which led to changing borders) and to a decrease in the natural increase of population. This decrease was due to falling birth rate and increased mortality. The sub period between 1955 and 1966 marked the demographic transition in Romania. In 1957 Decree no. 463 was issued which legalized abortion on demand. According to experts from the Centre for Statistics of the Ministry of Health, the record regarding the number of abortions was registered in 1965. As a result, in 1966

Decree no 770 was adopted and it resulted in a rather 'forced' increase in the birth rate in Romania.

- *The period between 1967 and 1978* showed a change in the population natural increase rate. In 1967 and 1968, natural increase was about three times higher than in the years 1964 to 1966. Maintaining a birth rate of around 20 and a death rate of about 9 , resulted in high natural increases. In 1978 Romania's population reached 21,914,163 people, which meant a total increase of nearly 2.8 million people from 1966.
- *The period 1979-1991* marks an atypical development of the Romanian population. Continuous reduction of natural increase (from 8.7 to 1) was due to a decrease in death rates. It reached 11.9 in 1991, compared to 18.6 in 1979. Whatever the real causes of these dynamics in the period 1979-1991, the population increased by almost 1.3 million people. The year 1991 represents a turning point in changing the direction of development of the population of Romania.
- *During 1992-2002*, natural increase was negative both due to lower birth rates and increasing mortality. This trend has continued to the present. Romania shows a relatively unusual development because, after 1992, the birth rate began to decline, while mortality (favored by an aging population) increased (Figure 5.2.). The literature reveals that when the curves of the two variables meet, a new phase of demographic transition begins [3]. Therefore, the analysis of this period begins with 1992.
- *During 2002-2013* the population decline continued.

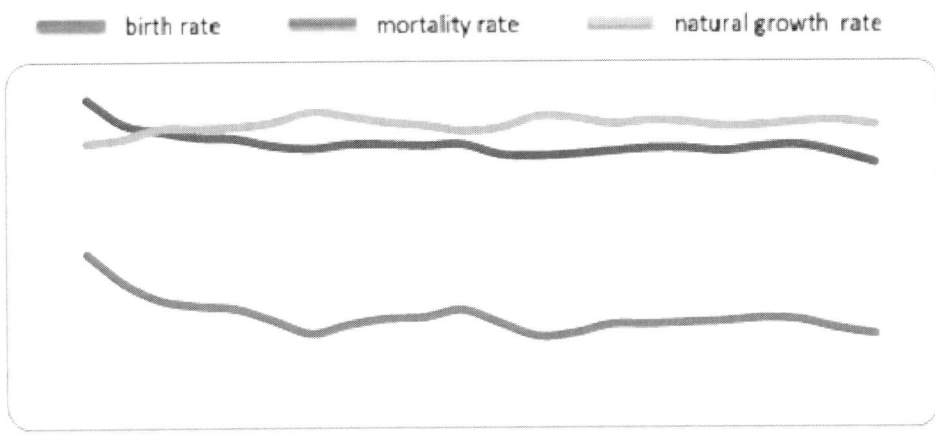

Source: www.inse.ro.

Figure 5.2. The dynamics of birth rate, mortality and natural growth of the population of Romania between 1990 and 2011.

In the period between 1990 and 2013 the population of Romania has registered a declining trend (Figure 5.3), a trend which is expected to be maintained in the future, if current conditions remain unchanged. The stable population of Romania decreased based on external migration as well. There was an increase in the share of women in total because of a higher mortality rate among male population. Average life expectancy for women is 7.4 years older. According to the *Population and Housing Census* in 2002 the Romanian population was 21,890,910 people, being lower by 1,504,110 persons compared to 1991, and on October 20, 2011, the population recorded a total of 20,121,641 people, of which 51.4% women and 48.6% men [4].

During the period 2007 to 2011, the stable population decreased by 7.2% (1,559.3 thousand people) mainly due to external migration gain. The drop in population affected both sexes almost equally, the structure remaining relatively the same between the last two censuses.

Romania is facing a severe demographic crisis that raises and will continue to raise and generate new problems. According to the latest census of population and households in 2011 compared to 1990, Romania's current population is approximately 19 million people [5].

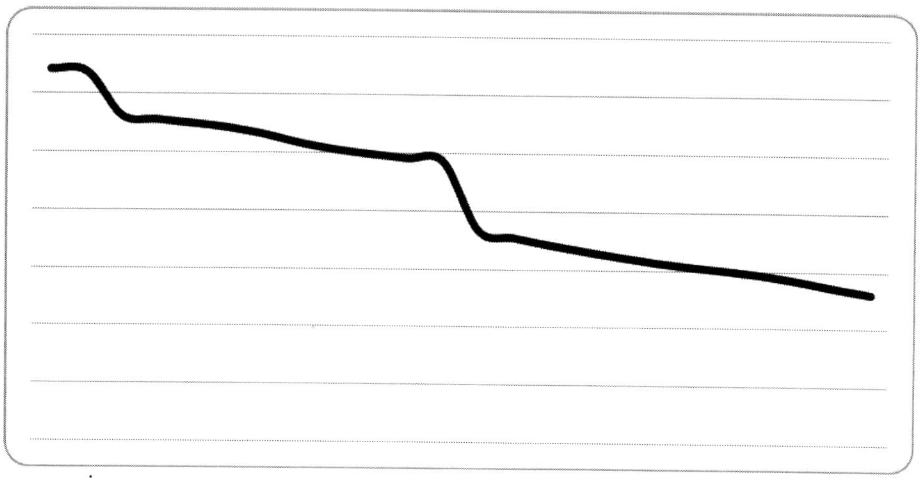

Source: www.insse.ro.

Figure 5.3. Population Dynamics in Romania between 1990 and 2013.

The deterioration of the demographic situation of the country is the direct or indirect result of a complex political, economic and social context that is specific to transitions. The demographic crisis expresses the cumulative result of some distorted dynamics of birth (fertility), mortality and external migration that have occurred in the last 23 years.

Population dynamics in Romania in the period between 1990 and 2013 is explained primarily by a reduced birth rate. This was deepened after 1990, both as a result of increased family freedom to decide the number of children, but also as a result of the empowerment of women, who have given more attention to career and become involved in activities which implied reduced family time. The reproductive model that emerged in Western Europe in the 70s has influenced the reproductive pattern in Romania, especially in the last three decades. According to this model couples want a small number of children and they are brought into the world by mothers at a later age [4]. The year 2013 was the year with the fewest births for Romania as a modern state, with 2014 as the 22nd consecutive year of population decline. Romania loses about 30,000 inhabitants every year. If this rate is maintained in the long term, then in 2030 the Romanian population will be equal to that of 1946.

Demographic projections show an aggravating unprecedented demographic crisis in Romania. Romania's continuing demographic decline, at least until 2050, is being confirmed by studies and forecasts conducted by experts and Romanian researchers, primarily by the

National Institute of Statistics, the Centre for Demographic Research "Vladimir Trebici" of the Romanian Academy and the reports submitted by some institutions authorized by international organizations: the United Nations Development Programme-UNDP / Population Division; OECD; World Bank and European Union. Figure 5.4 highlights both the growth of the Romanian population since 1990 and some projections that anticipate continued population decline until 2050 at least.

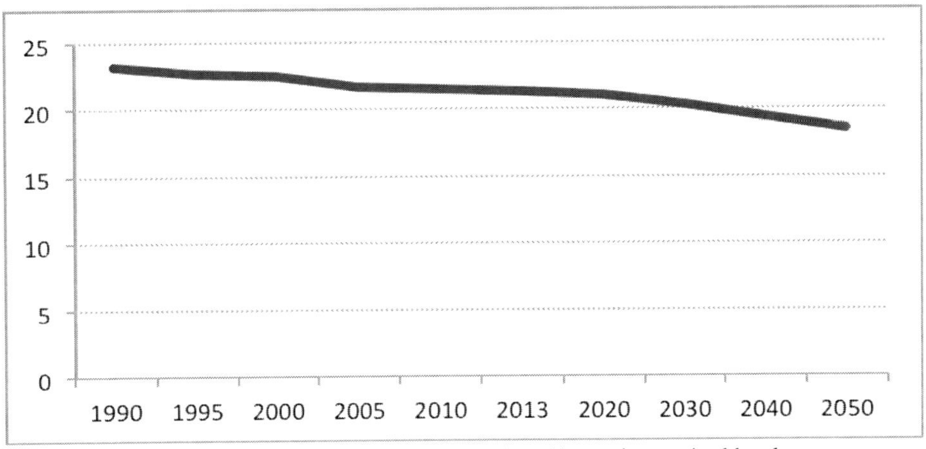

Source: http://epp.eurostat.ec.europa.eu; www.insse.ro; http://www.ince.ro/ccd.html.

Figure 5.4. Population Dynamics in Romania starting 1990 and some projections to be achieved by 2050.

According to a study by the United Nations [6] it is estimated that if the fertility rate remains at the level recorded in recent years, the Romanian population will reach 16.8 million in 2050 and 8.5 million in the year 2100, respectively. The situation is particularly worrying if we take into account the spillover effects they may generate medium to long term.

The evolution of natural increase is the cumulative result of birth and death dynamics:

- birth rate has declined continuously since 1990. In 1990 there were 314,746 births while in 2000 that number dropped to 234,600, and in 2009 to 222,388. The trend continued in 2010, when there were over ten thousand fewer births than the previous year. Couples want a decreasing number of children and women decide to give birth to children at ages increasingly advanced. For example, in 2010 the average maternal age was 27.6 years. With a rate of 9.9 births per thousand population in 2010 and 9.4 in 2012, the birth rate in Romania is below the average recorded in the European Union (EU). In the EU-27 countries best positioned against this indictor are: Ireland (16.7%) and France (12.8%). At the opposite pole are: Austria (9.1%), Italy, Hungary and Portugal (9.4-9.6‰).
- In Romania, there are developments which are territorially differentiated: the counties with better birth rates are: Botosani, Iasi, Suceava, Vaslui and Bacău; areas that also have the highest share of young population (0-14 years), over 18%. One of the factors that have contributed to the birth rate in Romania is the continuously decreasing number of marriages and the increasing average age of partners who are more and more career-oriented. In 1990 the average age at marriage was 26.9 for

husbands and 23.7 for wives, while in 2010, it was 29.9 and 26.4, respectively. The latest available data highlights the age of 31 for men and 28 for women. Furthermore, the number of divorces has increased. However, compared to Europe, the divorce rate in Romania is relatively low. After 1989, both the number and the percentage of children born outside marriages has grown rapidly - from 15% in the first half of the 1990s, to nearly 30% in recent years.

- mortality has remained consistently high. The mortality rate in Romania (12.1% - deaths per thousand inhabitants) is among the highest in Europe, surpassed by Bulgaria (14.2%), Latvia and Hungary (13%). Cardiovascular diseases and tumors are major causes of death for 79% of the deceased. For comparison purposes, in developed countries the percentage is only 30-40%. Infant mortality, with 10 deaths per 1,000 births, is the highest in the European Union, being three times higher than that recorded in countries such as the Czech Republic, Greece and Slovenia. However, compared with 1990, when infant mortality rate was 30, in 2013 it was lower. Romania's position in the EU remains critical in terms of mortality rate of mothers at birth. However, a significant improvement in this indicator has been noticed and also a reduction in the rate from 170 in 1990 to 72 in 1995 and 27 in 2012, respectively [7].

The demographic crisis in Romania has direct consequences on the whole socio-economic development. Romania faces a decrease in the employment-population ratio and the aggravation of unemployment (*Chapter 3*). Currently, the working age population economically active in Romania is made up especially of people born until 1967-1970. Retirement of this generation will generate extensive consequences for pension and social security systems, as well as for tax policies (*Chapter 4*).

We anticipate a possible increase in taxes that will be paid by active people, due mainly to the sharp drop in the number of taxpayers. Future generations will feel the painful consequences of acute demographic crisis.

Romania is currently facing and will face increasingly unprecedented demographic phenomena in the future. The main characteristics that shape the demographic profile and demographic crisis in Romania are:

- Low fertility rate. In Romania, according to data from the Population Division of the United Nations Development Programme [6], the fertility rate dropped from 1.9 in 1990 to 1.4 in 2010 and 1.25 in 2012. Exception among Rroma women who give birth, on average, to 3 children;
- Negative natural growth. Natural increase has been negative since 1992 and remains so until today. In 1992 there were 3,462 more deaths than births. The year 2010 marked the beginning of demographic collapse because, for the first time, population growth was negative throughout the year [8].
- Increase in average life expectancy at birth in 1990, from 66 years for men, to 73 years for women, while in 2010 it went up from 70 years for men to 77 for women [7]. The average life expectancy in Romania - 73.5 years - is among the lowest in Europe, ranking with Baltic neighbors. In Denmark, Germany, Spain, Italy, Finland and Sweden, the average life expectancy is over 80 years;

- High international migration levels, especially among working-age population, women of childbearing age and especially emigration of young well-trained people ("brain-drain") remains at high levels, with a number of over 10,000 Romanian leaving the country to work abroad. Over 60% of migrants are women. Leaving their home, in many cases their families fall apart, causing consequent lower birth rates [9].

In conclusion, *the diagnosis of the status quo* in Romania, as a result of the dynamics of demographic phenomena that characterized the period 1990-2013 can be presented synthetically as follows: *acute demographic crisis.*

The demographic crisis manifests mainly in:

- acute negative natural increase due to: reduced fertility rate; plummeting birth rate one of the highest mortality rates in Europe;
- a relatively low average life expectancy;
- increased international migration.

It is anticipated that the decline will continue in the future [8]. The effects are not only economic, but they also involve social risks that have demographic impact [10]. As a basis for coherent *development of policies and programs dedicated to reducing long-term demographic crisis,* we consider it necessary to examine in depth *the structure of the population by various criteria: age, gender, territorial distribution, etc.*

2. Dynamics of Population per Age Groups

Romania's population is aging. The "Green Chart of Population" states that: "Not the decrease in the number of population is the most worrying, but the fact that this development is associated with a continuous decline of the age structure. There is danger of serious demographic imbalance in the country, which causes serious economic and social imbalances" [11].

We are witnessing:

- reduction in the share of young people, aged 0-14 years, from 23.7% in 1990 to 15.0% in 2013. According to studies and projections carried out at the *Centre for Demographic Research "Vladimir Trebici" of the Romanian Academy,* we will continue to witness an increasing decline in the young population aged 3-20 years (from 5 million today to 2.7 million in the year 2050);
- increase in the share of elderly population 65 years and over - from 10.3% in 1990 to 15.0% in 2013. In 2000, for the first time in Romania, *the population over 60 years has grown to surpass the population under 15 years old.* In recent years, the number of elderly aged 75 years and over has gone up. In 1990-2012, the older population grew by 822,400 people, where more than 60.4% belongs to the age group 75 years and above. In 2013, the population group 85 years and over, represented 8% of the population aged 65 and over, with an increase comparable to 1990 (5.1%).

In relation to *population structure in terms of background, gender and territorial profile* in Romania, the highest percentage of people over 60 come from rural areas, especially counties of southern Wallachia and central Transylvania. In *rural areas we can notice a feminization of the population.*

In 1990, the share of population aged 65 and over in rural areas was 13.5% of the total population and it increased in 2012 to 18.3%. The *"feminization of old age"* manifests through an increase in the number and percentage of women in the elderly population; women tend to live longer, their number is two times higher than that of men. By residence, population dynamics has followed the same downward trend (figure 5.5) and there has been a marked aging of the population in rural areas.

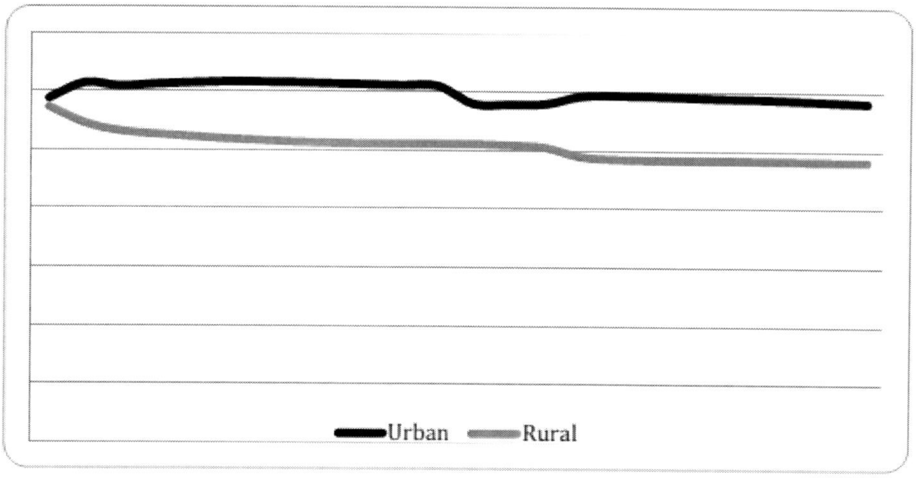

Source: www.insse.ro.

Figure 5.5. Population dynamics based on residence, 1990-2013.

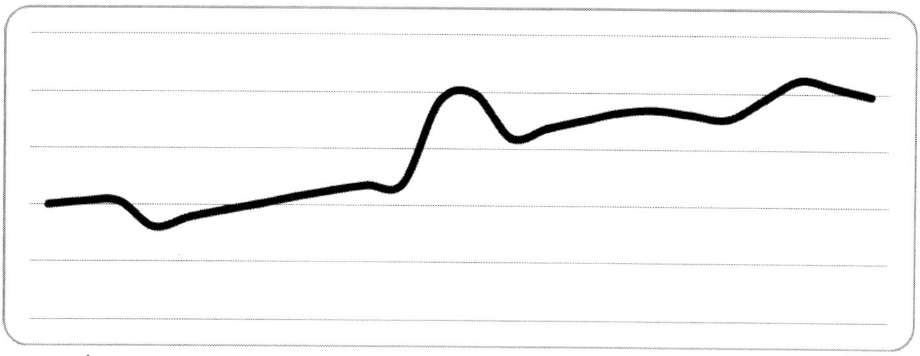

Source: www.insse.ro.

Figure 5.6. Population dynamics based on working-age. 1990-2013.

The *share of adult population*, aged 15-64 years, increased steadily from 66% (in 1990) to 70% (in 2013). For the first time in four decades, from January 1, 2013 the share of young population is equal to the share of elderly population (15.0%).

Over half the population of Romania (55.7%) is represented by mature people, aged between 25 and 64 years. The *average age of the Romanian population has* increased from 32.5 years (1992) to 39.1 years. The evolution of the working-age population is captured in figure 5.6, which shows a decrease in this category, particularly after 2011.

Vert has analyzed the aging of a population with the *aging index* that is calculated as the ratio between the number of persons aged 65 years and over, on the one hand and the number of those aged under 20, on the other hand [12]. It is believed that a country's population is young if the population aged under 20 years is 1.3 of the total population. In Romania, *the aging index of the population* has doubled between 1990 and 2014 (figure 5.7). Values of more than 70% of this index (2008) show enhanced aging.

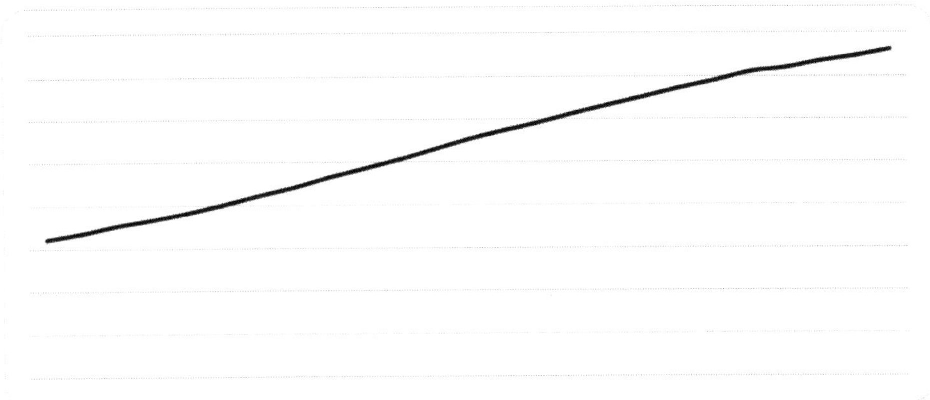

Source: www.insse.ro.

Figure 5.7. Dynamics of ageing index in Romania. 1990-2014.

Population ageing mainly affects the labor market, the social protection systems (especially pensions and social assistance), the health care system and public/private expenditure. Population ageing impacts and causes mutations in school population, fertile population and active one.

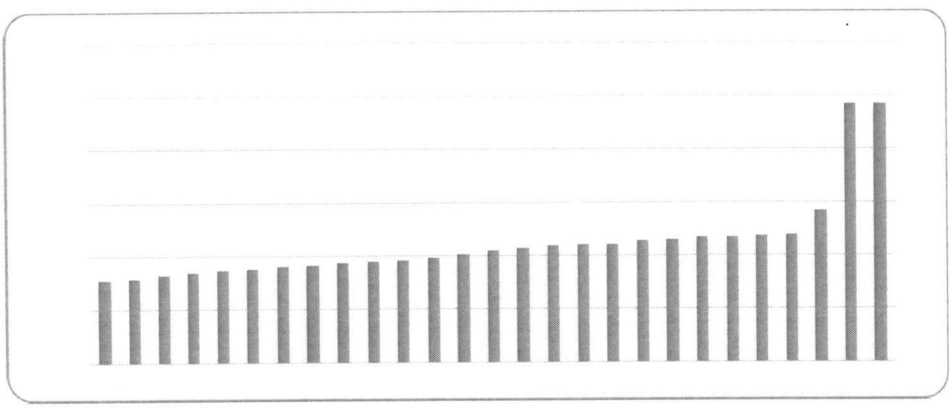

Source: Eurostat- Old age dependency ratio and Projected, http://epp.eurostat.ec.europa.eu/

Figure 5.8. Dynamics of dependency ratio in Romania between 1990 and 2013 and a projection until 2080.

Dependency ratio shows the pressure on those who work, who need to "support" both younger generations that are part of the educational systems and retirees who want to benefit from the health and social care. Thus, in 2012, one thousand adults backed 430 people, young and old (including the elderly representing 50%), compared to 515 young and old people in 1990 (when the share of the elderly population was 30%). This reduction was achieved primarily on account of the decline in the young population (0-14 years).

The number of elderly people aged 65 and over per 1,000 adults increased from 156 in 1990 to 215 in 2012, resulting in increased social pressure for adults.

Figure 5.8 highlights the evolution of the elderly dependency ratio (which according to *Eurostat* is the ratio between the total number of elderly people - 65 and over - and the number of people of working-age, 15-64 years - starting in 2009 and the projection of the rate in the year 2050 when this ratio exceeds 50% [8].

For Romania, the dependency ratio highlights a crisis of social security, that, in order to be solved, does not only require to proceed to a reform of the pension system, but also to restore the relationship between the productively employed and the retired ones. In this regard, one has to consider stimulating employment and an increase in jobs, particularly in the private sector, to stimulate investment policies (Chapter 3).

The ageing of the population and the rise in the dependency ratio is a phenomenon present in all countries of the EU-27, a phenomenon that will worsen in 2050 according to forecasts available both in Romania and the EU on average (Figure 5.9).

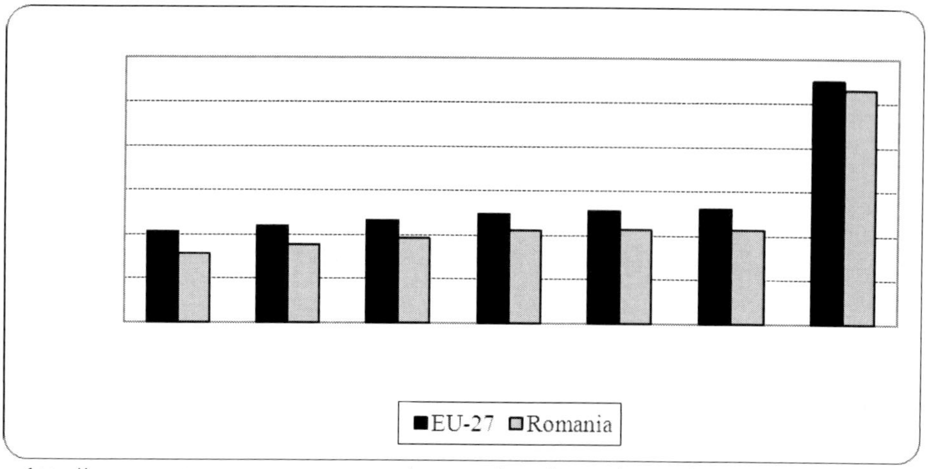

Source: http://epp.eurostat.ec.europa.eu; www.insse.ro; http://www.ince.ro/ccd.html.

Figure 5.9. Comparative analysis between the dependency ratio of elderly people (%), in Romania and the UE-27, between 1990-2010 and an estimation of its evolution by 2050.

The EU-27 projections show that the share of population under 25 years will fall from 30% of the total population in 2000 to 23% in 2050. This will cause a reduction in the working-age population (25-64 years).

In 2040, the EU-27 working-age population will be less than half of the total population [13]. Population structure by age will continue to change [14]. Ageing population results not only in labor supply reduction and *an increase in the dependency ratio of the elderly*, but also in a *decrease in the labor supply of young workers, which is expected to* affect the future welfare of the EU -27 [15].

Among the factors that highlight the *impact of demographic ageing* on *the labor market* we consider, in particular:

- economic resources necessary to support the elderly will become insufficient due to decline of overall activity and decreasing employment. In addition, labor productivity will be reduced, because usually older people have lower productivity;
- long-term growth of elderly dependency ratio will affect pension, social insurance, medical care etc.

Predicted values for birth and fertility in Romania [11] reveal that in 2050 Romania's demographic picture will look different: pensioners will represent more than half of the population and there will be relatively few adults and children.

These projections have started from the hypothesis according to which, as stated in the literature [16], an increase in fertility level to replace generations is not possible yet.

3. Some Features of Demographic Phenomena in the Territorial Profile of Romania

Between 1990-1991 North-West, North-East, South-East and Bucharest-Ilfov has shown an increase in the stable population of working-age. In 1993, the population decreased regionally with a few exceptions: North-East, South-Muntenia and South-West Oltenia.

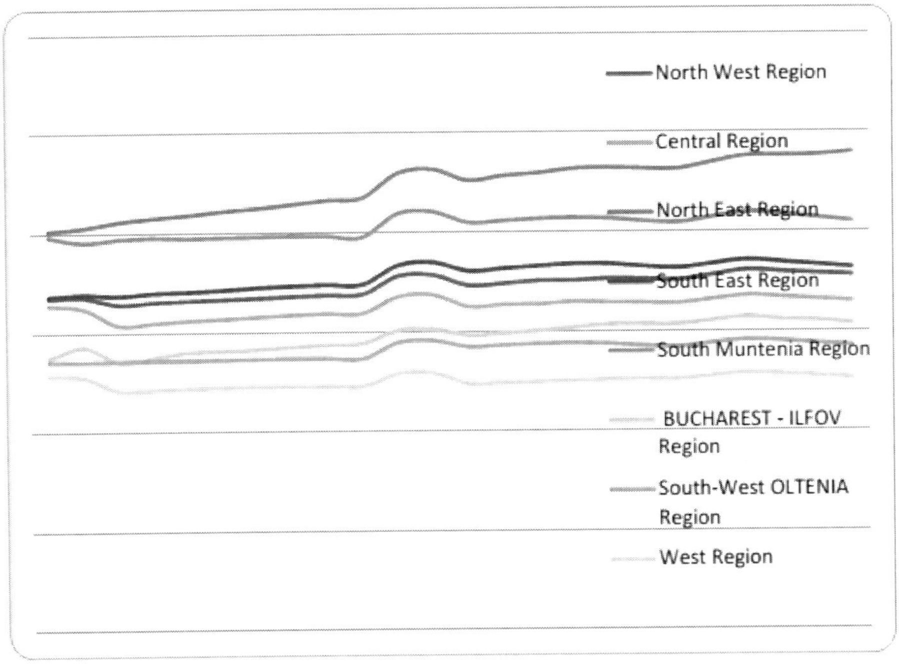

Source: www.insee.ro.

Figure 5.10. Dynamics of stable working-age population on 1 January at regional level (no. of people) 1990-2014.

In the period 1994-2002, the population of working age increased across the country, and, since 2003, all regions have recorded a decrease of this indicator. The next year it fluctuated in all regions. In 2014, the stable population decreased with the exception of the North-East.

In 2014, most of the working age population is found in the North East region, followed by the South Muntenia region, and the opposite is found in the western region (Figure 5.10).

Regarding territorial distribution, natural growth in Romania, in 2011, here are the counties that have experienced an increase in the young population: Bistrita, Iasi, Suceava, Brasov and Bucharest-Ilfov. The lowest value was in the county of Teleorman (Figure 5.11). These developments are summarized in the following two figures, which capture the color coded scale of natural growth and fertility rates in the territories. The closer the color is to red, the higher the indicator and, as the intensity of the color approaches blue, the analyzed indicator shows a lower value.

Rate of natural growth

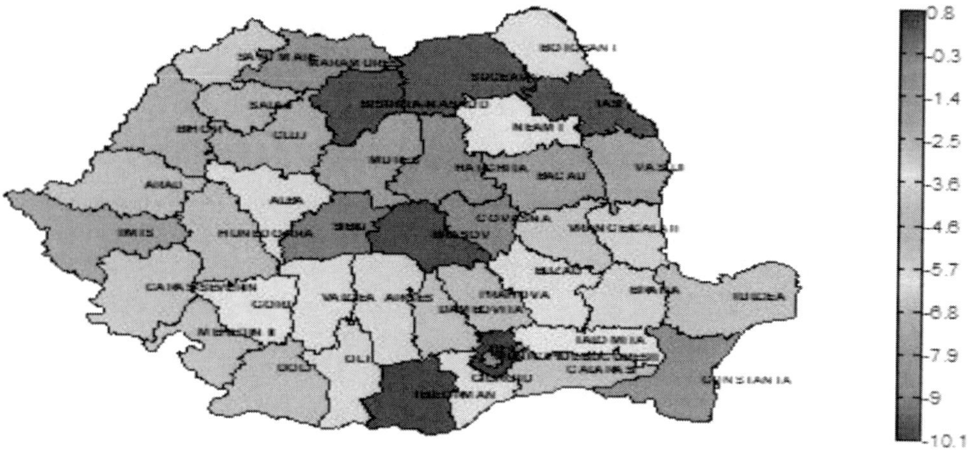

Source: personal representation based on INSSE data.

Figure 5.11. Distribution of natural growth in the territories of Romania in 2011.

Source: personal representation based on INSSE data.

Figure 5.12. Distribution of fertility rate in the territories of Romania in 2011.

To facilitate understanding of the natural growth developments in the territories, for the same year, there have been identified local differences between fertility rates showing frequency of live births compared to the number of women of childbearing age (Figure 5.12).

Regionally, in 2011, Suceava County recorded the highest fertility rate per 1,000 women of childbearing potential, age of 15-49 years. The following counties came next: Ialomita, Mures, Iasi, Harghita, Salaj. At the opposite pole we have Hunedoara, Gorj, Galaţi.

4. International Migration of the Romanian Population

After 1990, the Romanian economy has turned into a market economy through reforms, restructuring and privatization, generating high unemployment, surplus of labor that could not be absorbed in the absence of a sustained rate of investment and efficient agriculture. Many have chosen migration to Europe.

In the years 1990 and 1991, the Romanian population decline was due primarily to external migration that exceeded natural increase. Since 1992, the decline in population due to migration has been followed by natural population decline principally due to reduced fertility. Emigrants are most prevalent among active people, both economically and demographically. Official statistics show that the 1.775 million decreases in the total number of population from 1990 to 2010, is 33.6% due to negative natural growth of the population and 66.4% rate to emigration.

The highest number of immigrants registered in 1990, 1996 respectively, was of 9,000 people, and the largest number of immigrants reached in 1998 was 11,900 people (Table 5.1). Please note, however, that this is only permanent migration (i.e., those who permanently leave home changing residence). Although there are difficulties related to statistical information that we have about migration, recent studies show that, since 1989, between 10 and 15% of the Romanian population has participated in international migration flows, particularly to countries in the western part of the continent, after the early years when there were significant flows to the USA and Canada. There are not enough statistics to allow capturing characteristics of the Romanian migration in all its complexity and dynamics, with the exception of permanent migration. Romanian statistical information on the dynamics of migration flows starts with 1991. Temporary migration for work has become the most dominant category of migration.

Some studies have analyzed the Romanian migration in the last two decades [17] and identified four waves of migration from Romania to other countries in Europe (mainly Germany, Greece, Hungary, Switzerland, Italy, Spain, France, United Kingdom), North America (Canada, USA) and Middle East (Turkey, Israel):

- *first wave,* between 1990-1995 with a migration rate of of 3%;
- *second wave* between 1996-2001, with a migration rate of 7%;
- *third wave* between 2002-2006, with a migration rate of 28%
- *fourth wave* since 2007, when Romania became a member state of the European Union. Since then, Romanian EU labor migration has turned into a phenomenon of labor mobility within the Community.

According to the above study, the first three waves of migration were Romanian socio-economic development opportunities through potential migration of the unemployed in the local labor market and thus financing of the national economy through remittances.

Instead, the fourth wave of Romanian migration is described as a phenomenon that leads to a loss of skilled or highly skilled human capital who is attracted by better conditions of pay and living standards in the countries of absorption.

This category of migrants registered particularly after 2007 is highly specific to Western European routes and specific to the brain drain phenomenon. It is believed that migration of Romanians for work converted to labor mobility within the Community is a mass phenomenon that affects all aspects of Romanian society.

Some authors claim that, in the future, Romania might compensate for the lack of Romanian specialists by attracting and encouraging the settlement in our country of highly qualified immigrants from third countries. But immigration is a relatively new phenomenon known to Romanian society and it has greatly increased especially in the last decade after Romania became a member state of the European Union.

Unlike Romanian migration quantified at approximately 10% of the Romanian population [18], the phenomenon of immigration in Romania has been relatively modest. Data available at the end of 2010 show that legal immigration holds 0.3% of the total population (total non-EU immigrants / total population). According to the National Prognosis Commission, in 2013-2015, the number of immigrants is likely to increase to 200,000 to 300,000 immigrants, which would mean 1% - 1.4% of the population.

Over the last decade the influx of foreigners to Romania has been on an upward trend, accompanied by a diversification in the composition of migrating flows. However, some experts believe that Romania's status as an EU member state can render it a more attractive destination for immigrants. Analysis of migration flows to and from Romania over the past two decades shows that Romania maintains its principal feature of emigration country that may become, besides a transit country, one increasingly attractive for immigrants. According to Eurostat forecast for the period 2008-2060, Romania will register at least one net immigration rate of 18.4 per thousand.

The drop in population in Romania due to more intense international migration is a complex phenomenon that involves consideration of factors of influence such as:

- income gap between the country of destination and that of origin (influenced by the possibility of finding a well-paid job). Mansoor and Quillin [19] estimated an average difference of wages of at least 30-40% between country of origin and destination;
- the potential of migrant education;
- age of migrant.

The evolution of future external migration is unpredictable, being dependent on the economic and social development of Romania and the immigration policies of developed countries. It is necessary to analyze the causes and effects of this phenomenon, taking into account the indicators calculated by the specialized agencies and the opportunities gained by Romania through membership in the European Union [3]. Romanian migration for work, whether it is called migration or labor mobility within the Community (after 2007 when

Romania became a member state of the European Union) is a mass phenomenon that affects all aspects of the Romanian society.

Table 5.1. The contribution of the natural growth and the migrating growth to the overall population in Romania between 1990 and 2011

Year	Overall Population	Natural growth	Emigrants	Immigrants	Migration balance	Contribution to population decline	Contribution to population decline (%)
1990	23206720	67660	96929		-96929		
1991	22788969	23515	44160	1602	-42558	-19043	-0,08%
1992	22755260	-3462	31152	1753	-29399	-51904	-0,23%
1993	22755260	-13329	18446	1269	-17177	-82410	-0,36%
1994	22730622	-19365	17146	878	-16268	-118043	-0,52%
1995	22680951	-35032	25675	4458	-21217	-174292	-0,77%
1996	22607620	-54810	21526	2053	-19473	-248575	-1,10%
1997	22545925	-42424	19945	6600	-13345	-304344	-1,35%
1998	22502803	-31869	17536	11907	-5629	-341842	-1,52%
1999	22458022	-30594	12594	10078	-2516	-374952	-1,67%
2000	22435205	-21299	14753	11024	-3729	-399980	-1,78%
2001	22408393	-39235	9921	10350	429	-438786	-1,96%
2002	21794793	-59137	8154	6582	-1572	-499495	-2,23%
2003	21733556	-54116	10673	3267	-7406	-561017	-2,57%
2004	21673328	-42629	13082	2987	-10095	-613741	-2,82%
2005	21623849	-41081	10938	3704	-7234	-662056	-3,05%
2006	21584365	-38611	14197	7714	-6483	-707150	-3,27%
2007	21537563	-37237	8830	9575	745	-743642	-3,45%
2008	21504442	-31302	8739	10030	1291	-773653	-3,59%
2009	21469959	-34825	10211	8606	-1605	-810083	-3,77%
2010	21431298	-47524	7906	7059	-847	-858454	-4,00%
2011	21354396	-55197	18307	15538	-2769	-916420	-4,28%

Source: personal representation based on INSSE data.

Figure 5.13 presents the dynamics of external migration of the Romanian population between 1991 and 2011.

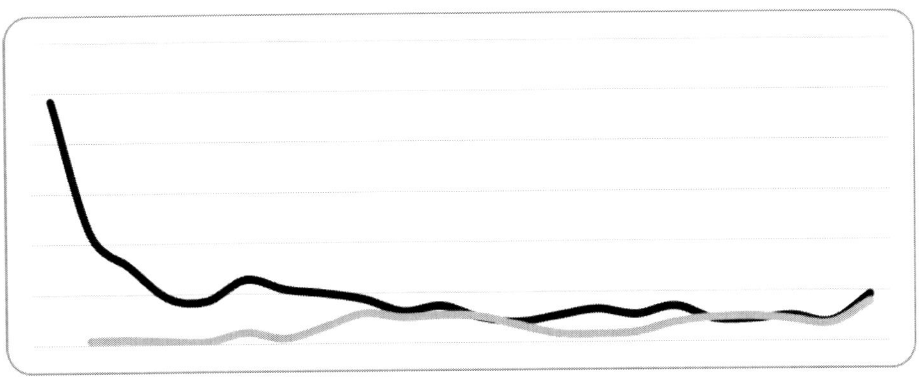

Source: www.insse.ro.

Figure 5.13. Dynamics of external migration of Romanian population 1991-2011.

Main aspects:

- maximum number of emigrants (96,900 persons) in 1990 due to economic, social, political and legal contexts. During this period, *ethnic migration* was the main factor of external mobility of the population. The total number of immigrants was *61% German and 11% of Hungarian origin.* In relation to the country of destination, most immigrants preferred Germany, Hungary, USA, Austria etc.;
- in 1995,the number of migrants increased by 49% over the previous year (1994), and most (35%) preferred *Germany* as the country of destination. This is an example of *temporary migration*, facilitated by the entry into force of the Convention implementing the *Schengen Agreement;*
- in the period 1996-1999 the number of immigrants experienced a relative decline;
- in 2000 the number of emigrants increased especially due to economic motivations;
- in 2002-2007, *Schengen visa exemption* has resulted in increased labor migration;
- according to *Eurostat*, in 2008 Romania was the EU country with the highest number of emigrants, 46% of them going to Italy and 19% to Spain. The profile of the Romanians who headed toward southern European countries is that of low-skilled migrants (negative selection according to the level of education), while the USA and Australia attract mostly highly skilled Romanians (positive selection), while Western European countries attract all Romanian migrant categories. Romanian migration since 2009 has seen a number of visible developments, which have become increasingly clear in recent years.

The changes relate to the typology of the Romanian migrant and migration: highly qualified specialists migrate from areas such as health, education, IT, and this migration is viewed as a long-term project with a character that tends to become permanent.

These issues are reflected in the increases of Romanian migrants in destination countries like Britain, France, the Nordic countries (from Europe) or non-EU destinations: Canada, United States.

Table 5.2. Evolution of international migration in Romania between 1990 and 2010

	1990	2010
International migrants (000)	143	133
% female among migrants 0-19	47	50
% female among migrants 20-64	53	42
% female among migrants 65+	60	62
Number of refugees	n.a.	1,021
Number of internally displaced persons	n.a.	n.a.
Annual inflow of remittances ($000)	11 (1994)	3,811 (2011)

Source: Romania country profile, UNDP, July 2012, p. 4.

Both *temporary and permanent migrations* have complex effects economically and socially in the short, medium and long term.

Decisive for Romanian migration is moving abroad for work, most migrants being listed as active population (15-64 years), women and men alike. It is also a circular migration, with a temporary profile: construction worker if male, or domestic services if female. Over the whole period 1990-2010 (Table 6.2) the number and percentage of women, in terms of migration was higher because men and women are turning to different jobs. If in 2010, the number of Romanian migrants who were working abroad was estimated at 2.8 million, the main destinations being Spain and Italy [20], current estimates of the number of Romanians working abroad now stands at three million people, mainly going to the same destinations.

The economic crisis has led to rising unemployment and immigrants have been the most affected. The economic crisis *has affected women and men differently*. Journalists from Newsweek (2010) have called the current crisis "*mancession*," because women have coped better than men. In 2010, due to the crisis, some areas dedicated to men (construction, agriculture) declined, while activities for women (family support) increased. The share of women *over 65 years is higher than that of men* (35% in 2010 compared to 22% for men of the same age).

According to the OECD [21], the effects of the crisis on migration are unlikely to reduce the motivation to migrate because of the economic crisis. Statistics of the *International Organization for Migration* [22] indicate that, overall, since the beginning of the economic crisis in the European Union in 2007, net migration flows have remained positive.

A component of the migration flows aimed at Romania, closely related to labor mobility is return migration. In Romania, 2008-2010 has generated controversy related to return migration – the economic financial crisis was thought of as a cause of such a circulatory phenomenon. In the fall of 2009 experts in migration management systems denied such a mass return.

A massive return migration of a number of about 2.5 million Romanian workers abroad would have created a nationally unbearable social pressure. Eurostat statistics show that in 2010 there were approximately 2 million workers of Romanian nationality in the EU [23].

According to NIS, Romanians' preferred destination countries in 2011were: Spain, Israel, Germany, Italy, Austria, and USA. Most job applications focused on the following sectors: agriculture, construction, hospitality, family assistance [24].

There is a strong correlation between migration analysis and the analysis of quality of life, because there can be two-way effects and conditionality between them.. On the one hand, low quality of life leads individuals to migrate temporarily or permanently, in search of better living conditions. On the other hand, emigration to more developed areas can help improve quality of life for some individuals, those who emigrate.

In Romania, the main cause of migration is the existence of economic gaps between Romania and developed countries. Receiving countries seek to attract well-trained and / or cheap workforce by making use of information and communication technologies to provide useful information by the employer to potential employees without having proper face-to-face meeting [25].

Inclination towards international migration is influenced by the *individual characteristics of the person who migrates.*

Young people are more willing to go than the elderly; men more than women; unmarried more than married people; high skilled versus unskilled ones.

Regarding the number of Romanians who have left to work abroad (*temporary migration*), different data is being circulated.

It is estimated that about 10% of Romanians, aged 15-64 years are working abroad (about 2.7 million people). Some authors report that *"Romania lacks the link between migration policy and development policy"* [20].

The same author reported possible directions for Romanian migration:

- policies focused on working abroad;
- rethinking the impact of migration on regional development
- immigration and policies regarding the correlation between migration and development.

Diagnosis of demographic crisis in Romania reveals acuteness. We analyzed aspects mainly related to ageing and international migration. Active population decline and increasing dependence for Romania (in 2011, 23.7 dependents per 100 employees), produces economic effects such as:

- reduction of potential GDP (potential GDP of Romania fell to 1.3% in 2013 from 5% in 2004) by reducing the contribution of the labor force;
- the economic downturn;
- increasing the long-term pressure on the state budget both on the revenue side (by affecting growth) and on the expenditure side (by increasing spending for social assistance and health);
- maintaining dependence on foreign capital and the current account deficit.

Long-term consequences of these developments will worsen, as illustrated by some of the projections made by experts from home and abroad.

Conclusion

In conclusion, within Romania, over the last two decades, between 1990-2013, there was a demographic transition from a demographic structure characteristic of a country with a relatively young population, growing, to one characteristic of a country whose decline is of increasing concern, while the proportion of older people is increasing. The main contribution to the increase of population demographic decline after 1990 has been the migration abroad mainly of active people, both economically and demographically.

The demographic decline has been caused by falling birth rates and natural growth rates; the latter becoming negative year after year since 1992.

The impact of the demographic crisis in Romania is felt in the labor market, mainly by reducing the employed population or by increasing pressure on the need to support both a growing elderly population, and a young population group that is not working but is dependent on the working population. As a consequence, besides the economic risks, there are social ones mainly related to pension and social security. Seniors need not only pensions but also special care systems [26]. Demographic imbalances have profound implications on the functioning of the economy as a whole and on other social services, such as for example: providing housing conditions, education, health and other protection systems and social security [27]. According to available data, between 1990 and 2010 the share of young population between 0 and 19, dropped dramatically, from 31.7% in 1990 to 25.7% in 2000 to 20.8% in 2010, thus affecting the education system, but having effects that propagate in the whole socio-economic development of Romania.

Meanwhile, during the same period, the share of elderly population over 64 years increased from 10.4% in 1990 to 13.3% in 2000 to 14.9% in 2010. Population ageing is stronger in rural areas where there is a relative phenomenon of feminization of the population as well.

During the same period, the share of the active population (aged 20 and 64) of the total Romanian population increased from 57.9% in 1990 to 61.0% in 2000 and to 64.3% in 2010.

The demographic crisis is affecting the economic and social development of Romania on short, but particularly medium and long term. Long term projections prepared by experts and institutions from home and abroad show that at least until 2050, our population will continue to decline. Alarming as well are the aspects that show a structural-qualitative degradation in relation to variables such as:

- changing population structure by age, gender, backgrounds (urban / rural);
- widening of gaps related to distinctive dynamics of demographic variables at territorial level;
- reducing the stock and quality of human capital due to widening effects of international migration of labor, especially related to phenomena of "brain drain" and "brain circulation"

Population ageing, characteristic that is found at most EU-27, [28] has worsened and will cause a series of economic and social problems. Under these circumstances, the emphasis will be placed on the adoption of a *mix of coherent policies* designed to defuse possible pressures on the labor market and educational systems, social security, health etc. *Proactive* measures of employment and social protection can play an important role, especially on medium and long term basis to reduce unwanted adverse effects. *The ageing effect* is found in other European countries, too. The literature highlights a *pattern of non-conditional β convergence for the variable total fertility rate* (TFR) in the presence of phenomena such as:

- the "*catching down*" phenomenon, where RTF showed rapid decreases compared with other countries or periods respectively (as is the case of Romania after 1990);
- the "*catching up*" is a phenomenon analyzing variable dynamics *average age when women decide to give birth to a child* (a trend indicator steadily increasing, including in Romania after 1990).

Some Elements That Highlight the Economic and Social Impact of the Demographic Crisis

Population is a central element of any consistent strategy for sustainable economic and social development.

Population dynamics, age structure, fertility, mortality and migration affect every aspect of economic, social and human development.

The aging process in conjunction with the birth rate mainly affects: the balance between generations; the labor market; social protection systems (especially pensions and social assistance); the health care system and, by extension, public and private expenditure.

There are already large imbalances in the age structure of the population between urban and rural areas, the largest share of the elderly population being found in rural areas.

In the labor market, demographic changes affect employment both in terms of structure and development of the active population and inactive population.

The relationship between employment, employees and retirees, labor market balance affects a significant proportion, taking into account the principle that pensions are paid by contributions from those working. The ratio of the average number of pensioners and the unemployed, on the one hand, and employment and number of employees, on the other hand, expresses the pressure that manifests on the income of those working. These aspects are captured by the indicator dependency ratio.

Dependency rate dynamics in Romania over the past two decades show increasingly higher pressure on the shoulders of workers due to an ageing population and the increasing number of retirees.

The current pension system is characterized by a high rate of addiction, it cannot properly support the elderly (the elderly population in rural areas, previously working in farming cooperatives, being particularly affected). A ratio of almost one active person that backs a retired one shows that we are in a deep crisis of social security insurance schemes. This crisis does not require as only solution reforming pensions and social security, but it also requires restoring the relationship between the employed and retired by stimulating productive direct and strong jobs growth, especially in the private business sector, through policies to encourage investment.

The aging process of the population requires reform of social security and health care, including the development of health and social security assistance for elderly people.

In the short term, paradoxically, low birth rate does not have negative economic implications. Those specialized in this field are more inclined to consider this level exclusively efficient when it comes to economic aspects because for both young couples and for society, it does not require an increase in economic resources geared toward pregnancy, childbirth, child rearing, education and health.

Demographic phenomena involve an analysis to consider the medium and especially *long term effects*. Long term population decline, caused by decreased fertility will affect more than the age structure of the population and it will generate economic and social imbalances. The volume of public spending and society spending would be higher under conditions of older populations, especially now that there are large gaps (7-8 years) when compared with developed countries in terms of health status, life expectancy, health state at birth, the average active life.

Due to deepening demographic decline of the continuous downward trend in birth and growth of external migration, an improvement of demographics in our state would require efforts to reconsider the basis for a long-term sustainable project by adopting strategies and policies leading to both a recovery of fertility and birth and a better quality of life that will contribute to reduction of external migration.

The impact of aging on the economy envisages, in particular the following:

- low labor and, consequently, an acute shortage of economic resources necessary to support the elderly. In addition, there are influences on labor productivity: an aging population has lower productivity;
- even if on short term, there may be some "*apparent*" positive effects of population decline (reducing the expenditures made by the state for family and medical leave pre and post-natal, child allowances, medical care, schooling), but on long-term it would increase elderly dependency ratio and thus affect the social insurance system, health and education systems etc.;
- the multiple and complex influences of demographic aging on healthcare systems, social protection, education or infrastructure, public and private expenditure on medium and long term are influenced implicitly. With age, the cost of individual health care grows;
- amplifying the importance of investment in lifelong learning, by focusing on non-formal and informal axis thus leading to changing lifestyles by promoting healthy lifestyles.

International practice and, in particular, experience in EU-27 countries facing an acute demographic crisis has highlighted the trend towards a set of proactive measures which have an important role in reducing the undesirable effects of deepening demographic crisis. On this basis we have outlined, some possible solutions that could be taken into account by different levels of decision makers in Romania to mitigate the adverse effects of the deepening demographic crisis.

Among the courses of action that decision makers in Romania may consider are:

- *birthrate recovery*, which would contribute to a decrease in long-term aging. To increase the birth rate they would need to consider the important role of reconciliation between family and professional life; greater accessibility and better quality of specialty services (social, health, education, etc.); improve reintegration policies of mothers in the labor market;
- *improvement of investment in people* (especially those related to health insurance and lifelong learning) in order to significantly improve labor productivity as a prerequisite for sustainable development, smart and inclusive, in relation to "Euro 2020" requirements
- *improving educational-system responsiveness to labor market needs* through flexibility and security ("*felexisecurity*") to consider adopting new forms of employment and social protection. We note, for example, silver universities ("*3rd Age Universities*") which is a common practice in countries that have tried to identify proactive solutions for elderly people. Such alternatives, however, involve a profound change of mentality and attitude, which involves a reconstruction on new foundations of the entire educational system in terms of education, carried out throughout life;
- *revising the pension and health systems* to provide such long-term sustainability;

- *promoting economic and social development policies to ensure quality of life and standard of living that can help keep in the country at least some of the professionally trained young people.* . In this way investments in people (especially related to health and education) can be exploited in the country without the amplified loss caused by the international migration of the most qualified and trained young people.

This set of actions have to be correlated with those provided in "*Europe 2020 Strategy for Romania.*" For this purpose it is intended to achieve, by 2020, a 70% employment rate for the age group 20-64 years compared to the target of the EU that envisages an average rate of 75%. In this context, to support the economic and social development of Romania, we have applied a *mix of strategies and policies* that entail measures facilitating synchronization and coherent articulation of possible policies and strategies, both at regional and at national and European level.

REFERENCES

[1] Suciu M.C, Gheţău, V., Roman, M., (2009), Demographics and Higher Education in Europe. Romanian Study Case, chapter in "*Demography and Higher Education in Europe: An Institutional Perspective*," published in CEPES series - UNESCO *"Higher Education for A Knowledge Society*," UNESCO-CEPES publications.

[2] Aceleanu, M. I., (2012). Links Between Education, Employment And Quality Of Life. The Case of Romania, *Management and Marketing Journal. Challenges for the Knowledge Society*, Vol. 7, No. 4/2012, http://www.managementmarketing.ro/pdf/articole/293.pdf

[3] Trebici, V., (1996). Demography, *Encyclopedic Publishing House*, Bucharest.

[4] Collection Romanian Statistical Yearbook, National Institute of Statistics.

[5] Gheţău, V., (2012). Demographic Drama, *Compania Publishing*, Bucharest.

[6] UN Population Division (2010), "World urbanization prospects: The 2009 revision," Department of Economics and Social Affairs of the United Nations (UNDESA), Geneva.

[7] United Nations Population Fund - Romania. Country implementation profile, 2012.

[8] Gheţău, V. (coord.), (2011). Îmbătrânirea activă a populaţiei: de la provocări la beneficii /Active aging of the population: from challenge to benefits, National Economic Research Institute of the Romanian Academy, Center for Demographic Research Vladimir Trebici.

[9] Anghel R.G., Horvath I., (2009), The sociology of migration. Romanian Theories and Case Studies, *Polirom Publishing House*, Iasi.

[10] Risks and social inequities in Romania, (2009) Report of the Presidential Commission for the Analysis of Social and Demographic Risk, September 2009.

[11] Green Paper on Population, (2006), National Commission on Population and Development.

[12] Vert, C., (2001). Geography of population, theory and methodology, *Mirton Publishing*, Timişoara.

[13] Report of CEDEFOP (2010) Working and ageing. Emerging theories and empirical perspectives, European Centre for the Development of Vocational Training, Luxembourg Publications Office of the European Union.
[14] Gronqvist H., (2009). Essay in labor and demographic economics, The Institute for Labor Market Policy Evaluation (IFAU), Uppsala, Sweden.
[15] Fertig, M., Schmidt, C. M., Sinning, M. G., (2009). The impact of demographic change on human capital accumulation, *Labor Economics*, 16, pp. 659–668.
[16] Trebici, V., (1990). Let's talk about the demographic dynamics, Economic Tribune.
[17] The Fourth Wave. Brain drain-West route - SOROS Foundation.
[18] Sandu D., (2006). Sojourne Abroad: Economic migration of Romanians 1990-2006, Open Society Foundation.
[19] Mansoor, A., Quillin, B., (2007). Migration and Remittances: Eastern Europe and the Former Soviet Union, World Bank, Washington, D.C.
[20] Sandu D., (2010). The social worlds of the Romanian migration, *Polirom Publishing House*, Iasi.
[21] OECD (2009) International Migration and the Economic Crisis: Understanding the Links and Shaping Policy in Responses in International Migration Outlook.
[22] Koehler, J., Laczko, F., Aghazarm, C., Schad, J., (2010). Migration and the economic crisis in the European Union, Research and Publications Division, IOM.
[23] Eurostat (2011) Population and Social Condition. Statistics in focus.
[24] Census results in 1992, 2002, 2011, 2012, 2013, The National Institute of Statistics, Romania.
[25] Bădescu, G., (2005). Romanian labor migration and citizenship, www.cenpo.ro/files/01%Migration.pdf; CENPO = Centre for European Non-for-Profit Organization.
[26] Balasa A., 2005, Ageing: Challenges and Responses in Europe, *Calitatea Vietii Journal*, XVI, no. 3–4, 2005, pp. 273–288.
[27] Sime, A. V., Eşanu, G., (2005), Migration and globalization, Detectiv Publishing House, Bucharest.
[28] Active ageing and solidarity between generations, a statistical portrait of the European Union (2012), http://ec.europa.eu/health/reports/european/ statistics/index_en.htm

In: What/Who Are We After the Transition? Focus on Romania ISBN: 978-1-63483-947-1
Editors: M. Dinu, D. Ailenei, A. Dachin et al.

Chapter 6

THE RESTITUTION OF TRANSFORMATION

Marin Dinu**, PhD, Dragoş Huru, PhD, Gabriela Molănescu, PhD, Anca Paraschiv, PhD and Cristina Voicu, PhD
Bucharest University of Economics Studies, Bucharest, Romania

ABSTRACT

The first chapter of this book looks at the meanings of the greatest societal correction in history, namely the collapse of the communist system in Central and Eastern Europe and the return to capitalist market economy and rule of law. Precisely it was a matter of putting an end to a nearly continental scale experiment which had been imposed on the grounds of ideological imperialism, and resuming the interrupted history course of globalized world evolution.

Central and Eastern European (CEE) countries experienced an abnormal loop in their evolution. The correction of their course supposed both cutting off their geopolitical causal ties, and adjusting on-the-fly to two complicated processes: the first of these consisted of restoring the functional structure of the individual's cost-effective and well-fare motivated actions, while the second of reactivating the free decision-making societal innovation experience which was brutally interrupted by the mid 20th century.

The result is a type of post-communist capitalism, as it looks like today, after two and a half decades of transformation. Its content is an approximation of: (i) elements of pre-communist experience, which social memory brought back to the fore, (ii) and the reification of the reflexes conditioned by the communist social experiment (iii) the taking over of the recent capitalist breakthroughs from the Western World. The post-communist transformation therefore is entitled to a separate study.

The last chapter renders the particularities of transformations and their manner to shape reality in this side of the world. Consequently, it provides the answer to this book's question-title.

* Corresponding author: dinumarin@gmail.com.

6.1. What/Who are We after the Transition?

It is not entirely correct to take the post-communist transition for a laboratory transformation whose results were previously provided by the system change general theory. For instance, CEE countries have witnessed a double transformation for half a century but to the opposite direction. Their modernity cycle is different from that of Western countries. Unusually as it may seem, the double transformation did not spell progress for the CEE countries but returning/coming back to a societal experience point that they departed from when communist rule took over. Their return takes place under certain circumstances which cannot be eliminated by simply quitting the communist societal model. It is kind of a backward-forward movement in an attempt at going back to tradition with a legacy of experiences that are not always congruent with the hope to advance.

The temporal aspect reflected by the backward-forward ambiguity is hard to ignore. Disambiguation can only be achieved by establishing an invariable stake, i.e., to revert to progress, to make future a guiding light for escaping the trap of living on the fringe of development for so many centuries. This involves removing the historical loop overburdened by the education-induced ethos as well as by the societal experience as an alternative to normality.

Within the universe of nuances of the CEE shift, transformation is a re-transformation of the societal system meaning the return to a previously natural state after an artificial state had been forcefully imposed. Technically speaking, re-transformation is similar to re-formatting a society's system in order to turn back to the a previous state in which the hardware was not troubled and the software was not virused. We are speaking precisely about the the states' liberties' administration hardware and software. Re-formatting is a managerial strategy of a top-down enforcement process [1].

As far as CEE countries are concerned, the societal system re-formatting strategy may well correct the course of history that veered off the mainstream. Seen from this perspective, it is an exceptional transformation, similar to the positively phased discontinuance periods when trend reversal consequences are offset one step at a time, the abandoned trend is resumed and the deviant trend is dissolved. This period of times features breaks and speedy rebounds to the natural and rational mechanism of society's life, in order to make things not looking like a societal experiment. It is a transitory evolution stage by the logic of natural order so as to restore natural order.

For the CEE countries, entering the post-communist era is a return to the pattern of normalcy, a transformation via consensualized reform, as the societal system distances itself from the option of violent changes referred to as the 'revolutionary path' or the 'path of revolutions'. The wind of change blows towards exiting the communist dystopia reality.

Aside from this abnormal form of a societal system, the CEE area re-enters thus the natural path of transformation followed until the late 1940s. By their rational attempt to reach the democratic acceptance of the social contexts and by learning procedures of avoiding or correcting errors, the CEE countries return to their previous route [2].

Viewing the post-communist path as a re-transformation ensures the successful avoidance of another societal experiment, possibly by treating transition as a memory-free process. What we are dealing with is basically a return to the freedom of making history that was brutally interrupted by Soviet occupation. In brief, post-communist transition is about rendering back the transformation that the peoples in CEE countries had experienced in line with the Western Europe prior to being left behind the Iron Curtain.

The restitution of transformation takes the value of a signposted road along which development comes in stages.

6.2. The Outcome of Reverting to the Capitalist Economic and Societal Model

The transformation movement that swept across Central and Eastern Europe was geopolitically driven by the values of democracy. The break with the communist regime orchestrated in the region in the aftermath of post-war geopolitical conventions occurred amid the weakening controlling power of the Soviet Union. What followed this episode is seen as the CEE countries' effort aimed at resuming the trends of the Western society model.

Despite some biased interpretations, the post-communist transformation was fuelled by two sources: the Euro-Atlantic economic and societal model (as a real target) and textbook theoretical projections. The outcome of transformations becomes relevant in reference to the two sources, without any precise dosage rule regarding what was inspired by the Western-style reality or the transfer of expertise in managing societal affairs via advisors, on the one hand, and the solutions arising from conceptual schemes of transformational strategies produced by global logistics institutions, on the other hand.

For certain these sources, fully trust by the actors of changes, have been augmented in terms of transformation power by what is referred to as the social memory of an alternative to communism.

In fact, all transition strategies featured typically Western society experience elements undertaken directly by the transformation actors from the radical idea system tank, no matter this was known by the large public or only by the chancelleries. These strategies included action plans and ideas promoted by persons or politically-active groups during the pre-communist years, which returned to the foreground of economic and political life. The transformations, such as liberalization and privatization, unfolded under the impact of the pre-communist social memory, i.e., a capitalist-type society, consonant with Western trends by the time CEE countries fell under the Soviet army occupation. The social forces from the pre-communist period had a decisive influence on the post-communist evolution as well.

The CEE countries experienced two antagonistic processes that not always sprang from rational and democratic sources. There was a process of destruction aimed at the *manu forte* Soviet-type control exerted for half a century, of the collectivist idea that social projects were wrapped in. Another process was the construction of democratic power structures, social relationships encouraging free entrepreneurship and a functioning market economy, private property and the rule of law. The true measure of implementing post-communist transition is the successful management of the two processes by avoiding the critical mass of violence by a hair's breadth. This fact is supported by the disparity between two types of effects: the effects of constructing the new well-being mechanism and the effects of destroying the former social and economic mechanism [3].

The real challenge of transformation is, in the long term, the dismantling of the domestic and external dependencies of society and the country, as well as of the individuals who had been shaped in the belief that the totalitarian state should guide them for as long as they live. Paternalism has conditioned in both public and private terms the mindsets resistant to the necessary change for shaping social relations built on the free judgment of actions. The potential for violence incorporated in the paternalistic dependence involved, in order to counter its effects resistant to change, subtle strategies, not always feasible to the actors who had to recalibrate their views and behaviors.

The post-communist transformation consisted of at least two stages: the first one was aimed at repositioning domestic developments onto the strategic lines of the Washington Consensus and the second one focused on regional political and economic integration into the European project of capturing globalization. For the CEE countries, both stages implied their resuming the global trends toward a model combining the capitalist market economy functionality with the patterning of a society based on democracy and rule-of-law principles. This model of society paves the way for a global civilization.

Formally, as depicted in the previous chapters, the post-communist transformation implies to launch and implement certain packages of processes, among which, in the first stage, liberalization and privatization, together with stabilization, played the key role in shaping an economy whose regulatory mechanism is the market. Transformations basically bring about free entrepreneurship and its corollary, private property. The functioning of this mix of processes and the achievement of their goals, as proved by Thatcher's project of expanding the market's scope and regulatory force, were deemed as valid for the post-communist period as well.

The transition theory in a post-communist version was inevitably corrected on the fly, chiefly in terms of the transforming function: to reinvent the capitalist market economy fundamentals. This function involved the creation from scratch of market mechanisms and the related genetic conditions, i.e., the freedom to decide and act in terms of the right of ownership. The situation is different from the previous examples, among others the United Kingdom in the ninth decade of the past century, where we dealt with the enlargement and consolidation of the potential of a market functionalized during the uninterrupted capitalist history. In order to expand the market, according to Thatcher, the trade union spirit characterized by Owen's 'harmonies' had to be replaced by the privatization of heavily unionized public industries. Post-communist transition destructured real socialism, which had become government policy, thus closing history's deviant loop that prevented freedom structures and actors from re-emerging. The transformation model is, in the first case, on a continuity track, toward enlarging market, whereas in the second case it means discontinuity, a radical break, the destruction of an artificially-introduced societal system and the re-construction of the abandoned system. The Thatcherism-inspired model induced a linear change with normal fluctuations; the post-communist change is undoubtedly headed in another direction: the non-linearity that resurfaced after the centralized system volatility takes a giant leap in the beginning, before posting cascade-like swings until the linear pattern of the re-built system becomes manifest.

The above diagram illustrates the complex nature of post-communist transformations and reveals the magnitude of a project stretching well beyond the economic framework, like the inspiring force of a theory checked in a different context. The spontaneity of the revived social creativity leaves the transition project open, as the entire world is undergoing a model transition. The nascent long cycle of the second modernity heralds a reality that coagulates the experience of postmodernist transition, whose components derive from the experience of the change in the societal model.

The functional link between the post-communist transition, which broadly covered almost half of the countries in the world, and the final goal of transformation is global in nature. It means the closure of a cycle knot of the social evolution that began three centuries ago and the opening of very long cycles. To exit the postmodernist transition means to abandon the logic of irreducible and violent ideological adversity, implying to invent appropriate forms of freedom management and to deal with the problems of subsistence in a totally different way than it had occurred in the previous societies. The nascent world already feels the dynamic effects of the third industrial revolution that brings about momentous changes in the manner one lives and thinks, including the creation and management of the means for well-being.

The stake of post-communist transformations has also put to the test the CEE countries' capacity of utterly exiting the consequences of the post-war geopolitical influences and resuming the path of developments compatible with what was characterized as the Western-style economic and societal model. The second stage of the transformation vouchsafes the political, economic and military anchors for this goal. The CEE countries joining NATO and their later inclusion into the European integration project are, thus, the pillars of a successful exit from the post-communist transition. The former communist countries are, in other words, building up strength for properly addressing the transformation challenges specific to a societal project meant to pass the test of globalization.

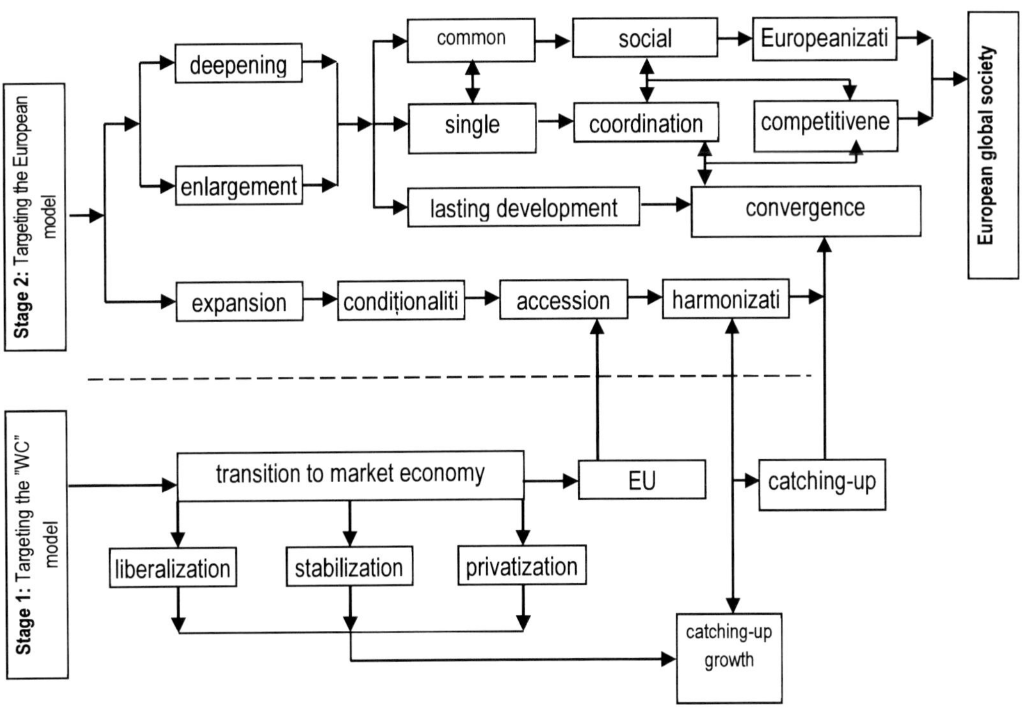

Figure 6.1. Stages of post-communist transformation.

A number of countries in Southeast Europe are still in the first stage of transformations, the same as those in Eastern Europe, but some of them will most likely follow the current

Russian integration project. Every country experienced specific episodes, including that of the first months since the communist party lost its supremacy, when attempts were made at orchestrating the changes in the Gorbatchev style, which is referred to as 'socialism with a human face'.

The differentiations between overall results occurred against the backdrop of a reactivation of the historical determinants of evolution in freedom and of each country's capacity to drive change, to keep up the pace, magnitude and depth of radical, complex transformations.

The odds of completely returning onto the capitalist development path are higher for the CEE countries that are members of both the European Union and NATO. The redesigning of a new world order by Russia's actions in Ukraine gives the NATO member state CEE countries the practical benefits of their capacity as North Atlantic Treaty Organization member. Until now only a specialized professional group was aware of this.

6.2.1. Stage One: Destruction – Construction

The public enthusiasm that accompanied the first moments of the change of the totalitarian communist system was the expression of abandoning an experiment that kept society away from the liberty and democracy practices. The economic and societal model imposed by the communist rule of the single party stymied free entrepreneurship and subdued the development of ideological illusions.

Quitting this model was thus the only way for CEE countries to resume the trend leading to real development as in the Western countries. Transition to the newly targeted model after the collapse of the communist regimes proved to be an intricate societal project whose understanding was the precise measure for the consistency of strategies and the substantiation in shaping reality.

In Romania, the same as in the other CEE countries, transformations are a case of formal alignment to the theoretical projection of the capitalist economic and societal model referred to as the Washington Consensus.

In fact, there could be no other way, despite the lack of unity of perceptions shortly after the communist dictatorship fall. Beyond the propensity of some people to preserve what was viewed to be good in socialism, the path of capitalism had at least one different version from the pattern of change suggested in the Washington Consensus. That was in line with the reality of the early 21st century capitalism: the return to the path of capitalist development that had been disrupted by the political options manifest after Romania's being occupied by the Soviet Army.

The two trends of transition, the former being prevalently restorative and the latter aiming to reach structural compatibility by following the latest capitalism trends, generated a burdensome, costly transformation model, including for the reason that none of them was very clearly separated from the post-communist transition theory. Quasi-permanent irresoluteness regarding the future vision/strategy led to high volatility in all major segments of society – from politics to economic and social life.

Transition debuted with a whirlwind of more or less coherently debated visions. It is certain that the first domestic stances as to where the post-revolution developments were headed were relatively quickly expressed. They focused on the wave which the country's new leaders biased on following Gorbatchev's instructions on one hand, and the ideated revival of the historical parties, on the other hand. These were laying stress on returning to the societal, economic and political practices of the former society before Socialism.

The relevant thing is the shift experienced by the decision-makers by adopting a Washington Consensus based government program. What seemed to be the road to defining the national post-communist trajectory marked by a comprehensive document describing the possible development directions, for which prominent economists of the time were handpicked, got stuck in blueprint mode. Confidence in foreign experts' high knowledge of the route from communism to capitalism rooted out almost any specific feature in designing/preparing a program of ideas. This program could have maximized the positive effects of creative destruction, especially since it referred to a deviant historical loop, i.e., the political experiment of socialism and communism forcefully imposed on the CEE countries after the signing of the peace treaties in 1945.

The fundamentals of a slow evolution have paradoxically emerged rather fast: within five months since the collapse of the communist regime, the legal elements for free entrepreneurship were enacted [4]. Unfortunately, their enforcement saw various distortions or delays. Political hesitations and turbulences bordered a trend toward clinging to the former practices of nipping in the bud any freedom. There were some rifts whereby major decisions were taken by a strong reluctance against the Washington Consensus-recommended shock therapy. The explanation of this kind of attitude is not necessarily connected to the mere resistance to change, but to the distortion manifest in describing the projected changes to large public. These were introduced as being irreducibly in competition with each other. Public debate was thus replaced by expressing agreement or disagreement, equivalent to labelling affiliation or adversity to the only ideological stream capable of washing away the past, judging by the Proletkult pros and cons.

The consequence in terms of genuine action was not long in coming, and this was a waste of time as to properly understand and cleverly implement the key elements of a successful change. In many ways, post-communist transition in Romania took the inverted form of post-capitalist transition in the aftermath of World War Two. A recurrent feature of the transition strategy embedded in government programs was, above all, an awful amount of improvisation and statements of intent. Furthermore, political wrangling, marked by the budding politicians' need to cut off any link to the ghosts of the recent past, caused the institutions/mechanisms operating in any economy to be removed from post-communist societal architecture as they seemed a legacy of former practices (see, for instance, industrial policy, development strategies, macroeconomic planning, and others). The effects on the economy were soon manifest as well, translating into a sudden drop in domestic supply, also augmented by the disengagement of industry executives coming under pressure of unions' claims and of a mainstream dubbed as "original democracy" that entailed successive changes of company managers under emotional pretexts. The direct outcome was a decline in GDP during the first two years after 1989. Social costs and the impact on consumption were partially offset by the return of enterprise shares to certain population categories bound by the communist regime to back financially the industrial sector.

The interesting part was that, at the beginning of the change, the transition policy makers ignored the theoretical suggestions on the mechanisms designed to obviate the after-effects of political wrangling on the economy. The lack of expertise in coordinating intricate processes, the policy makers' weak dedication to seize priorities and most of all the decisive importance of preserving economic stability fuelled the recessionary factors. With each cabinet the pattern of economic transformations changed, most often our of wrongly perceived ideological reasonings, leading to a destruction-construction cycle as related to the recent past, and not only to the communist command economy architecture alone.

Therefore, the beginning of the change disregarded any theoretical scheme, making emotional spontaneity the name of the game in transition management.

Perhaps the most striking feature of the early economic reform, judging by its persistently negative consequences, was taking things as a way to reap the benefits of the politically controlled economy. The explicit reflection of this perpetual attitude toward the economy after the change of the political regime shows that the great hindrance to post-communist transition was the absence of human factors able to lay the bases of the societal structures. This happened as Romania's communist regime annihilated over time any core of theoretical and practical experience typical for the economic individualism and free will.

The reified achievements of the CEE countries stand for their normally unfolded transformations on the condition to have had enough human resources who besides the good will to implement the change had also the experience of an alternative to the socialist economic model and to the political philosophy of the single Communist party. The fact that Poland had preserved a significant kernel of industrial private property, for example, made economic reform measures resonate not only to the legitimate expectations, but also to people who were receptive to and, of course, interested in steering the country toward a functioning market economy. There is no doubt that the rules of the transition game could be learned along the way, but where Western expertise had interlocutors who had already been accustomed to private property management, the post-communist transformation achievements emerged more saliently from early on.

No doubt that the theoretical scheme implemented during the post-communist transition, unlike the role it had played in approaching the market in the ninth decade of the past century, ran less smoothly because, in countries like Romania, the market had to be started from scratch. The necessary and sufficient conditions for putting in place the market had, in turn, to be created, including the human factors willing to work with market logic. If we talk about the birth of a new world, the post-communist transition played the mythical role of Genesis: to shape the man who would inhabit the economic rationality space and interweave his intentions with the return-generating transactional intersubjectivity performance.

There were also issues that had long remained challenges to transition strategies. In Romania, of all transformation processes recommended by the Washington Consensus economic stability met with the most contradictory results. The recessionary cycle fuelled by the entangled political decisions for the next decades is best seen in industrial production trends.

The most telling aspect of an improper stance in approaching transition to the market economy is that the falling down of governments brought about recessionary episodes that peaked after 1990 and 1997. To view them as transformational recessions is wrong. These bouts of recession should not definitely be seen as the result of a step-up in the renewal crisis. They were almost solely attributed to a political opinion reacting to the external environment, not to an economic analysis inspired by the real opportunities of changing the regulatory mechanism of the Romanian economy at that time.

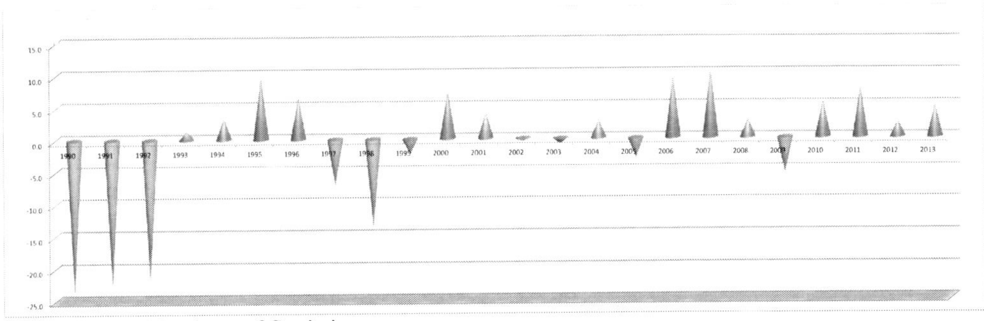

Source: National Institute of Statistics

Figure 6.2. Industrial Production in Romania (annual change, %).

The external pressure for carrying out radical reform failed to reach the competent receptor accustomed to substantiating the implementation of difficult measures aimed at system change. Complying with what was believed to be the external expectations replaced the effort to manage domestic change in terms of economic stability. The truth is that the effects of recession took hold concurrently with proceeding to reactive reform, i.e., only following external pressures, and made themselves felt in the long term, signalling something really alarming: the risk of curbing the initial enthusiasm for the change. The contraction was an alarm signal for the inadequate approach to economic reform, while the offsetting relation of the "destruction-construction" functioning binomial of the old and the new economic mechanism should have been kept in place.

The failure to stabilize production stood behind the slow changes in all areas and heralds the convergence potential shortfall in stage two of the transformation process. The economic substance losses, to an unreasonable extent, the dismantling of well-performing sub-sectors, the dereliction of entire sectors for which restructuring was not even an option, mitigated by the critical mass effect the chance for turning the market into a faster avenue to well-being, to getting out of the gutter.

Of course, over the long term, the restructuring effects on the industrial component of the transition economy, in line with the global economic trends, are becoming visible, though after two-and-a-half decades, under the force of traction of two factors, one pertaining to stage two of transition, namely European integration, and the other to productive capital relocation amid the global economic crisis. This is basically a repositioning of the functioning part of the economy, also involving broad-based reindustrialization, especially under the impact of global demand.

Literally, the void manifest in Romania's industrial landscape prior to the EU accession paved the way for the risk of covering it with transfer costs that prompted a decrease, during stage one of the transformation process, in the benefits of entering the market age at full speed. The preference for suboptimal formulas such as borrowing to meet domestic demand for goods was only natural.

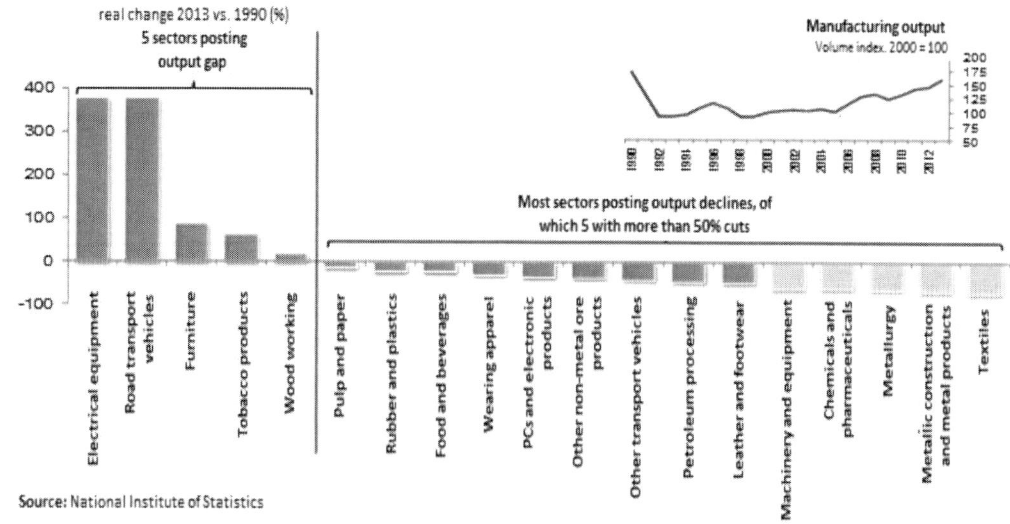

Source: authors' adaptation after National Institute of Statistics' data

Figure 6.3. Industrial production restructuring.

Romania went through a recession of a different nature, which was related to the efficiency of the working population patterning, i.e., an almost 10 percentage point increase in the share of laborers employed in agricultural activities to the detriment of the workforce in the industrial sector in stage one of the transformation. It may be considered, and it actually was, a correction of excess industrialization that displaced workers from the agricultural sector and relocated them to typically urban activities. But its magnitude also denotes a misconception about the ability of reform to preserve the social convenience gains of modernity stemming from industrial revolutions and social emancipation movements.

The liberalization, of prices above all, unfolded against the backdrop of economic instability and translated into companies' propensity for covering their economic substance losses and inefficient resource use by upping costs. The economy hence witnessed rampant inflation and domestic and external imbalances veered completely off track. These trends started to flatten out in stage two of the transformation process, once the talks on joining the EU had been launched in the latter half of 2000 and after Romania's Medium-term Economic Strategy was passed. In late 2003, capital account liberalization marked, despite the consequences of the social costs accompanying transition, the successful completion of a crucial process of enhancing market economy functioning and opened up the economy engaged in the effort of integration into the European market.

Long-term transformation was accompanied by the disadvantage of multiple imbalances, on which the poorly-coordinated economic policy decisions had little impact. Imbalance signals continued incessantly and were most often perceived by international financial markets in particular.

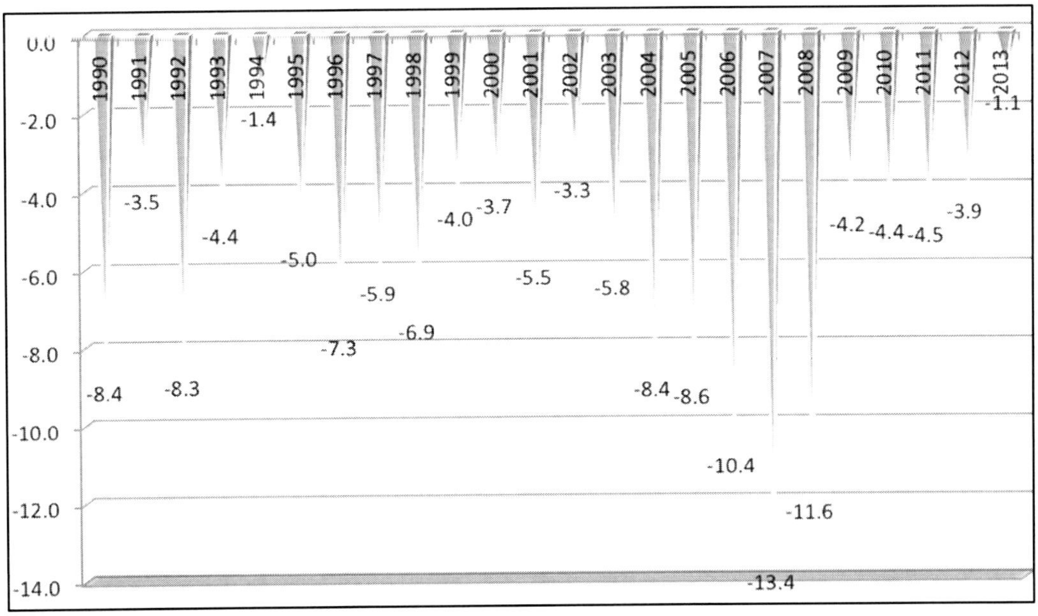

Source: National Institute of Statistics

Figure 6.4. Current account as share in GDP (%).

The status of sensitive external balances can be associated with the slow-moving, frequently faulty functioning of the market economy. The inclination to consume more than the economy produces is a reality with deeper cultural determinants than the situation arising from a shallow substantiation of transformations. Some kind of complacency in addressing these issues justifies the poor decisions taken in support of the actual reform.

Nevertheless, Romanians' spirit of entrepreneurship was not turned to account by an appropriate promotion of entrepreneurial culture, just as election cycles fell short of people's expectations and caused paternalist behaviors to linger. The inconsistency in consolidating the local value added-generating factors entailed the pressing need to resort to imports in order to satisfy domestic demand. Adding to this were the negative effects of the borrowings made to bridge the yawning government deficits as well as of the speculative capital inflows triggered by the interest-rate differential and the high exchange rate of the local currency.

Much of the external imbalance, as reflected by the trade gap, occurred amid the persistence of competitiveness differences. The state-of-affairs is relevantly summarised by the developments in the current account throughout the review period.

Property restructuring, the cornerstone of transformation with the highest stake, incurred the highest social costs, but made a somewhat spectacular headway as well. The reversal in the weights of ownership type in favor of private property occurred in 1996, when the post-communist transformation witnessed the U-turn to a market economy. Reaching the critical mass of the post-communist shift in terms of its major element of transition shows, however, that the costs associated with the country's change in the social fabric had been accepted.

Social adherence to the post-communist transition project has proved, from this perspective, an extraordinary achievement, in spite of the social tension emerging after the separation of the public perception of losers and winners as regards the change in the rules of access to resources.

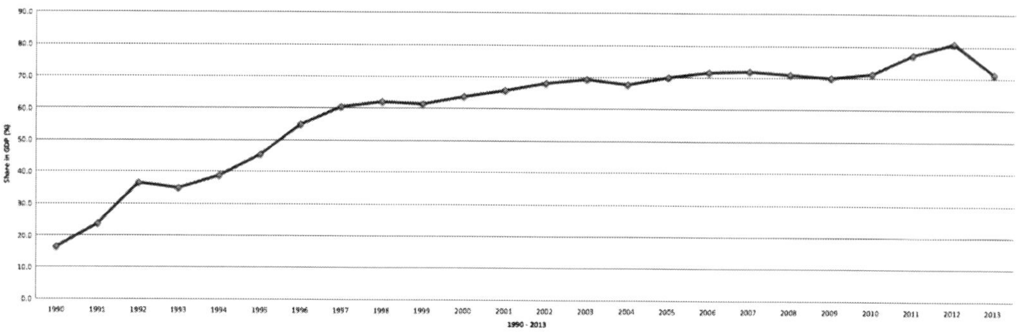

Source: National Institute of Statistics, European's Commission European Economic Forecast, autumn 2014.

Figure 6.5. Private sector as share in GDP (%).

The shaping of a social class inextricably linked to the strength of private entrepreneurship within a relatively short time testifies to the fact that the change potential allowed actually a transition patterned on the shock therapy. The evolution of the private sector as a share in GDP followed the trends seen in the CEE countries, which pinpoints that Romania, despite the views expressed herein, is no exception to the unvarying pattern of post-communist transition.

The European anchor, as shown further on, brings along a radical change, as the three essential processes of transition, i.e., liberalization, stabilization and privatization, have become increasingly effective in shaping a functioning market economy. Domestic and external balances have been gradually restored amid the growing investment potential, chiefly as a result of improved access to foreign funding sources.

Resumption of GDP growth proceeded slowly and no significant shocks occurred. From this perspective too, it became certain that effective transition must ultimately be confirmed as a good economic growth strategy. Developments in the GDP illustrate the in-depth transformations in economic fundamentals and the increasingly efficient restructuring along the lines of a market economy.

The reliance on external resources, entailing larger imports than exports (by volume), was a persistent trend, but in early 2014 exports made a net contribution to GDP growth. In the same vein, gross fixed capital formation increased its share in GDP.

The actual outcome of the transition can definitely be seen as a gain, even though one cannot overlook the wasted creative effort that took its toll. The most relevant aspect of the post-communist path toward everyday reality is the feeling that it could get better. Of course, this feeling proceeded from the longer-than-expected persistence of welfare effects.

The sentiment of an economic cycle with short-lived boom-and-bust periods prevailed during the transition in Romania. The evolution of the economy can suggestively be defined as a worthless stake, the positive effects of expansion being swiftly swept away by the economic crises that were partly generated by the transformation recessions following the change, in part as a contagion effect of an external environment mired in uncertainty. The transition boasted few big winners, yet many unsatisfied players with uncertain welfare gains [5].

There is no doubt that the transition was as deep as the degree of awareness experienced by the general public and the elites in regard to the objectives and the means of transition. Relative to the huge expectations that fuelled the initial enthusiasm for a radical change of direction, the contingent reality appears unsatisfactory. To a large extent, the outcome corresponds to people's habit of seeing themselves winners collectively, especially through their own efforts, in a performance-driven world marked however by development gaps ascribed not only to diversity. The Romanian economy has to fight an uphill battle in order to re-enter the global trends. The most challenging part of transformations is the weak capacity of a functional anchoring of the national economy to the *modus operandi* typical of the global economy, where competition rules are made by the advanced economies.

6.2.1.1. Lack of Initiative

Dedicated analyses show that the weaker-than-expected effects regarding the swift transformations also stem from a certain weakness of the reform scheme based on the philosophy of the Washington Consensus, which failed to take into account the specific initial conditions that could ensure real transition.

First and foremost, in the case of an almost entirely nationalized economy, the expected self-generated completion of the transformation processes, primarily concerning the market, is merely wishful thinking. It was impossible for the market to emerge concurrently with the major transformation processes. As the Romanian society had just escaped the communist dictatorship, it lacked experience in opting for an appropriate economic and political alternative. The only possible way of taking the efficient option for shaping a new reality was to stimulate the spontaneity of embracing the radical solution suggested by the regime change. This would have shaken the conditioned reflex of domestic and external dependencies cultivated by the communist education. It would have generated a natural reform, by consensual human action and free will.

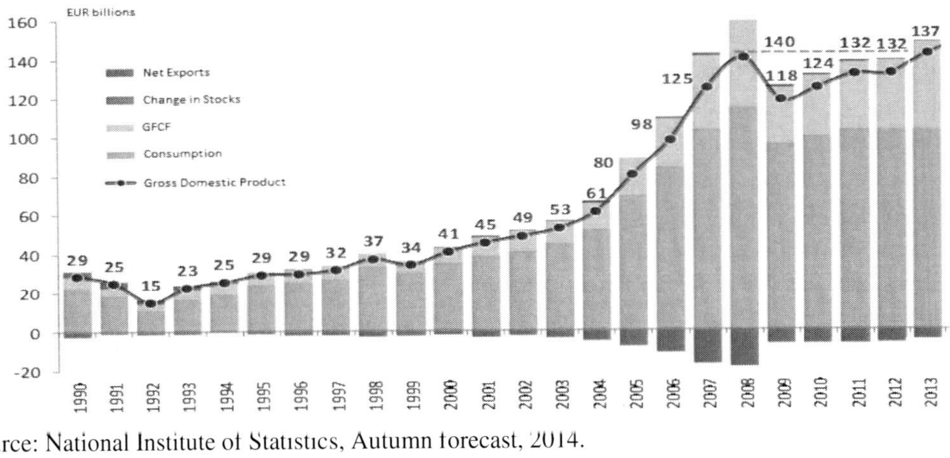

Source: National Institute of Statistics, Autumn forecast, 2014.

Figure 6.6. Gross Domestic Product's Evolution.

The key to the change in the regulatory mechanism of the economy was the creation of social and economic conditions for individuals' decisions and actions favorable to taking the risk of running their own business, by taking the initiative and using the available resources [6]. In fact, the logic of transformation reversed completely: abstract processes should shape people, not the other way round! In other words, liberalization was to focus primarily on destroying the social and economic context of paternalism, capable of generating the actors meant to bring about the private property. To a large extent, it was all about the transformation of the human factor that was actually invited to take charge of advancing on the path to the market economy. Thus, it was not a process or a set of processes triggered by bureaucratic decisions that could produce a swift result but making people act in compliance with the law, thus accelerating the transformation processes in order to meet the objectives of creating a functioning market.

The shocks of automatic price liberalization on certain market-unfriendly structures and on individuals who acted under strict command structures turned violent and led to rejection responses, including the indifference coming from the self-preservation instinct. The persistent lack of spontaneous implication in the transition stages, mainly those defining the fire triangle of the post-communist transformation of the economy – liberalization, privatization and stabilization – is not fortuitous. In the absence of external stimuli meant to help attain the strategic and stage objectives, namely the EU accession and the IMF-WB accords, it would have taken even more than around two decades for the transition to come to an end.

The lack of initiative and the failure to include the initial conditions into the transformation model also destroyed the coherence of the public policies designed/implemented during transition. The transformation models ignored the constraints specific to Romania and generated an algorithm tested in Western Europe but impossible to implement in Eastern Europe. It was wrong to believe that the model that had been efficient for decades in the West could be swiftly put in place in Romania. It was wrong to bet on burning certain stages of institution-building, a decision whose negative consequences are visible even today. As a matter of fact, all CEE countries missed the example of societal creativity, of innovating the adequate post-communist transformation model meant to secure the quick return to the capitalist development model.

After December 1989, the lack of initiative translated into ample economic cycles, with booms being almost offset by recessions and sharp increases alternating with abrupt declines in industrial production. The slow convergence process was also stimulated by the strongly pro-cyclical policies defying any fundamental(s) revealed by the macroeconomic theory and practice in advanced economies.

The inhibited free entrepreneurship actually left room for the uncertainty surrounding public policies, the short term being preferable to the long term. The consistency of a societal project could not be achieved in the absence of a political consensus concerning the main structural issues of the Romanian economy.

6.2.2. Stage Two: The EU Anchor

Romania's accession to the EU, preliminarily exercised including by association prior to 1989, followed the entry into the Western geostrategic project (NATO) and was solely the result of the political decision regarding the enlargement of the Euro-Atlantic structures toward Central and Eastern Europe.

Integration is a long-lasting process and its path is defined by the continuation of the post-communist transformations targeting a capitalist world economy model, i.e., the model designed by the European construction. The EU enlargement to the CEE countries actually implied the use of an admission grid certifying the advance on the path of post-communist transformations. They are assessed in the minimal version of the political criterion, which requires the functioning of democracy and the rule of law, of the economic criterion, which focuses on the existence of a functioning market economy and its capacity to cope with competition forces on the single European market, as well as of the technical criterion on the capacity to assume the obligations incumbent upon a Member State.

As a matter of fact, the analysis based on these criteria illustrates the stage of post-communist transformations. A certain degree of tolerance for the presumed integration standards can also be noticed as regards the criteria for joining the euro area, the requirements focusing on the attainment of exclusively nominal parameters illustrating financial and fiscal stability, as well as public finance sustainability.

In 2014, Romania made significant progress toward the nominal criteria standards for joining the euro area. The indicators on government deficit, public debt, exchange rate volatility and long-term interest rates range within the limits set by the criteria, and the inflation rate is likely to reach the appropriate level within one year. The tendencies may strengthen the more so as the euro adoption date was postponed by nearly four years.

It is common knowledge that the real aspects of social and economic developments are not euro-area-accession criteria to be observed by the CEE countries. The situation is somewhat more complicated as real convergence gaps are still quite wide, which renders difficult the efficient integration of the economies into the EMU. Thus, if we refer to a synthetic real indicator, i.e., GDP per capita, expressed in terms of purchasing power parity standards, Romania posted around 49% of the average EU level in 2012, compared with 69% in Estonia and 62% in Latvia, the latest euro-area newcomers. Complex calculations show that attaining a GDP per capita ratio similar to that of the countries that have achieved monetary integration will be feasible during a period of 5 to 10 years, provided that economic growth accelerates by 4 percentage points per annum or 2 percentage points per annum.

The notable differences in terms of income represent the major stake of real convergence with the well-performing European economic model. The growing tendency of incomes, particularly wages, is uncertain, as transformations especially in industry do not support this process.

The overwhelming share of small wages in total payrolls is a long-term challenge in terms of industrialization based on the FDI attracted by Romania due to the low labor costs. To a great extent, the structure of wages also explains the economic migration of important categories of population toward the EU countries paying higher wages. All in all, more than 53% of the workforce earn less than 230 euro (*lei* 1,000), which is the subsistence level.

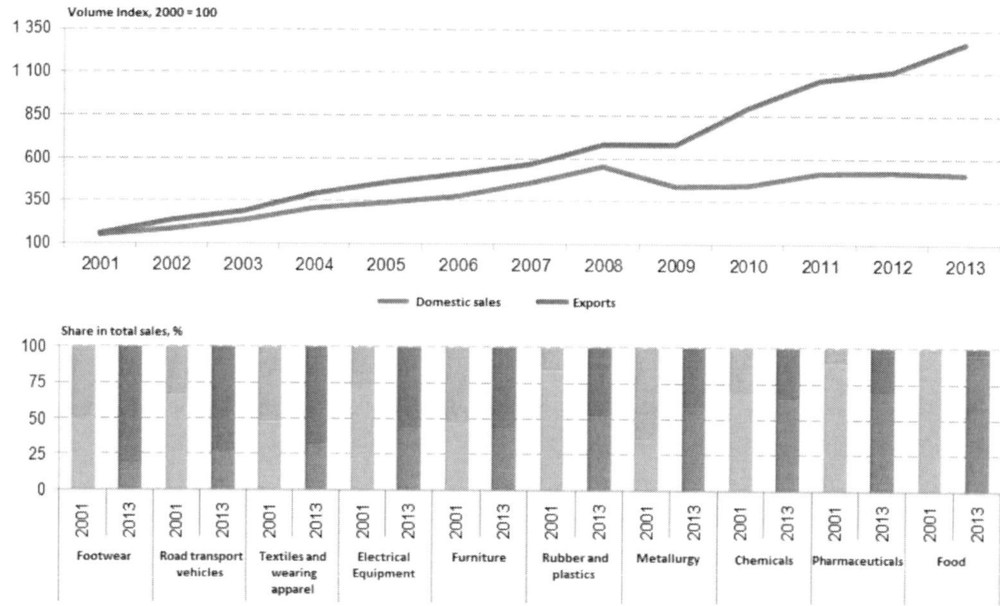

Source: Eurostat, NBR calculations.

Figure 6.7. Access to external markets and the impact on industrial development.

The better-paid categories increased more expeditiously over the recent period and the trend will most likely continue, on the back of FDI inflows to industries using highly skilled labor. Convergence of wages is still a rather intricate strategic issue, especially given the faster convergence, almost nearing completion, of energy and staples prices.

Nevertheless, the real complications come from the weak profitability of the companies operating in Romania. Actually, on a quasi-permanent basis, about half of these companies incur losses. Under such circumstances, companies are wary of increasing wages.

Profitability will definitely improve once the effects of the EU economic crisis have been overcome and the relocation strategies regarding the economic activities in a global environment have been recalibrated. The entrepreneurs who have gained experience in the European developed countries and the government programs meant to support young people who want to start up a business should make a substantial contribution. More precisely, to solve this problem requires the correction of the transition path by massive resort to FDI.

The opening up of the economy concurrently with the start of the EU membership negotiations, apart from the continuation of liberalization as the engine of strengthening transition to a market economy, translated into the increase of quality transformation effects on industrial output.

The new degree of economy openness generated stronger tendencies of redefining the functioning structure of the economy, with integration supporting liberalization – the main transformation instrument specific to post-communism transition, but also fuelled the continuation, in another area, more consistent with global challenges, of the restructuring process, by targeting the performance of the European economic model. In fact, the sweeping economic changes destined to enhance the capacity to cope with market forces, start to emerge concurrently with the adoption of the European targets in the post-communist transformation in Romania.

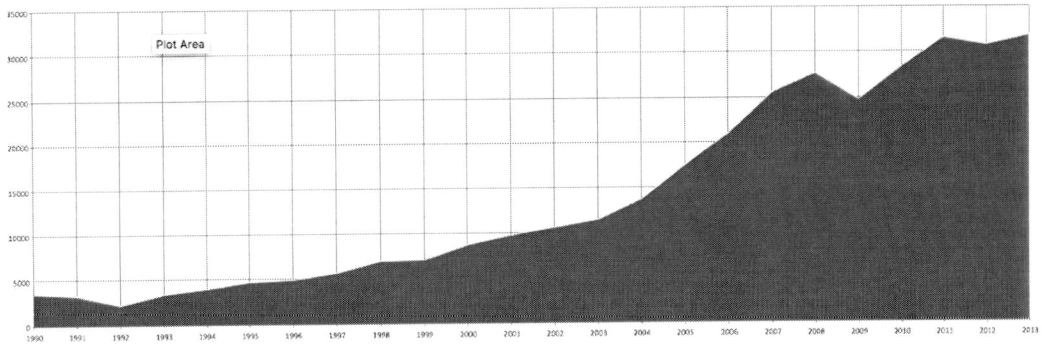

Source: National Institute of Statistics, Eurostat.

Figure 6.8. GDP per wage earner (EUR).

The GDP per employee trend, albeit on the rise, points to the structural causes, from technical endowment to wages and profitability, which are really pivotal for the sustainable integration of the Romanian economy into the EU economy. The indicators that give a clear picture of the strategic goals of integration are, beyond any doubt, real convergence indicators.

The clear uptrend in the GDP per employee ratio seen after EU accession shows the benefits of adhering to the single market mechanism, the turning to account of Romania's economic performance being given an impetus whose magnitude alleviated, to a large extent, the effects of the crisis shortly after accession. In fact, since the signing of the Accession Treaty until today, GDP per employee has witnessed a twofold increase and the rising trend continues once economic growth has resumed.

The most difficult objective to fulfill is to strike a social balance, which requires the achievement of a support economy as a basis for social stability. The wide gaps between incomes in Romania and those in the euro area represent the signal for a more cautious approach to economic developments, at least in the area of creating better paid jobs and supporting social-oriented investment projects, such as those focusing on road infrastructure. The GINI coefficient is still disconnected from the trend seen in the countries that joined the EU after 2004, these countries having already attained the EU performance standards. Income polarization in Romania was aggravated by the belt-tightening measures taken during the crisis. Subsequently, polarization alleviated following the economic rebound, as its reduction has been ranked among the major domestic policy goals. In the case of lower-than-expected incomes, one should not overlook the possibility of a more pronounced loss of the sentiment favorable to the EU integration. With 15% of the population accounting for 85% of the total economic gain, negative economic, social and political effects are to be expected in the period ahead.

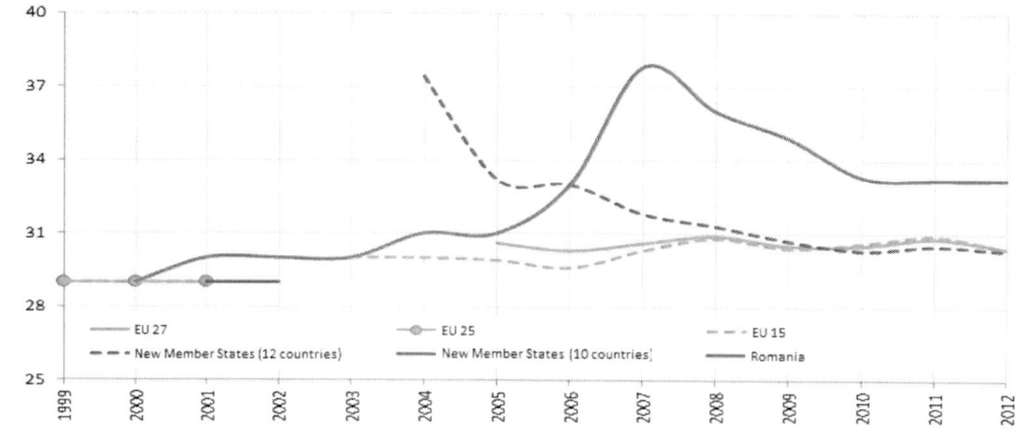

Source: Eurostat.

Figure 6.9. GINI coefficient.

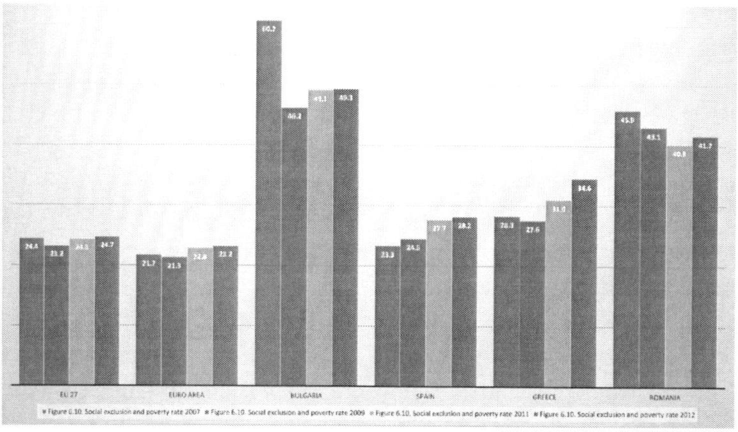

Source: Eurostat.

Figure 6.10. Social exclusion and poverty rate.

Table 6.1. GDP disparities (%)

Geographical area or country/Year	2008	2009	2010	2011	2012
EU27/28	2.0	2.0	2.0	1.9	1.9
Euro area	2.2	2.2	2.1	2.1	2.0
Czech Republic	1.7	1.7	1.6	1.6	1.5
Slovakia	1.5	1.5	1.5	1.5	1.4
Hungary	1.3	1.3	1.3	1.3	1.3
Poland	1.2	1.2	1.2	1.3	1.3
Romania	1.0	1.0	1.0	1.0	1.0
Bulgaria	0.9	0.9	0.9	0.9	0.9

Source: National Commission of Prognosis.

The weak point of the convergence performance is correlated with the social cohesion whose main elements fall into the category of strong motivational factors in favor of change and also represents the political stake providing economic support to individual emancipation. The category of population living in poverty and social exclusion is much too large so as not to regard real convergence in Romania otherwise than the basic process helping integration and the daily concern of decision-makers.

Real convergence is the toughest challenge during stage two of the post-communist transition in Romania. The real convergence performance in Romania lags way behind the European model performance and it needs to address the deep social-oriented aspect of integration.

The medium-term targets of this stage focus on catching up with the CEE countries faring better, yet it is decisive to attain, in the appropriate long run, the average level of EU-wide GDP. The target is clearly linked to the transition project as an assumed process aimed at the development and modernization of Romania, the soft spots relative to the standards of living representing the sensitive measure of the transformation model in operation.

Both in a global sense, as GDP per capita, and in a structural sense, as a share of poverty-stricken population, Romania needs to make a tremendous transformation, i.e., a twofold increase in GDP per capita and a halving of the social exclusion and poverty rate. This can only be achieved by speeding up the transformation processes required by the EU integration.

The improved social and economic performance translates into the conclusion of the processes specific to stage one of the post-communist transition, implying the completion of the transformation triangle consisting in liberalization, stabilization and restructuring, as well as the speeding-up of the processes specific to stage two. Among the latter processes, convergence is pivotal in ensuring the success for breaking certain historical patterns regarding Romanians' approach to fast-paced development.

The harmonization of the Romanian society and economy with that of the EU appears reasonable and certifies the validity of the national strategic option for EU integration, if several structural elements are considered.

The above scoreboard indicators, setting forth a comparison between financial stability developments, place Romania onto a relatively balanced position compared to the CEE countries. It is obvious that since it has joined the EU, Romania carried on the transformations, even consolidated some transformation achievements illustrated by the low inflation rate and the markedly narrower current account deficit.

The real concern for generating an appropriate trend of developments is the enhanced investment effort in the field of reindustrialization in step with the world market requirements and the long-term consolidation of domestic and external macroeconomic balances. The Romanian economy still faces balance potential issues, as consumption exceeds production.

The EU anchor starts impacting economic stability in Romania on a corridor comprising all the post-communist countries that have joined the EU. Really great strides were made as concerns mainly the functionality of the modified economic mechanism, the capacity of the economy to function in a stable environment. The efforts to consolidate the structural balance tendencies are in an incipient stage but the advance compared with the pre-accession stability potential is the best proof that the positive influence of integration on transformations is a fact.

Table 6.2. Scoreboard indicators on the structural stability in Romania and other EU countries in 2012-2014

Evolutive indicator		Current account balance	International account balance	Real effective exchange rate calculated based on HICP	Market share of exports of goods and services	Nominal unit labor cost	House price index	Private sector debt	Loans to the private sector	Public debt	Unemployment rate	Total liabilities of the financial sector
Country		% of GDP, 3 year average	% of GDP	3 year percentage change	5 year percentage change	3 year percentage change	annual percentage change	% of GDP	% of GDP	% of GDP	%; 3 year average	annual percentage change
	Year	-4%/+6% of GDP	-35% of GDP	+/-5% (Euro Area); +/- 11% (non-EA)	-6%	+9% (EA); +12% (non-EA)	6%	160% of GDP	+15% of GDP	60% of GDP	10%	16.50%
Bulgaria	2011	-3.4	-85.9	1.9	17.0	21.3	-9.7	133.4	1.8	16.3	9.4	4.9
	2012	-0.9	-79.7	-4.0	4.8	7.4	-5.3	131.8	2.5	18.5	11.3	10.1
	2013	0.4	-76.2	-1.0	5.7	12.7	-0.3	n.a.	n.a.	18.9	12.2	n.a.
Ireland	2011	0.0	-112.2	-9.7	-12.2	-12.7	-15.4	300.7	15.4	104.1	13.5	-0.7
	2012	2.3	-112.0	-12.2	-16.3	-10.4	-11.7	306.4	-1.6	117.4	14.4	-0.7
	2013	4.0	-104.9	-3.9	-7.2	-3.0	1.3	n.a.	n.a.	123.7	14.2	n.a.
Greece	2011	-10.4	-84.5	1.8	-18.8	4.1	-8.6	129.2	-3.6	170.3	13.2	-3.4
	2012	-7.5	-108.8	-4.5	-26.7	-8.1	-12.4	129.1	-6.8	156.9	18.2	-3.4
	2013	-3.8	-119.3	-4.5	-27.3	-13.2	-8.9	129.3	-5.9	175.1	23.3	-16.8
Spain	2011	-4.4	-90.3	-2.6	-7.8	-1.3	-9.9	205.7	-4.7	70.5	19.9	3.7
	2012	-3.1	-91.4	-5.2	-14.6	-5.6	-16.9	194.4	-10.5	86.0	22.3	3.3
	2013	-1.4	-98.2	-0.4	-7.1	-5.5	-10.4	n.a.	n.a.	93.9	24.1	n.a.
Italy	2011	-2.9	-21.7	-3.3	-18.4	4.8	-2.1	125.8	3.0	120.7	8.2	3.9
	2012	-2.3	-26.4	-6.2	-23.8	3.1	-5.4	126.4	-1.0	127.0	9.2	7.1
	2013	-0.7	-29.5	0.0	-17.8	4.5	-7.0	n.a.	n.a.	132.6	10.4	n.a.

Evolutive indicator		Current account balance	International account balance	Real effective exchange rate calculated based on HICP	Market share of exports of goods and services	Nominal unit labor cost	House price index	Private sector debt	Loans to the private sector	Public debt	Unemployment rate	Total liabilities of the financial sector
Country		% of GDP, 3 year average	% of GDP	3 year percentage change	5 year percentage change	3 year percentage change	annual percentage change	% of GDP	% of GDP	% of GDP	%; 3 year average	annual percentage change
	Year	-4%/+6% of GDP	-35% of GDP	+/-5% (Euro Area); +/- 11% (non-EA)	-6%	+9% (EA); +12% (non-EA)	6%	160% of GDP	+15% of GDP	60% of GDP	10%	16.50%
Cyprus	2011	-8.0	-71.7	-3.0	-16.5	7.8	-9.6	286.6	19.9	71.5	6.6	0.1
	2012	-6.7	-82.4	-5.8	-26.6	0.8	-2.2	299.2	10.0	86.6	8.7	-1.9
	2013	n.a.	n.a.	n.a.	n.a.	n.a.	n.a.	n.a.	n.a.	n.a.	n.a.	n.a.
Hungary	2011	0.1	-106.9	-4.2	-3.6	4.6	-7.4	147.2	7.8	82.1	10.7	-2.6
	2012	0.6	-103.1	-1.2	-17.8	4.4	-9.2	131.0	-6.1	79.8	11.0	-8.3
	2013	1.4	-92.6	-4.0	-19.0	9.0	-4.6	120.9	-3.9	79.3	10.7	3.5
Poland	2011	-4.7	-64.0	-11.6	12.7	4.6	-5.4	76.4	7.1	56.2	9.2	4.3
	2012	-4.6	-66.6	1.3	1.3	4.2	-5.9	74.7	3.4	55.6	9.8	9.6
	2013	-3.4	-69.3	-4.4	-0.4	4.4 (a)	-4.2	n.a.	n.a.	57.0	10.0	n.a.
Portugal	2011	-9.5	-104.8	-3.1	-8.8	0.8	-4.1	222.1	-1.6	108.2	11.9	-0.4
	2012	-6.5	-115.4	-4.0	-16.0	-5.3	-8.6	223.7	-5.4	124.1	13.6	-3.6
	2013	-2.8	-118.7	-0.6	-7.3	-2.1	-2.2	217.6	-4.2	128.9	15.0	-5.9
Romania	2011	-4.5	-64.2	-3.3	23.2	-6.4	-17.7	74.0	2.3	34.7	7.2	4.4
	2012	-4.4	-67.9	-2.0	5.9	-5.2	-9.2	72.9	0.9	37.9	7.2	5.3
	2013	-3.3	-62.3	0.3	10.5	-0.5	-4.5	n.a.	n.a.	38.4	7.2	n.a.

Table 6.2. (Continued)

Evolutive indicator		Current account balance	International account balance	Real effective exchange rate calculated based on HICP	Market share of exports of goods and services	Nominal unit labor cost	House price index	Private sector debt	Loans to the private sector	Public debt	Unemployment rate	Total liabilities of the financial sector
Country		% of GDP, 3 year average	% of GDP	3 year percentage change	5 year percentage change	3 year percentage change	annual percentage change	% of GDP	% of GDP	% of GDP	%; 3 year average	annual percentage change
	Year	-4%/+6% of GDP	-35% of GDP	+/-5% (Euro Area); +/- 11% (non-EA)	-6%	+9% (EA); +12% (non-EA)	6%	160% of GDP	+15% of GDP	60% of GDP	10%	16.50%
Slovenia	2011	-0.1	-40.8	-1.1	-6.7	8.3	1.0	115.4	0.5	47.1	7.1	-1.3
	2012	1.2	-44.9	-4.5	-19.9	0.4	-8.4	113.6	-2.9	54.4	8.1	-0.8
	2013	3.1	-38.7	-0.7	-16.6	-0.8	-6.1	103.6	-3.9	71.7	9.1	-10.4
Slovakia	2011	-3.4	-65.5	3.4	21.5	5.6	-5.2	73.2	2.6	43.4	13.4	1.2
	2012	-1.7	-64.1	-3.2	4.2	0.9	-5.9	73.1	3.2	52.4	14.0	2.6
	2013	0.2	-65.1	2.0	-2.2	0.9	-0.4	n.a.	n.a.	55.4	14.0	n.a.

Notes:

- the table was created with the data available in 2014;
- Indicators do not meet the reference levels;
- stands for discontinued data series;
- n.a. stands for data that were not available until the 1st of November 2014.

Source: EUROSTAT, National Bank of Romania calculations.

The recent achievements in Eastern Europe enhance the role of the EU as an engine for the new Member States' potential to consolidate development in a secure economic environment. Structural vulnerabilities came under strong speculation from Russia's new propensity to control the economies that had previously been in its area of influence in order to satisfy its imperial aspirations revived via financial instruments. The only guarantee for breaking away from the former geopolitical system, including any post-communist dependencies, is the structural consolidation of the transformations in stage one and stage two of transition to the market economy and to the Western-style democracy.

Catching up in terms of productivity against the European competitors is vital in this respect. Integration into the single European market means the harmonization of all performance levels, primarily efficiency levels. The transfers of value added, profitability and population toward the euro area are actually losses of real convergence potential, which postpone *sine die* the functional and sustainable integration of the social development and modernization of Romania. They will come to a halt only when the efficiency indicators equal those in the EU.

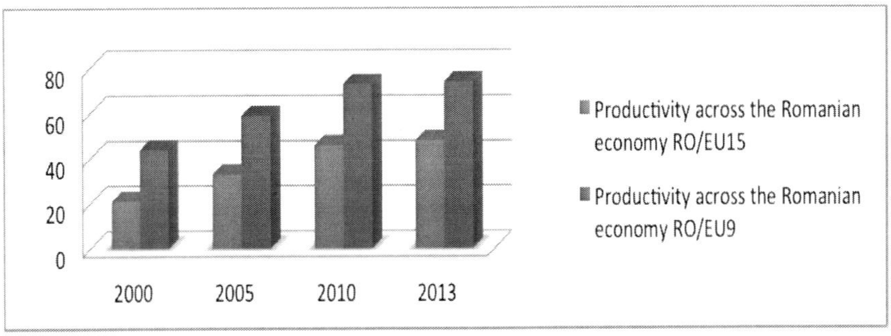

Note: EU9 – BG, CZ, EE, HU, LV, LT, PL, SI, SK.
Source: EUROSTAT, National Bank of Romania's calculations.

Figure 6.11. Productivity across the Romanian economy (%).

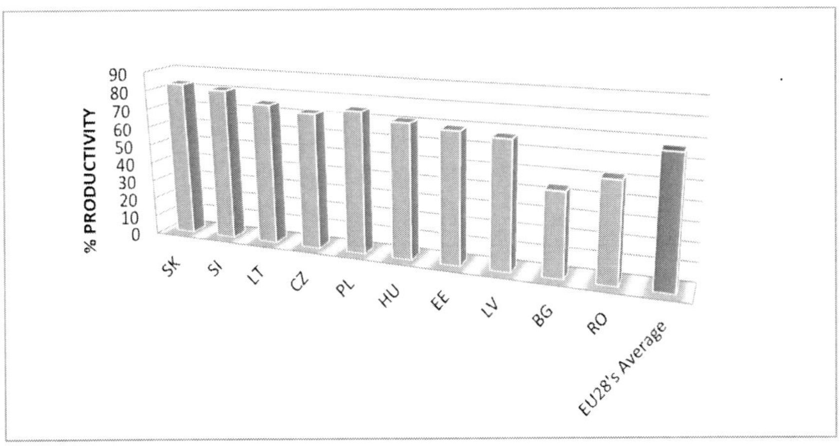

Note: GDP in PPS/working population.
Source: EUROSTAT, National Bank of Romania's calculations.

Figure 6.12. Productivity across selected countries of the EU in 2013.

Basically, the European project, or stage two of the post-communist transformations in Romania, by connecting long-term trends to the Western economic model has the capacity to ensure real anchoring in spite of its rather slow pace and certain mentality issues. The EU umbrella protects the sound tendencies focusing on the restructuring of the deep-rooted mentalities manifest in a society that was subject to communization for more than five decades.

The EU anchor provided the reason for accelerating the structural reforms imperative for the modernization of society. Despite certain costs, the pressure from competitive forces determined by the free movement of production factors, goods and capital prompted the economic system to reject the inefficient components and to converge toward a model similar to the Western-style model. Romania today boasts more efficiently patterned economic growth than in the past, an industrial model based on competitiveness clusters with value added via a technological upgrade of production. Industrial production is being restored on a more competitive basis [7] The economic growth pattern is less energy-intensive and more focused on producing medium and high value added.

6.3. The Test of Assimilating Alternatives

The trend of staying trapped in an automatically implemented, invariable strategy has been for centuries a feature of the Romanians' way to make history. With stage one of the post-communist transition being inspired by the Washington Consensus and stage two consisting in the European integration, there were no comprehensive analyses of possible options. To find an alternative to the path is beside the point, the additional means for reinforcing the transformational power of the strategic change model set as a target should be multiplied instead. Alternative strategies encompass many possible solutions to the pending issues on the development of the Romanian economy that the strategies applied during the two stages of the transformation cannot deal with or do not envisage to resolve.

In a decisive way, the basic option for the transformation path is congruent to any tactical and operational elements that would foster the completion of processes specific to the two transition schemes used in stage one and stage two. For instance, the reform strategy put forth by the Vienna-based AGENDA group [6], replicating the transition scheme of the Washington Consensus, should have been attached more attention in substantiating the decisions to implement the liberalization and privatization programs. At least the recommendation to encourage change actors' involvement by putting in place the social and economic context fostering individual action and decision risk taking, boosting entrepreneurship and the detachment from state dependence would have ensured from the very beginning the chance of a thriving, property-creating environment.

The prevailing emphasis on the entrepreneurship effect in shaping the market economy structure could take some pressure off of acquiring public property without an equivalent in terms of value, implementing non-economic privatization methods or designing privatization otherwise than as a business sale. The entrepreneurship boosted by the liberalized environment would have brought about accumulation of capital that would have, in turn, supported the fair ownership transfer from the state into private hands. The capitalist market economy begins with the formation of capitalists, the capital owners. Any other option resembles an experiment that does not lead to a smooth-running market economy, but to a huge dispute over the rightfulness to become a property owner. Market creation means, according to the Vienna-based AGENDA group, putting in place the market actors by liberalizing the operational framework, as described in "The Market Shock." Private property would have emerged naturally, in the spirit of market economy, consistent with the performance requirements imposed by the free play of supply and demand. State ownership privatization was, under the circumstances, a natural consequence of the market created by actors trained in its logic.

It should be pointed out that there had not been talk of another final target, another economic and societal model, but of transformations meant to shape a capitalist-type market economy, with an option to turn to better account the domestic resources and help the individuals' entrepreneurial inclinations materialize. In fact, the negative side of the balance sheet of capitalist transformations made in line with the Washington Consensus recipe includes a weak domestic entrepreneurial class, an overly shallow middle class and a society reliant on a consumer market underpinned by other economies.

An alternative to the Washington Consensus is the New Developmentalism that came up as an interesting transformation matrix at the turn of the 21st century. It defines the development path for some countries in Asia running at a swift convergence speed based on export-oriented growth in particular [8].

The principles of this transformation-based vision are grounded in the fact that markets remain the main pillar of development and the state secures an appropriate institutional structure for obviating and removing market failures and a financial system supportive of the development of innovative industries. These principles ensure greater moderation in managing the destruction of the former economy and fostering the trends leading to modernization and integration of transition economies into the global economy.

The mentors of the new developmentalism model put the spotlight on the development strategy, with industrial policy playing a prevaling part, and underscore the contribution of domestic demand to growth, together with enhancing revenue policy, in contradistinction to the Washington Consensus. The development policies funded chiefly from domestic saving, taking the exchange rate as an indicator of the monetary policy stance, using the industrial sector as a means to balance the current account, as well as the institutionalization of the banking sector operating under the "patient capital" paradigm, providing long-term financing so as to establish a competitive industrial sector are the alternatives to mitigating the neomonetarist transformation scheme slippages.

New Developmentalism concepts attempt to find the right answer to the challenges of the economies that followed the transformation recipe recommended by the Washington Consensus, especially in terms of changing the capital structure weight by repositioning into the top spot the domestic capital that could be more sensitive to supporting social development, to the ever-increasing individuals' expectations about the access to the results of using domestic resources. More precisely, New Developmentalism brings back to the fore the issue of economic democracy, amid an excessive concentration of economic power and oligopolistic control over the global market. New Developmentalism points to corrections in the global market integration strategies by raising the share of domestic capital in total capital of an economy.

6.4. The New Transformation Challenges

The IMF got more involved in CEE countries from 1990 onwards, in view of the intricate transition they were facing. Along with the noticeable financial assistance, the emerging economies in Europe have benefitted from the IMF's technical assistance and expertise on a variety of issues such as monetary and budgetary policies, financial market operation, external debt management, macroeconomic statistics and, generally, the establishment and strengthening of market economy-related institutions. In the early years of transition, when Romania, similarly to most countries in the region, still grappled with the after-effects of being disconnected by the communist rulers from the international flow of ideas and information, the expertise transferred from the IMF to Romanian officials has, in turn, been a kind of nonmonetary assistance.

Macroeconomic consolidation can be reinforced solely by stepping up structural reform. To improve corporate governance in state-owned enterprises, to implement pension system reform and to make structural adjustments in areas such as revenue collection, employment, energy and the agricultural sector are the major challenges of the post-communist transformation in the years ahead. The switch from purely macroeconomic adjustment programs (which governments prefer, as they are more neutral) to complex structural reform programs (which are, in certain cases, closer to vested interests) is imperative. The paradigm shift implies a better correlation of macroeconomic issues with structural issues, amid a reasonable acceptance from a social perspective.

For example, the latest precautionary Stand-By Arrangement that Romania signed with the International Monetary Fund, the World Bank and the European Commission includes a consistent structural reform package, starting from state-owned enterprise restructuring, privatization of energy companies, clamp-down on tax avoidance to pension system and social assistance reform. The need to increase the multiplication effect by streamlining state-owned enterprises is cited as a sound reason [9].

Private management in public enterprises has been a solution implemented mostly in developing countries as a protection and an insurance against slippages owing to political clout or poor managerial skills. This method comes with benefits and costs and their assessment should be accompanied by the pros and cons relative to the substantiation and implementation of this method. The pros include *inter alia* firmer discipline in public enterprises, lower reliance on the political clout of these entities, and a cut in their arrears to the government budget. Alternatively, the cons refer to this process being highly intricate – performance contracts should be assessed by applying complicated formulas, whereas private managers could be a suboptimal solution and the state might lose control over resources and the access to them without benefitting from a capital increase, as is the case of privatizing companies. If applied in a politicized environment, private management will be able to bring about substantial changes only for an extended period of time.

6.4.1. Resourceless Strategies and the Risks of Transformational Recession

The shock therapy being implemented via the magic triangle – deregulation, restructuring, privatization – has led to realizing new processes such as transformational recessions. The period 1990-93 experienced the first ever transformational recession rife with high inflation, plunging domestic supply, unemployment, extreme poverty and social exclusion. The second transformational recession of 1997-99 left an imprint on collective memory because of the nearly endless list of companies slated for liquidation, high inflation, joblessness and, even worse, massive layoffs, the severe crisis, bank runs, and growing poverty and social exclusion [10].

Empirical studies have shown that a consolidated industrial sector is less prone to macroeconomic volatility. The so-called "race for resources" has been sweeping across the world seemingly defending the proper timing for Washington Consensus 2. The reform package constituting the conditionality for the borrowing relative to the privatization of strategic companies, especially in the energy sector, the tight fiscal and monetary policies, and the brisk energy price deregulation means that the ceiling of the conditionalities embedded in the Washington Consensus 1 recipe has already been reached. The resource issue is *the* great challenge of the new conditionalities. The successful completion of the transformations relies today on the complicated issue of resources, as their control has become a discretionary function of the economic forces driving globalization.

For the emerging economies, as Romania, the third transformational recession is likely to take the form of low growth rates, the return to the vicious circle of elevated public debt, inflation persistence and a spike in structural unemployment.

From a geostrategic perspective, the test of post-communist transformation was part of a broad-based global movement to overcome the consequences of an ideological adversity typical of the first modernity triggered by the first industrial revolution, against the backdrop of individual and national emancipation revolutions. In fact, the transformation test preceded the whole world's entering the age of globalization. The logic of the globalization test is different, as this test is being passed incessantly, with globalization reinventing itself as the second modernity super-cycle. In technical terms, this cycle is driven by the third industrial revolution that inevitably entails the approximation of freedom management formulas and the emergence of other, post-national societal structures.

The true critical point of this new test type is to force a country like Romania undergo new transformations, after the previously unfinished ones. These new transformations are difficult to be accepted, not because of an exhausted national will, but because the global economy structure replicates itself through radical paradigm shifts which, however, can be dealt with only by the countries where development has been a historical feature for centuries.

REFERENCES

[1] Dinu, M. (2014). *Un sfert de secol de restaurare a economiei de piață în România. Transformarea postcomunistă. Peisajul funcționalității*, www.dinumarin.ro

[2] Aslund, A. (2010). *Cum s-a construit capitalismul. Transformarea Europei Centrale şi de Est, a Rusieişia Asiei Centrale*, Moldova Tipo Publishing, Iaşi

[3] Dinu, M. et al. (2005). *Economia României. O viziune asupra tranziției postcomuniste*, Economica Publishing, Bucharest.

[4] Dinu, M. & Brateş, T. (2014). *Răzbunarea trecutului. Capitalismul în cinci luni postdecembriste*, Economica Publishing, Bucharest.

[5] Dinu, M. (2013). *După tranziţie. Avatarurile dezvoltării (Interogare a ceea ce suntem prin ceea ce facem),* presentation for Academica BNR, 04 September 2013, www.bnr.ro

[6] Kregel, J., Matzner, E. & Grabher, G. (1995). *Şocul pieţei. O agendă pentru reconstrucţia economică şi socială în Europa Centrală şide Est*, Economica Publishing, Bucharest.

[7] Iorga, E. (2014). *Mozaicul modificărilor structurale:câteva piese,* prezentare în cadrul Conferinţei Băncii Naţionale a României – *Transformări în economia românească,* http:// www.bnro.ro/ Simpozion-Transformari-in-economia-romaneasca-10812.aspx

[8] Bresser-Pereira, L. C. (2013). *Development, progress and economic growth,* Textos para discussão 350, Escola de Economia de São Paulo, Getulio Vargas Foundation (Brazil).

[9] Weiner, R. S. (2002). *Romania ,the IMF, and Economic Reform: 1996-2002*, disponibil pe http:// isanet.ccit.arizona.edu/ noarchive/ robertweiner.html

[10] Socol, C. (2009). *Macroeconomie*, Economica Publishing, Bucharest.

CONCLUSION

Marin Dinu, PhD, and Dumitru-Alexandru Bodislav, PhD*

Bucharest University of Economics Studies, Bucharest, Romania

What/Who are we after the transition?. The answer awaits and it reconfigures at the same pace with the text. The characteristics that are in tune with expectance are reaching the will for the conditions that motivated the change. Is unstructured a social experiment that created conditional reflections difficult to surpass with high speed, going forward being in line with the change of direction. The delicate part is that the post-communist vehicle's driver is and isn't highly experienced, and also too tired for the obstacles race of the transformation.

Of course, on a more profound plan, the answer is designed on the path of involvement in highlighting societal transformations. The landscape is changing. In blunt terms of the transformation's system, the answer could be more cynical: the outputs depend on the volume and the quality of the inputs. When local resources enter prematurely in a global system, the effects, sadly, dissipate worldwide. The principle of communicating vessels specific for the global economy covers the whole input gap, but also overtakes too much from the output flow. Countries with economies that are on the path towards market functionality mark this way a deficit for development resources.

* * *

The difficulty of rationally managing a unique experiment – the transition from the communist economy to capitalism – has put pressure on the evolution of the post-communist countries during the last two and half decades. The convenience offered by the use of the principle "seeing and doing" instead of implementing an articulate strategy has resulted in an increased volatility, the up/down evolutions materializing in a slow convergence if compared to the standards of the developed countries. The lack of a consistent theory of transition has rendered the process of transformation even more difficult.

The explanatory model of transition can hardly be outlined. It seems that the specific mechanisms of the transformation have not overlapped in due time with the social changes, such occurring a conflict between the regulations and the reality, between micro and macro.

* corresponding author: dinumarin@gmail.com

The main cause of the almost permanent wire walking has been the inconsistent theoretical schemes related to this process. The obvious feeling is that, even after 25 years, the citizens of the former communist countries have not understood what is happening to them, how much was rational, how much emotional, how much consistent or not, how appropriate or contrary to expectations.

This book includes the elements of added value in understanding the economic, social and political transformations in Romania. We can comprehensively notice the post-communist transition as a transformation process, the movement of the Eastern European economies between the independence of path and an innovative path of convergence towards a model of sustainable development. The deficit of experience and the lack of vision have led to the occurrence of a crisis of transformation, thus generating high economic and social costs. The low knowledge of the Western management, the difficulty of shaping a strategy for the minimization of the costs with de-industrialization and the institutional fragility have been the main elements which have resulted in a winding road of the transformation of the economic, social and political system.

In 1989 the premises of development were mixed, as the initial conditions were heterogeneous among the former communist countries. The starting point supposed not only differences in the degree of centralization of economies and the entrepreneurial capacity in the private sector, but also different amplitudes of understanding the mechanisms the market economy is based on. Assuming that the initial conditions have represented the main explanations for different progresses during the first part of the transition period (1990-1997), the implementation of consistent public policies provides the key to understanding the different convergence speed during the second period of transition, after 1998.

Strictly quantitatively, the permanence of the post-communist transformations should be praised – the analysed CEE countries reached a level of GDP/capita of approximately 3 – 7 times higher than in 1990. Even though the initial conditions have been unfavourable, Romania reached however a stage of development based on the improvement of efficiency in using the production factors during the European Union pre-accession period.

The structural adjustment has not resulted in a sufficient increase of productivity. The structural rigidities arising just by misapplication of the principle of competitive advantage have caused the degradation of the economic structure especially during the first decade of the post-communist transition. The mechanisms adjusted for the entry/exit on/from the market of the companies have not been successful. The last decade has brought, however, sustainable changes in the economic structure, as the processes of re-industrialization and development of services have been obvious.

One of the essential elements of the transition, the reform of property has been a difficult process, as it has been impregnated with the cultural heritage of the communist society. The ambiguous legislation of property rights has transformed the process of the reform into a general rush after enrichment, thus seriously affecting the ethical and moral standards of the new Romanian society and enhancing the level of corruption.

The attempt of the State to use privatization also as an instrument of macroeconomic stabilization has failed to a large extent, as the gains of financial sustainability have been neutralized by the subsequent poor performance of most of the entities in the private sector. The fact that the economic importance of the property reform had not been understood when the transfer of property to investors with doubtful entrepreneurial experiences, with methods and practices to the limits of the law, was accepted to a too large extent. The principle of privatization of profit and nationalization of losses gives a suggestive explanation for the way in which the reform of property has been made in Romania.

The economic and social success of the reform of property in Romania can be validated only on a long term and it depends, to a large extent, on the social recognition of the new property rights.

The shock of transition, the conjuncture fiscal decisions, and also the three periods of economic downturn in Romania have contributed to the permanent structural problems in terms of budget and also to the low degree of collection of the tax revenue, the increase in the tax burden and evasion, the increase of the arrears to the state budget, and the low efficiency of the public investments and the budget waste. In this context, there has not been a significant gain of attractiveness for the business environment, despite the introduction of the single tax or of the increase of government investment expenditure. Moreover, the situation of the private sector has been negatively affected by the effects of the pro-cyclical fiscal policy from the period before the economic crisis, when there was no concern about reducing the budget deficits and creating budgetary reserves for the periods of recession.

Thus, the exhaustion of the fiscal maneuver space during the period of economic boom represented the main constraint of the fiscal policy management which needed to adopt fiscal consolidation measures, such as increasing taxation and decreasing public expenditure. The authors propose a series of intelligent solutions, which can mitigate the trade-off between the consolidation of the public finances and the economic growth in Romania, arguing the need to adopt qualitative measures to improve the situation of the public finances, to the detriment of the quantitative ones.

The conditionalities specific to the process of transition of Romania to a functional market economy have the value of a matrix diagram of the cross influences of the internal factors and of the external forces on the main social and economic aggregates. The analysis shows that the mentality, the corruption and the quality of the political class have represented obstacles in the economic development, while the European integration, the agreements with the international financial institutions and with the multinational companies have had a net positive effect. Thus, the accession to the European Union has represented an efficient conditionality not only in terms of the funds allocated and of the access to a larger market for the Romanian products, but also by limiting the access to annuities of the groups of interests in Romania. The accession to the European project has made possible the adoption by consensus of a national strategy of reform, but it also revealed the conformism and mimetism regarding the implementation of the community aquis. The conditionalities of the international bodies, falling into the vision known as Washington Consensus I and II, have been many times respected too late or in a wrong manner, including due to the controversial nature of some of the transition and development models settled for the emerging economies.

A problem which will severely affect the future evolution of the countries in transition is the demographic crisis and its effects upon the labour market. Romania's demographic profile, in relation to some aspects specific to the demographic transition, indicates the existence of two trends, which will be worse in the next 40-50 years – the decrease in population and the degradation of the age structure of the population. Thus, over the last two decades, the demographic stricture has turned from one with a relatively increasing young population to one with a declining population, in which the proportion of the older persons is increasing. The demographic dynamics have negative effects both upon the real economy, by reducing the labour force and the potential production, and also upon the sustainability of the pension system, of the social security and of the medical care, as a result of the increase of the dependence rate of the older persons. The demographic crisis is further enhances by the migration of the active persons outside the borders. The structure of the migrants has turned, during the last years, from one dominated mostly by poorly qualified persons, before the economic crisis, to another one in which the proportion of the highly qualified persons in field such as health, IT and education increases. The current wave of the Romanian migration is described as a phenomenon leading to a loss of qualified or highly qualified human capital that is attracted by the better conditions of the salaries and of living standards from the countries of absorption.

The specificity of the transformations and the way in which they have set up the reality in this part of the world lie in a double transformation, a return/coming-back/regression to a point of the societal experience left by the initiation of the communist experiment. This transformation was actually a re-transformation, a process applied from top to bottom, in strategic formulas with some risk of experiment, in order to hasten the return of the CEE countries in terms of development to the natural way followed by the West.

Looking forward toward the future, Romania must propose the entry in the second modernity. Besides the accession to the Euro area by simultaneously increasing the nominal and the real convergence, it is necessary to change the development paradigm – passing from the stage of development based on efficiency to the stage of development based on innovation. The structural reforms will be targeted to the institutional development, the macroeconomic environment, the development of the financial market, the technological endowment, the complexity of business and innovation, the infrastructure, the access to health and education, the efficiency of the goods market and the investment in human capital.

The consistency of the development could be provided by means of an intelligent economic growth. The innovation of new mechanisms to encourage capitalization will result in the increase of the economic potential through the transfer from the exogenous economic growth – with unstable and volatile growth engines – to the endogenous economic growth (supported by engines such as research-development, innovation, IT&C, start-ups, technological improvement, investment in human capital, institutional consolidation, etc.)

The decrease of the macroeconomic volatility can be achieved through the consolidation of the aggressive industrial policy: passing from industries intensive in poorly qualified labour force and industries with a low processing degree to innovative industries, energy and eco-industries; conditional subsidies, polycentric approach and focus on the clusters of competitiveness, and also on the development of the technological and industrial parks, cooperation between the private sector, universities and research centres. Moreover, it is necessary to attract foreign investments with high added value, including by stimulating the investments with multiplier effects, the creation of new jobs and social value added in the areas where they settle.

The recovery economic growth is sustainable only under the terms of a high discipline of the public finances and by improving the corporate governance in the public companies. Moreover, it is necessary that the process of economic growth is inclusive. The creation of new jobs is the active form of social protection, which should be targeted to the vulnerable categories.

It is certain that a high economic growth rate would lead to the dissemination of its benefits to the entire structure of the global social system, thus creating a level of welfare resembling that of the core of EU countries. Development would mean that, practically, transition reached its targets, the social pressures would be minimised and the factors reinforcing the stability of the rational construction of a new society and economy would be get stronger.

The sustainable economic development should be the defining element of the transition finality, so that the transformation process is not only an end in itself.

* * *

The catching up, as an end of the post-communist transition, has a two-way sense: in line with internal development, and also in line with stopping external adversity. Both strategic objectives target tempering – if not erasing – the conditions for re-entering in a deviant loop of history. Post-communist countries strengthen their impulse of escaping periphery, Western countries demolish their barricades for violent bipolarization of the post-war world. How each succeeds is the exact measure of the chance of ECE countries to have a safe future.

From the vantage point of the results reported to the initial status, the reality seems to look better, but comparing with the targeted model's performance it shows gaps that need extended period of time to recover.

Between accomplishments and expectations there settled in layers the damage of the geopolitical challenges from the ECE countries.

Editors' Contact Information

Professor Marin Dinu, PhD
Chair of R.E.A.C./D.E.E.P.
Bucharest University of Economic Studies
Department of Economics and Economic Policies,
Calea Dorobanti, no. 15-17, district 1,
Bucharest, Romania
Email: dinumarin@gmail.com

Professor Dorel Ailenei, PhD
Bucharest University of Economic Studies,
Bucharest, Romania
Email: dorulilenei@gmail.com

Professor Anca Dachin, PhD
Bucharest University of Economic Studies,
Bucharest, Romania
Email: ancadachin@yahoo.com

Professor Cătălin Huidumac-Petrescu, PhD
Bucharest University of Economic Studies,
Bucharest, Romania
Email: catalinhuidumac@yahoo.com

Professor Mariana Iovițu, PhD
Bucharest University of Economic Studies,
Bucharest, Romania
Email: marianaiovitu@yahoo.com

Professor Marius Corneliu Marinaş, PhD
Bucharest University of Economic Studies,
Bucharest, Romania
Email: mariusmarinas@gmail.com

Professor Christina-Marta Suciu, PhD
Bucharest University of Economic Studies,
Bucharest, Romania
Email: christina.suciu@economie.ase.ro

Postdoctoral Research Fellow Dumitru-Alexandru Bodislav, PhD
Bucharest University of Economic Studies,
Bucharest, Romania
Email: dumitru.bodislav@economie.ase.ro

INDEX